Mr Crippen, Cora and the Body in the Basement

For Mum and Dad, who taught me to resent injustice

Mr Crippen, Cora and the Body in the Basement

Matthew Coniam

PEN & SWORD
TRUE CRIME

First published in Great Britain in 2021 by
Pen & Sword True Crime
An imprint of
Pen & Sword Books Ltd
Yorkshire – Philadelphia

ISBN 978 1 39900 972 0

A CIP catalogue record for this book is
available from the British Library.

Typeset by Mac Style
Printed and bound by CPI Group (UK) Ltd,
Croydon, CR0 4YY

Pen & Sword Books Limited incorporates the imprints of Atlas,
Archaeology, Aviation, Discovery, Family History, Fiction, History,
Maritime, Military, Military Classics, Politics, Select, Transport,
True Crime, Air World, Frontline Publishing, Leo Cooper, Remember
When, Seaforth Publishing, The Praetorian Press, Wharncliffe
Local History, Wharncliffe Transport, Wharncliffe True Crime
and White Owl.

For a complete list of Pen & Sword titles please contact

PEN & SWORD BOOKS LIMITED
47 Church Street, Barnsley, South Yorkshire, S70 2AS, England
E-mail: enquiries@pen-and-sword.co.uk
Website: www.pen-and-sword.co.uk

Or

PEN AND SWORD BOOKS
1950 Lawrence Rd, Havertown, PA 19083, USA
E-mail: Uspen-and-sword@casematepublishers.com
Website: www.penandswordbooks.com

'The people of 1910 might be indifferent to the worsening relations between the Liberals and the Lords, but they were eager to accept the tiniest detail in the story of the pursuit and arrest of "Dr" Crippen. It was hot news indeed; something was happening for the first time in world history. I am no connoisseur of murder, but I fancy that in its grisly annals Crippen and his actual crime would not be given a prominent place; it is what happened afterwards that is important.'

J.B. Priestley, *The Edwardians*

'There is nothing you can tell me about Crippen that I don't already know.'

'So?'

'So, like Crippen... I am patient.'

Theo (Peter McEnery) and Reingard
(Diane Cilento), in *Negatives* (1968)

Contents

Prologue

Hawley Harvey Crippen was not the only one whose fate hung upon the result of his appeal for his conviction for murder. So, too, did that of his Madame Tussaud's waxwork. It had already been completed, to a chilling standard of accuracy, thanks in no small measure to those famous photographs of the accused in the dock: not an illegal practice at the time but strongly discouraged, and usually only permitted by prior arrangement. These had been taken, according to the legend, by Jack Tussaud, great-great-grandson of the original, using a camera hidden in a bowler hat.[1] But the museum was forbidden from displaying the result until the appeals procedure had been completed. If Crippen had been released, it would have been all for naught, and the figure would have been melted down. But of course, things did not go Crippen's way, and his surrogate stood in the museum's Chamber of Horrors for over a century, until the whole exhibit was permanently mothballed in 2016.[2] And somehow he has endured, long outlasting his shock value, into an age when the crime of which he was accused would be lucky to get a paragraph or two on page five, elected to that folkloric afterlife where fact and fiction can take turns without censure, keeping company with the likes of Dick Turpin, Guy Fawkes and Captain Kidd.

It was a not particularly complicated case, nor all that surprising, provided it was taken at face value. Murder in the family – for financial gain or to get rid of an encumbrance, and committed using poison – crowds out most other forms of murder in the literature. A henpecked husband, arsenic in the tea, the wife away visiting her sister, a new lump in the flower bed: the Crippen case deviates from these clichés only in its fine print. And in the years that followed there was Seddon (convicted in 1912) and Smith (1915), True (1922) and Heath (1946), Haigh (1949) and Christie (1953). Their crimes all made the headlines too, and equally gripped the nation as their trials unfolded. But never, quite, in that grim pantheon, did they displace his memory in the popular imagination. How many today would immediately link the name George Joseph Smith with the Brides in the Bath murders? Was it Haigh or Heath who had the acid bath? Few, I suspect, could tell you. But say 'Dr Crippen' and there again he stands in the mind's eye: small, quiet, mild-mannered, fastidious, his hair reddish, brilliantined, thinning, with fishlike eyes peering through round, gold-rimmed spectacles.

Three things above all made his story a sensation. The first was the gruesomeness of the discovery: a filleted, dismembered corpse, beneath the bricks of the coal cellar in a gloomy, three-storey London house. The second was a quite unexpected dash of wild and tragic romance: the fact of Crippen and his mistress, Ethel Le Neve, attempting to flee justice by ship to Canada, disguised as father and son. It was all so thrilling, so dramatic, it could easily have sprung from the yellow pages of some sensational work of fiction, and there were even those so caught up in the sheer melodrama of it as to wish quite openly that the fugitives be allowed to snatch victory from the jaws of certain defeat. The third was its accidental but intoxicating marriage of technological progress and audience participation – wireless telegraphy, a new invention that both secured Crippen's arrest and gave the newsreading public vicarious access to the thrill of the chase in real time, as the villains rushed, oblivious, not to freedom but into the waiting arms of the law. An Edwardian version of O.J. Simpson's 'white Bronco chase', if you will.

If Crippen is the dark saint of British crime, his simple, haunting effigy at Madame Tussaud's was surely the sacred relic. For decades, and still when I first visited him in the early 1980s, he was situated in the dock at his arraignment, the faithful Ethel by his side. More recently he stood alone in a prison cell. Would he have been pleased or saddened to have been parted from his loved one? Saddened, perhaps, at the thought of facing eternity without her; pleased that she was no longer ignominiously on show in a so-called 'chamber of horrors' (a peculiar place for anyone who had been found unequivocally not guilty to have ended up in the first place). Apparently, she was removed in 1996.

Crippen the martyr, the role in which he cast himself in his plaintive final letters, makes more sense without the reassuring presence of his lady love in any case: *En ma fin gît mon commencement* (In my end is my beginning). And amidst all the bleak evidences of man's inhumanity on display all around, he stood apart even before he stood alone. A small man, seemingly weary and resigned; not elderly yet somehow frail; well dressed: frock-coated (grey, with shiny lapels); hands folded (neatness, composure); his stare glassy, and fixed at some indistinct distant spot. There was a genuine uncanniness about it; it is as if it had something it wanted to tell you. Some twist in the tail, maybe; some final act, still unwritten, to offset the anti-climax of a jury taking only twenty-seven minutes to find him guilty as charged. Something bizarre and incredible, some evidence of unbelievable error, or oversight, or coincidence, unacknowledged by all who took it knowingly or obliviously to the grave...

But if so, where was it to be located? Not still hidden in that dingy, gaslit, Edwardian house of secrets, at any rate. The house, like all who passed through it, is a ghost, a memory, an idea; its end hastened by the bomb that landed in its garden on the night of 8 September 1940. It was the first major air raid of the Second World War.

The same raids struck Madame Tussaud's, destroying over 300 head moulds and leaving many figures scattered and broken, like dead bodies. But Crippen, sad and watchful, survived. Unlike its utterly luckless real-life counterpart, the wax figure had twice withstood catastrophe already. It was untouched in the 1925 fire that destroyed many of the other figures, closing the museum for two years, and drawing a crowd 10,000 strong to watch the salvage operations. 'How are Deeming, Price and Crippen?' they called to the firemen exiting the building.[3] According to a correspondent of Inspector Dew's whose letters are preserved in the police files, 'a lusty cheer went up' among the crowd who had assembled at the conflagration when the news was received that Crippen had survived.[4] Because of its basement location, the Chamber of Horrors, in which the water from the fire department's hoses collected, was the least damaged part of the exhibition. The *Illustrated Police News* published a delightful drawing of Crippen's figure being lifted from the flood, titled 'Dr Crippen Saved from a Watery Grave'. Then, in 1931, he narrowly avoided destruction again when the Dogger Bank earthquake, Britain's severest ever, had sent his wax head tumbling to the floor at his feet. According to some reports the head split in two,[5] one portion falling and the other 'remaining lying on his shoulder, adding a new horror to the Chamber of Horrors'.[6] But again the icon was preserved; again Saint Crippen was delivered safe from harm, as if in restitution for some unknown injustice. Now he bides his time in the gloom of some locked storeroom, still awaiting the day – and he was sure it *would* arrive – when new evidence came to clear him, and he might again come out of the darkness and into the light.

The enduring fascination of the Crippen case to armchair detectives, I think, is attributable to the sheer mass of contradictions it is required to support. There is its strange mixture of the mundane and the exotic: a conventional domestic murder, buried in the heart of respectable suburbia, yet peopled with a cast of characters fit for any melodrama, headed by a failed music hall artiste as victim, and a huckster selling patent medicines as chief suspect. The mild-mannered husband who wouldn't harm a fly not merely poisoning his wife but dismembering and filleting her. The careful killer who obliterated all means of identification from the corpse, then wrapped what was left of the remains in his own pyjama jacket and threw in the victim's hair curlers. The ingenious fiend who successfully removed head, limbs, skeleton and genitals, spiriting them away to somewhere they have never been found, then opted to leave a lump of leftover flesh in the cellar of his rented house, complete with an incriminating scar. The fugitive who compelled his mistress to pretend to be his son, knowing that the world was looking for them. Then, at his trial, his dogged protestation of innocence in the face of seemingly incontrovertible evidence, when he might perhaps have made a sympathetically heard case for accidental death, and received a sentence for manslaughter. And that strange feeling – they all sensed it – that the man had no fight in him, that he was almost willing his own conviction, or at least not so much as lifting a finger to prevent it. The only logical reading was that here was a man stupefied with guilt – yet he went to his grave proclaiming his complete and absolute innocence.

All of these remained tantalising puzzles for just under a century, and looked set to remain so for all the centuries to follow. But then, in 2007, came another bombshell. Scientists in America had uncovered evidence that turned the whole case utterly on its head, just as Crippen had predicted. It was a bigger explosive for sure than the one that landed on the house over half a century before, and its debris scattered over an infinitely wider area. Some of the pieces remain in motion, descending still, and it is yet to be seen exactly how they land, and in what arrangements. But enough of the smoke has cleared already, and enough of the dust settled, to establish that almost everything we thought we knew about the body in the cellar, the henpecked husband, the harridan wife and the saintly lover was wrong. In some cases, we have merely been looking at it from the wrong angle, as if mistaking a reflection in the mirror for the person stood in front of it. Here, all that is needed is a minor change in emphasis, a shift in perspective, a slight widening of the range of possibilities, and all the known facts gently step back, allow the new insight to settle into place, and then easily coalesce around it as before. But in other cases, the new evidence is so transfiguring, so entirely disruptive of the very bedrock of the case as we have understood it until now, as to suggest that what we took for a true image was in reality the grotesque, wilful distortions of a funfair hall of mirrors. This is that story – what we thought we knew about Dr Crippen and the secret in his basement, what we know now, and whether there is any way, over a hundred years later, that we can join these two seemingly contradictory histories into one coherent account, one that tells us what might *really* have happened at number 39 Hilldrop Crescent, Holloway, North London, in the cold months of January and February 1910.

What did Crippen know? One thing that we can now say for certain that he knew, and that likely *only* he knew, was that the truth was *not* being revealed in court, merely a yellow journalism version of it that he had no means of countering. The Crown's case was not disingenuous, and those who advanced it, like the jury, were sure it was correct. But it was for all that a glib and convenient fiction. So maybe *that* was what we read in the expression on his effigy and the source of that strange sense of fatalism he conveyed to those around him: his understanding of the one thing we supposedly all know about fiction, yet forget all too easily. That the truth is often stranger.

It is necessary to look a little below the surface of things to find a reason for the fact that Dr Crippen and his companion have become objects of international interest, and that there has gathered at the Canadian port where the ship carrying them will touch a little army of high police officials and a much larger one of reporters, those efficient and infallible representatives of public emotion.

Crippen himself is a wholly commonplace person, notable only, apart from the crime of which he is more than suspected, as a member of an honourable profession who has for many years disgraced it by putting his knowledge and his degree at the service of quackery and charlatanism. Of the woman with him little could and nothing need be said, while the murder – admitting that there has been one, which is not quite certain – contained nothing of the romantic or the unusual to give it more than a narrowly restricted notoriety. Yet no small part of the civilised world has a considerable fraction of its attention fixed on these fugitive travellers, and is awaiting their arrest with thrilled impatience.

The explanation of this queer phenomenon doubtless is to be found in the present existence of a true dramatic 'situation' that is fast approaching a logical climax. And for once chance has arranged scene and circumstances in strict accord with a rule or principle well known to playwrights and always used by theme with confident assurance of its effectiveness. That rule is to let the audience or the spectators know exactly what is going to happen, while the people on the stage, or those of them upon whom interest is fastened, move forward to their predestined sorrow or joy in complete ignorance of coming events. The theory is that this gives to the observers a pleasant sense of superiority – of ability to see things hidden from others. That must be at least an approximation to the truth.

In this case, however, a feeling something like pity may be mingled with the other – a feeling that it is not quite fair to hunt down and capture a murderer by means of a device, wireless telegraphy, with which other murderers as bad as he have not had to contend. Of course, when dragged out into the light, that is instantly seen to be an absurd compunction or resentment, but it has an obvious analogy with the equally absurd antagonism which new methods of warfare excite among nations that do not at all recoil from the employment of those with which they are familiar. As if it made any difference from what direction comes that shot that kills!

New York Times, 30 July 1910

Chapter 1

The Discovery

Crime is a social activity, and inevitably thrives in and around centres of civilisation. More than half the memorable murders of Britain have happened in London, and many notable killers have had London associations. Patterns of crime associate with patterns of housing. Murders show which parts of London had the largest servant population. Fraud and bigamy lead to homicide in middle-class areas and western suburbs; street-fighting and gang activities prove lethal in the East End and Clerkenwell. Murder preserves respectability in Holloway; youth kills for kicks in South London.

Martin Fido, *The Murder Guide to London*

By the above matrix, the Crippen case was clearly a middle-class murder mystery, inseparable from the suburbia in which it played out. The suburbs are centres of relative affluence, quiet comfort, workday routine and weekend leisure, and – most central to their fascination as a locus of crime – hotbeds of secrets, at least one really juicy one lurking behind every identikit door. Suburbia is where the curtains twitch and gossip never goes hungry. From wife-swapping to satanism, any Sunday tabloid could tell you that deceptively respectable suburbia is where it's *really* all going on. A popular cliché defined it as the place where everybody comes from and nobody wants to return to (such was H.G. Wells's view of his childhood in Bromley), but in the aftermath of Victorian industrialisation it was a haven and a retreat for Londoners who came increasingly to view the city as a necessary evil, but no place in which to live. In the witness statements of the Crippen case you can practically see the beady little eyes, pair upon squinting pair of them, peeping around the lace curtains: 'Latterly there was a lady in black there, and last week there were also two lads staying with Dr Crippen… Both Mr and Mrs Crippen used to spend a great part of their time in the garden… Crippen had occasionally been seen in the company of a foreign-looking youth…'

The Crippens played out their scandal in the northward suburban spread that made neat, ordered brick worlds with names like Holloway, Highbury, St John's Wood, Hampstead and Swiss Cottage, and lonely green islands of Primrose Hill and Regent's Park, where fields and meadows were once the norm rather than the exception. Every day 'Dr' Crippen would set off for New Oxford Street; every evening he would return to Islington. You could have set your watch by the old boy. But appearances are often deceptive, and never more so than in the suburbs, starkly demarcated with wall and hedgerow to mark the boundary where one territory ends and the next begins, where each semi-detached villa is a man's castle, his uniformity without functioning as guarantor of his right to unrestrained individuality within. And even by the common standard, these were not your average English suburbanites. For one thing, both Mr and Mrs Crippen were American; for another, they were somewhat exotic blooms, trailing associations with the English music hall, sundry representatives of which they would entertain in gay parties, characterised by laughter, song, and that most unforgiven of suburban sins: slamming cab doors after midnight. Gaudy peacocks of the stage, relaxing after hours in the gaslit regularity of commuter-land: this was the first of the many juxtapositions the story would sustain.

The word 'suburb' is at least as old as Chaucer. Its nebulousness is baked into its very definition: it defines itself not by what it is, nor by where it is, but by what and where it is not. It is the somewhere that is nowhere, the is that isn't. At first suburbs were not discrete entities so much as a kind of topographical footnote: the bit that was left over when you discounted the country and the town. These suburbs were sinks for everything deemed too minacious or unwholesome to remain comfortably within the city walls, from hospitals for leprosy to brothels, gambling dens and, worst of all, theatres. By the seventeenth century it was being noted that the suburbs were growing exponentially and coming to sustain their own infrastructure and society, the first step on their road to self-sufficiency and respectability: writers likened them to the wide brim around a Jesuit's hat, far larger than the block. Once mass transport arrived, with its cheap workman's fares allowing easy and convenient daily movement in and out of the city, they took on their now-understood character, switching from sites of banishment to sites of escape. In 1891, the journalist Sidney Low, writing in *Contemporary Review*, noted: 'The Englishman of the future will be a suburb-dweller. The majority of the people of this island will live in the suburbs, and the suburban type will be the most widespread and characteristic of all.' As the Victorian gave way to the Edwardian, the pioneering to the consolidating, it is not hard to see why suburbia held so much appeal and so much promise: what Low described as a 'Sargasso sea of asphalt and paving', linked inextricably with the facelessness of financial transaction and its negation of commonality, inevitably paled beside these ordered expressions of humane compromise. The best thing about suburbia was its spirit of rapprochement: it rejected the city while at the same time accommodating it. Small wonder Low envisaged 'not one but a dozen Croydons' forming 'a circle of detached forts round the central stronghold' as the living shape of England's future. And as the nineteenth century gave way to the twentieth, suburbia replaced both the city and the country as the default locus of consensus normality. Life, *real* life, was lived on trams and buses and in municipal parks and cafés, and above all, *behind those curtains*, with their promise both of revelation and concealment.

An irony that Crippen exposed was that it was in the supposedly heartless city that everyone knew each other's business, and in the supposedly communal suburbs that horrors might be staged unsuspected behind respectable doors, and where neighbours, pressed for impotent comment after the fact, offered only banality and bewilderment. (*They seemed such a happy couple...*) And the suburbs, of course, soon became a place where murder was not only committed but consumed, in an ostensibly dubious but essentially innocent ritual of recreation, celebrated most famously by George Orwell in his essay 'Decline of the English Murder'. Orwell depicts a typical Sunday afternoon, with the suburbanite, well-fed and smoking his pipe, scanning the *News of the World* for a really good murder:

If one examines the murders which have given the greatest amount of pleasure to the British public, the murders whose story is known in its general outline to almost everyone and which have been made into novels and re-hashed over and over again by the Sunday papers, one finds a fairly strong family resemblance running through the greater number of them. Our great period in murder, our Elizabethan period, so to speak, seems to have been between roughly 1850 and 1925, and the murderers whose reputation has stood the test of time are the following: Dr Palmer of Rugely, Jack the Ripper, Neill Cream,

Mrs Maybrick, Dr Crippen, Seddon, Joseph Smith, Armstrong and Bywaters and Thompson...

In considering the nine murders I named above, one can start by excluding the Jack the Ripper case, which is in a class by itself. Of the other eight, six were poisoning cases, and eight of the ten criminals belonged to the middle class. In one way or another, sex was a powerful motive in all but two cases, and in at least four cases respectability – the desire to gain a secure position in life, or not to forfeit one's social position by some scandal such as a divorce – was one of the main reasons for committing murder. In more than half the cases, the object was to get hold of a certain known sum of money such as a legacy or an insurance policy, but the amount involved was nearly always small. In most of the cases the crime only came to light slowly, as the result of careful investigations which started off with the suspicions of neighbours or relatives; and in nearly every case there was some dramatic coincidence, in which the finger of Providence could be clearly seen, or one of those episodes that no novelist would dare to make up, such as Crippen's flight across the Atlantic with his mistress dressed as a boy, or Joseph Smith playing 'Nearer, my God, to Thee' on the harmonium while one of his wives was drowning in the next room. The background of all these crimes, except Neill Cream's, was essentially domestic; of twelve victims, seven were either wife or husband of the murderer.

With all this in mind one can construct what would be, from a *News of the World* reader's point of view, the 'perfect' murder. The murderer should be a little man of the professional class – a dentist or a solicitor, say – living an intensely respectable life somewhere in the suburbs, and preferably in a semi-detached house, which will allow the neighbours to hear suspicious sounds through the wall. He should be either chairman of the local Conservative Party branch, or a leading Nonconformist and strong Temperance advocate. He should go astray through cherishing a guilty passion for his secretary or the wife of a rival professional man, and should only bring himself to the point of murder after long and terrible wrestles with his conscience. Having decided on murder, he should plan it all with the utmost cunning, and only slip up over some tiny unforeseeable detail. The means chosen should, of course, be poison.

The Crippen case, clearly, conforms in virtually every detail to Orwell's ideal. In this context murder takes on a kind of surrogate function: it is the suburbanite's version of theatrical tragedy. To connoisseurs of murder, the parallels between this new drama and the more established sort could hardly have been more exact. A canonical murder, like a Shakespearean tragedy, has a classic five-act structure. There is the crime, the investigation, the apprehension, the trial and the punishment. Crippen was no more immune to the allure of crime than anybody else: he declared himself 'a reader of romances' at his trial, and during his flight from justice he was seen to be immersed in a copy of Edgar Wallace's *The Four Just Men*. And frequently in the Crippen affair we will catch its main players – especially Inspector Dew and Captain Kendall – in the act of playing to the gallery, as if presenting their best profile to the camera, carefully furnishing their place in posterity. As important as any professional commendation, or dressing down, was the verdict of the Sunday papers.

The first reports of the Crippen case broke on a Thursday. It was the fourteenth day of July 1910, a rare sunny day in what had been a fairly wet and cool summer. London's *Daily Mail* informed its readers of the discovery with a succinctness and sobriety that would be conspicuously absent from this point on:

> A discovery which was made late last night, after an exhaustive police search, at a large house in Hilldrop Crescent, Kentish Town, N.W., has led to the grave suspicion that a Mrs Crippen, who was well known in the music hall profession under the name of Belle Elmore, has been murdered and her body secretly buried.[1]

The find had been made by Scotland Yard's Chief Inspector Walter Dew, and the fact that he titled his autobiography *I Caught Crippen* may give some indication of how important he judged the case to be in terms of his lasting reputation. Hindsight is apt to make raconteurs out of all of us, as chance becomes presentiment, accidents acquire the pattern of design, the random becomes inevitable. We have no real way of knowing if Dew was *really* haunted by the image of Crippen's cellar prior to his triumphant assault upon it, only that he claimed to be when time came to make history out of it all. And yet, for one so fixated upon the cellar, it was a long time indeed before he made his breakthrough there. It was no short while, for that matter, before he was even inclined to take the case of Cora Crippen's disappearance all that seriously.

The first indications had come on 30 June. A colleague, Superintendent Frank Froest, had been consulted by John and Lilian Nash, the latter also known as Lil Hawthorne, a Nashville-born singer and principal boy in pantomime, noted for her spirited renditions of such favourites as 'Tessie, You are the Only, Only, Only' and 'Don't Cry Little Girl, Don't Cry'. The Nashes were concerned about their friend, Cora Crippen, treasurer of the Music Hall Ladies' Benevolent Fund, formerly a performer under the name by which they still knew her, Belle Elmore. She lived at 39, Hilldrop Crescent with her husband, a timid American medical man – the Nashes thought he might be a dentist – called Hawley Harvey Crippen, though in common with Cora and all their friends, they knew him as Peter.[2] It has been noted that but for their prior acquaintance with Froest, the Nashes would likely have taken the matter to their local police station rather than straight to Scotland Yard, where it could well have been buried beneath paperwork and more pressing concerns, never to have risen to the top. Another performer, Miriam Williams, aka Kate Roberts, aka Vulcana, a music hall strongwoman, had already done just that and been told that unless she was willing to make a charge there was nothing they could do. (Among the many eventful highlights of her long career, Williams was pronounced dead in 1939 after being hit by a car, and came round in the morgue in time to hear the last rites. This flavour of music hall hyperbole seemed to permeate the Crippen case, seeping outwards and reaching all in its orbit. According to a 1930 report in the *Sunday News*, Superintendent Froest was known as 'the man with the iron hands', and famed for his ability to tear packs of playing cards in two and snap sixpences as if they were biscuits. Cited without reservation even in some present-day accounts of the case, both talents are, of course, physically impossible for a person of any strength.[3])

Nash repeated his story to the Coroner's Court in July. The Coroner began by asking him when he last saw the Crippens:

> They had dinner at our house, on January 19, that was the last time. They seemed all right together, and had come on to our house after attending a meeting of the Music Hall Ladies' Guild. On Wednesday, February 2, I heard from my wife that Belle Elmore had resigned her post as treasurer of the guild. My wife thought it strange.
>
> On Saturday, February 5, we sent a note to Miss Elmore, saying that we would call that night. We wished to dissuade her from resigning.

On returning from Tottenham, where my wife was playing, we called at Hilldrop Crescent, but we could not gain admittance as the place was closed. Then on February 6 we heard from (Melinda) May, the secretary of the guild, that Belle Elmore had left for California. The news came as a surprise to everybody.

On February 27 there was a dinner of the Benevolent Institution, presided over by Mr Joe Elvin. I was surprised to see Mr Crippen enter with his typist. They sat opposite us. Mrs. Paul Martinetti (Mr Nash's hostess) recognised that she was wearing one of Belle Elmore's brooches. That made a great impression on me.

On March 23 we sailed for New York. During the first week in May there we received a letter from Mrs Martinetti, telling us that 'poor Belle had died'. About the middle of May we met Mrs. Fred Ginnett (president of the Music Hall Ladies' Guild) in New York. She was very much upset, did not like the look of affairs, and wrote to the authorities at Los Angeles, and, not receiving any satisfactory reply, got the New Jersey police to write on their official paper to Los Angeles. They received an official reply that no such person as Belle Elmore or Crippen had died in Los Angeles. We thought it very mysterious.

We sailed from New York on June 15, and, on June 28 I visited Dr Crippen at his offices. He seemed very much 'cut up', very nervous, and distressed, and sobbed. He gave out at first that she died in Los Angeles. When I questioned him, he said, 'Oh no, she died in some little town near San Francisco.' He did not know that I had lived there for some time, and said that the town had a Spanish name which he could not remember. At last I mentioned Alameda, and he said, 'I think it was that town.' I said, 'Peter, do you mean to say you don't know where your wife died?' And he answered, 'I think it was that town.'[4]

Dew, who wondered dourly if 'the Bohemian character of the persons concerned' might hold the key to the matter, began unenthusiastically following up the story at the Music Hall Ladies' Guild. There he met Paul Martinetti ('The Celebrated American Character Pantomimist, Clown and Ape Delineator', according to his publicity) and his wife Clara, who had a more detailed, but no less suspicious, account. As Paul Martinetti told the Coroner:

On one occasion – I cannot say the day – he called at my flat to tell me that his wife had gone to America on some very important business, that she might be away for months, and that he was going to sell his furniture. He said it was legal business and might lead to a title. Later on he wrote me a letter. I called on him the next day, and he told me that he was going to sell the house, as he did not like it. I said, 'Dr Crippen, if I were you I would take the first steamer and go home to America.' To this he made no reply. He told me that his wife had double pneumonia… Long after that I saw Dr Crippen at the music-ball Benevolent Fund with the lady typist. That was in the ballroom, and he looked very jolly. The next time I saw him he came to invite my wife and myself to go to dinner with him and to the theatre. We guessed it was also with the lady typist, and we refused. That was the last time I saw him.[5]

The Martinettis had dined with the Crippens on the night of 31 January: investigation would show that this was the last time Cora was seen alive. Through February Crippen had told various stories about Cora being called urgently to America, either to visit her family or on business on his behalf, then being stricken with pneumonia while there. But on 24 March he cabled Clara to tell her that he had received confirmation of Cora's death, and was leaving the country for a short while to collect his thoughts. On 26 March he placed a notification of her death in the theatrical newspaper *The Era*. He had told some who had enquired that she had died in the wilds of California; to the Nashes he nominated San Francisco, to yet others he claimed she had been with Otto, his son from his first marriage, at this point himself married and living in Los Angeles. Otto was contacted and expressed surprise and suspicion – she had not been with him, and his father had told him an entirely different story.

As well as Cora's strange disappearance, Dew was hearing more about the 'lady typist'. Her name was Ethel Neave, but she had taken to calling herself Ethel Le Neve: that in itself would doubtless have caused Dew's eyebrows to raise, though it was apparently her bluff and down-to earth-father who had first adopted the variation, during an unlikely spell in which he, too, had trod the boards. (Theatrical aspirations are epidemic in this story.) It seemed that Crippen had moved Miss Le Neve into Hilldrop Crescent more or less immediately after Cora's disappearance, and he was now dressing her in Cora's furs and jewellery, which they paraded together at public events. What's more, she had a habit of telling friends that she was the new Mrs Crippen. When Crippen had told Clara Martinetti he was spending some time away after Cora's death he had in fact rushed off to Dieppe with Ethel.[6] Meanwhile Crippen was tidying up his affairs and readying to leave. He gave his landlord notice of vacating Hilldrop Crescent by the end of June, though he later requested that the tenancy be extended until September.[7]

One reason why Dew may have been tempted to keep the business at arm's length is that from the first it was populated by figures from the English music hall, that unreliable and over-imaginative body of men and women with transient lifestyles and multiple names – neither conducive to the smooth running of a police enquiry – and little to do between performances except gossip bitchily about each other. There would have been every indication that this was just another petty intrigue between idle-minded players, many of them *American* to boot.

Music hall is one of those highly savoury ingredients of the Crippen story that have ensured its novelty, a century on; as potent as gaslight, flock wallpaper, velvet curtains. It was, to those raucously in its thrall, a world as unfussy, unpretentious, roguish, *joyous* and authentically working class as a Carry On film, yet for us somehow rendered eerie and faintly exotic by distance, and by transmutation through secondary representation. (If Walter Sickert had been around to paint Sid James and Barbara Windsor, our great-grandchildren may well feel the same about our own lowbrow diversions. Even without him, they may yet.) Music hall pulsed with energy, with life and with the love of life, but also with the *reality* of living, of living day to day and hand to mouth, with stoicism and pragmatism. Droll and dour, it was the only entertainment where the reality of working-class life was truly acknowledged, and by acknowledgement transcended. Half theatre, half pub, it offered an alternative home where the celebrated and glamorous earned their adoration not by the worship of difference but by the assertion of commonality.

Emerging from the humblest of starts in 'song and supper rooms' with such evocative names as the Cyder Cellars and the Coal Hole, the latter supposedly where the banjo was first heard in Britain, by the time the Crippens arrived in London music hall had grown into a vastly lucrative industry. As well as entertainment, it offered comfort of a sort rarely to be found elsewhere: performer Valantyne Napier observed that 'compared to the general living conditions of that time', the halls must have seemed truly palatial to 'the vast working-class audiences who filled the auditoriums'.[8]

From the first, however, it also attracted opprobrium, and a campaign against its affronts to decency led by one Laura Ormiston Chant gained a deal of traction in the 1890s. Chant especially objected to the prostitutes who openly plied their trade at the back of the auditorium: as a result of her crusade, the London County Council forced the Leicester Square Empire to erect a canvas covering shielding the prostitutes from the rest of the hall. In counter-protest, the audience promptly tore it down again. To those from the other side of the tracks who attended the halls in much the same way that well-to-do Americans in the 1920s frequented jazz clubs in Harlem, such occurrences only added to their authentic appeal. Sickert was far from the only representative of high culture to fall for this allure: it exercised a magnetic attraction to certain bohemian sensibilities, the type described by a rather discomfited Keats as engaged in 'a somewhat hectic search for… the rough accidents of life'. This kind of artist was, the poet summed up, 'searching sadly for his lost Philistinism, his heart full of an unsatisfied hunger for the commonplace'.[9] And search he did. As well as Sickert, taking notes and making pencil sketches in his box, there was poet and aesthete William Symons, who declared: 'I am an *aficionado*, as a Spaniard would say, of music halls.' Thackeray could apparently be seen at the Cyder Cellars at two in the morning. The young Winston Churchill was said to have been among those tearing down the canvas partition at the Leicester Square Empire.[10]

Cora Crippen, the legend has it, originally aspired to a career in opera. But her voice, angelically pure in comparison with those of her peers, was found wanting in the company of fellow aspirants. Music hall beckoned as lowly compensation, a refuge rather than a goal. Her ultimate tragedy, so the standard version has it, was the discovery of her inadequacy even here. The indefinable something that separates the beloved performer from the jobbing variety has resisted scientific isolation from the first, but presumably authenticity – indefinable, yet impossible to fake – has much to do with it. Audiences know, with an animal instinct that rightly terrifies all performers, when they are being condescended to. Cora Crippen knew her lines and had the moves, but there seems to have been no real connection, nothing of that bond of fellowship that carries over the footlights and into the stalls. Cora seems to have been one of those performers who never came alive on stage. Off stage she made friends easily with her vibrancy, her generosity and her vivacity. On stage she merely *performed*, and music hall audiences, ostensibly the least demanding, were in reality the first to spot the difference.

One of the minor fashions among historians intent on digging in their heels and retaining Crippen the Monster for posterity is an effort to show that Cora was not so disastrous a music hall performer as hitherto claimed (that being no doubt just one more calumny and slur emanating straight from the Demon Doctor's smear campaign). Nonetheless, Cora's professional record to some extent tells its own story: fame simply did not embrace her, for all her efforts to court it, and before long she recognised defeat and gave up the stage entirely, pouring her energies into the social world adjacent to it. *Here* she charmed; on stage, it would seem, she managed only competence. According to actor Scott Alexander, former colleague of Henry Irving and Herbert Beerbohm Tree, 'Belle Elmore was never the variety star she fondly imagined herself. Her act was simply a fill-in among the "wines and spirits" of music hall bills.'[11] Crippen does appear to have been supportive of her aspirations. Alexander recalled: 'We used to call Dr Crippen "the little man who carries the band parts". He was a charming little chap, apparently devoted to his wife, and he went everywhere with her, carrying her music when she appeared in music halls.'[12] In his statement to the police, Crippen seemed to have an instant recall of the details of her various assaults upon theatrical glory (in marked contrast to his inability to remember when his first wife died or his son was born):

> She got an engagement at the Town Hall, Teddington to sing, and then from time to time she got engagements at music halls. She went to the Oxford as a comedienne, and was there about a week. She also went to the Camberwell, and also at a hall at Balham. She also sang at the Empire, Northampton, and various towns. She would probably go away for about two weeks and return for about six weeks, but used to earn very little.

Despite this (or because of it), a number of gallant historians have rallied to her professional defence. A 2013 account claimed that she had appeared on the same bill as George Formby at the Dudley New Empire in 1902,[13] a suggestion apparently deriving from a *Daily Express* article from 1950. But the New Empire in Dudley didn't open until Christmas of 1902 (it had previously been the Dudley Empire) and Formby's bookings in December were at the Circus of Varieties in Rochdale, Gatti's in Charing Cross and the Middlesex and Sheffield Empires. In Rochdale he shared the bill with a Belle Harcourt, but that's as close as it gets. As for our Belle, she was finding work much scarcer than George that month. On 6 December, after a brief engagement in Camberwell (a bullseye for Crippen's account[14]), she put an advert in the theatrical paper *The Era* in forlorn search of bookings that didn't come.[15]

Her pouring of her excess energy into the Music Hall Ladies' Guild, again encouraged and supported by her husband, suggests to me recognition of the fact that the muse had visited but fitfully, if at all.[16] Her opportunistic exploiting of the 1907 Variety Artistes' Federation of England strike, during which many an otherwise unemployable turn was hurriedly conscripted to fill vacant halls, certainly rebounded, and suggests a well-founded desperation:

> Public sympathy was with the striking artist, and very few troubled the box office. The few who did enter the theatre went more for the purpose of 'guying' and to see the fun than to enjoy the show. At this particular music hall, the Euston, one night a sketch appeared, and when the leading lady and the heavy man appeared, the audience, such as it was, commenced to hiss and whistle so unmercifully that neither of them could be heard. They struggled for about five minutes to obtain a hearing, but all to no avail. Finally, the manager and owner of the sketch appeared upon the stage, and in a brief speech appealed to the audience, saying he trusted that their British spirit, fair play, would be strong enough to listen to the lady, even if they would not listen to the man. His appeal failed, and he left the stage amidst more noise than did his leading lady and the villain. Whether this sketch appeared again I do not know, but the villain of the piece was Weldon Atherstone... the leading lady was Belle Elmore, and the manager was Dr Crippen.[17]

The Era outlined as much as we will likely ever know of her performing career in a later obituary:

Miss Belle Elmore, who is supposed to have been the victim in the Crippen murder case, opened her career at the Old Marylebone Music Hall some twelve years or so ago, where she appeared in a small operetta and wore an embroidered gipsy gown. She appeared at the Grand, Clapham, and the Holborn. She also toured in the provinces. She last appeared at the Bedford Music Hall early in 1907, when she sang a song called 'Down Lovers' Walk', and also a coon song. She wore a short spangled dress. She also sang a costume song called 'The Major', and appeared in a musical duologue called 'The Unknown Quantity'. In one of the scenes she had to hold a sheaf of £5 notes. Crippen's desire for realism was so great that he gave her a bundle of genuine bank notes, which she left on stage the first night. Fortunately they were seen by her leading man, Mr Douglas. Others of her songs were 'She Never Went Further Than That' and 'Sister Mary Anne'. In the costume song called 'The Major' she appeared in full military costume.[18]

It is perhaps mildly curious that Crippen – who, despite his milquetoast appearance, was at heart a go-getter who tended to make his own luck – was not inspired to take up entrepreneurial or managerial work in the halls. He already had the entrées, the contacts, the backstage knowledge, along with much eminently importable business savvy from the by no means dissimilar art of drumming up public interest in bogus patent salves and tonics. He would have seen the money to be made, vastly greater than in the shabby world of mail order remedies. The Moss Empires chain, for instance, began with a few halls in Edinburgh, managed by the 25-year-old H.E. Moss in the 1870s. By 1899, not long after Crippen had arrived in London, Moss did likewise, opening Empires at Stratford, Holloway and New Cross. Moss employed eager young men on a mission just like Crippen to handle his growing business: Richard Thornton in Scotland eventually broke away to build up a separate chain in the North East. Managing director Oswald Stoll left to establish his own chain of Empires in 1910, the year of the Crippen tragedy. He died a knight of the realm in 1942.

Was Crippen never tempted to try his luck? We are told that he lost a lucrative position with Munyon's Homeopathic Remedies when 'Professor' Munyon was notified of a brief episode in which Crippen had moonlighted as Cora's theatrical manager. (At this point she was working under the suicidal professional name of Macka Motzki, supposedly at Crippen's own urging. She got her way and became Belle Elmore soon after, with no noticeable effect on her box office lure.) Even his nationality would like as not have worked in his favour. America, with its innate rejection of class distinction, was a kindred enterprise with the overtly democratising music hall; its own variations, vaudeville and burlesque, were equally popular and served the same social function. The States proved a natural source of music hall personalities, and many an American performer came to tour and stayed to reside. Cora, like her friends the Martinettis, should have made good use of this natural advantage, but she seems never to have found the essential reciprocity between audience and performer that, by necessity, preceded admiration and made it possible. In short, Cora Crippen was unfulfilled, and her quiet, undemonstrative husband offered precious little by way of distraction from a reality that had proved uncomfortable and disconsolate. Resentment was inevitably the child they bred, between them, in those cold, gaslit London evenings: Cora's absent ovaries ruled out any happier offspring.

This was not an environment Chief Inspector Dew had any great desire to penetrate. Showfolk were alien beings to him. Born in 1863, one year after Crippen, one of the eleven children of railway worker Walter Dew and his wife Eliza, he had left school without any distinction at 13 (he would later describe himself as 'an absolute dud' as an academic) and joined the police force at 19. There he had risen steadily through the ranks by the only sure means: unending, conscientious hard work. As a relatively minor officer he worked the streets at the time of the Whitechapel murders, and the force's failure to apprehend the killer remained with him like an unhealed wound, ever nagging; an injustice to be avenged.

His account of this period in his autobiography reveals an unbiased, street-level perspective that often works as useful counterbalance to the frequently tainted canonical version. (Dew, for instance, does not at all dismiss the evidence of grape seller Matthew Packer, the vital but ignored witness to the Liz Stride murder: he knows better than the Ripperologists because his boots were on the ground, not in an office.) But given that it is repeated without demur in most of the Ripper books, it is worth noting that his version of his *personal* involvement in the Ripper inquiry is entirely without corroboration anywhere else, and frequently reads as if

✂ DISCOVER MORE ABOUT PEN & SWORD BOOKS

Pen & Sword Books have over 4000 books currently available, our imprints include; Aviation, Naval, Military, Archaeology, Transport, Frontline, Seaforth and the Battleground series, and we cover all periods of history on land, sea and air.

Can we stay in touch? From time to time we'd like to send you our latest catalogues, promotions and special offers by post. If you would prefer not to receive these, please tick this box. ❑

We also think you'd enjoy some of the latest products and offers by post from our trusted partners: companies operating in the clothing, collectables, food & wine, gardening, gadgets & entertainment, health & beauty, household goods, and home interiors categories. If you would like to receive these by post, please tick this box. ❑

Mr/Mrs/Ms..

Address..

Postcode.................... Email address..............................

Website: www.pen-and-sword.co.uk Email: enquiries@pen-and-sword.co.uk
Telephone: 01226 734555   Fax: 01226 734438
Stay in touch: facebook.com/penandswordbooks or follow us on Twitter @penswordbooks

Freepost Plus RTKE-RGRJ-KTTX
Pen & Sword Books Ltd
47 Church Street
BARNSLEY
S70 2AS

Edgar Wallace was helping out with the narrative thread. His description of his own fevered state at the time is certainly worthy of a penny dreadful: 'The hunt became an obsession. I spent long, long hours on duty, only to return home worn out but sleepless. Night after night I tossed about on my bed seeing again and again the terrible sights I had witnessed.' Flash forward to the Crippen enquiry, and *plus ça change, plus c'est la même chose*: 'I was dog tired, yet sleep I could not. My mind refused to rest. The events of the day kept cropping up.'

Then there is his habit of placing himself repeatedly on the scene, often through sheer chance. Depending on his mood, he claimed to have seen some, most or all of the Ripper's victims. He professed to have known one of them, Mary Kelly, personally. He even claimed to have been the first policeman to arrive at the site of Kelly's murder: as he tells it, he just happened to be chatting to Inspector Beck at Commercial Street police station when Thomas Bowyer, who discovered the grisly spectacle, burst in to summon assistance. 'The thing of which I am about to write happened nearly fifty years ago,' Dew writes in his autobiography. 'Yet my mental picture of it remains as shockingly clear as though it were but yesterday.' But Bowyer, a pensioned soldier, late of India, with a heavy moustache and weathered face, is variously described by Dew as a 'youth' and a 'lad'. It is difficult to attribute such a discrepancy to the mental blurring of time: we all forget names and dates, but you don't suddenly remember a middle-aged former soldier as younger than you were, especially when you were only 25 at the time yourself. But Bowyer was employed by Kelly's landlord John McCarthy to collect the rent, and such rent collectors were *usually* young apprentices. In other words, it reads much more like an *error of assumption*, from someone who only read about what happened, than the faulty memory of one who was there.

Most of his recollections of the murders are simply those of the official account, often unchanged even in their wording. Occasionally he is caught out in the repetition of an official error. 'The girl's clothing had *nearly all been cut from her body* in the mad process of mutilation,' he writes of Kelly (my italics), repeating a falsehood in the record that persisted for a century and in some quarters stubbornly endures still, but which should have been obviously untrue to anyone actually in the room. (Kelly was nude.[19]) Strangest of all, he claims to have 'slipped and fallen on the awfulness of that floor'. This extraordinary *Grand Guignol* flourish is recalled by no other source, and must surely be pure invention, especially given the traction of policemen's boots, the roughness of the unpolished wooden floorboards, the size of the room (roughly 12 feet by 10 and cluttered with furniture and other people), and the incredibly measured pace at which anyone would have been moving about in there. Since entry to the room was not even made until some three hours after the discovery, and long after Scotland Yard's Detective Abberline and police surgeon Bagster Phillips had arrived, one has to wonder why the lowly constable who first attended the scene would be admitted at all, let alone allowed to tumble about in the evidence. But whether fantasising here or not, he would have been inevitably reminded of those days when he unearthed a different mass of mangled flesh, instituting still another mass media manhunt, in 1910. And unlike the Ripper investigation, this was a pursuit he was determined would end a triumph and a vindication for the forces of order.

That discovery was still a while away, however, when Dew decided, with no great excitement, to get Crippen's side of the story. With Sergeant Arthur Mitchell, he arrived at Hilldrop Crescent on the morning of 8 July, to be greeted at the door by Valentine Lecocq, a maid Crippen had obtained on a trip to France. They were then received by Ethel, who introduced herself as Crippen's housekeeper. When Dew asked her if she was, in fact, Miss Le Neve, she said yes and became tense and unresponsive. At his insistence she agreed to accompany them to the Yale Tooth Specialists, where Crippen was pretending to be a dental expert. In contrast to the jumpy and cagey Ethel, Dew found Crippen open, expansive, calm, and vastly more forthcoming than would have been expected of a man with something to hide. Over the course of the morning, and taking in an Italian lunch which Crippen devoured as if, Dew noted, he had not a care in the world, Crippen dictated a long statement that has from that day to this been the primary biographical resource on the Crippens and their marriage. Though Crippen seemed not at all unwilling to share the information he gave them, the information itself was in many ways troubling.

Most troubling of all, Crippen freely admitted that the stories he had told Cora's friends were untrue: 'Whatever I have said to other people in regard to her death is absolutely wrong… It is not true that she went away on legal business for me, or to see any relations in America. I did not receive any cables to say that she was ill, and it is not true that she was cremated at San Francisco, and that the ashes were sent to me, or that she sailed from Havre.' He had said those things, he explained, so as to draw a line under their marriage and discourage further attention and questioning, but the truth was very different: 'So far as I know, she did not die, but is still alive.'

He told Dew something of their peripatetic life, he moving from one pseudo-medical business to another, she attempting to become a theatrical personality under the name Belle Elmore. For some time now they had been resident in England, for the past five years at Hilldrop Crescent, living quietly, he keeping office hours and then often socialising with the friends Cora had made at the Music Hall Ladies' Guild in the evenings. What really happened, he claimed, was that she had left him, after the dinner with the Martinettis on 31 January. During the evening, Crippen explained, Paul Martinetti had asked to use the lavatory:

> As he had been to our house several times, I did not take the trouble to go and show him where it was. After they had left my wife blamed me for not taking him to the lavatory, and abused me, and said, 'This is the finish of it. I won't stand it any longer. I shall leave you tomorrow, and you will never hear of me again.' She had said this so often that I did not take much notice of it, but she did say one thing which she had never said before, viz, that I was to arrange to cover up any scandal with our mutual friends and the Guild the best way I could. Before this she had told me frequently that the man she would go to was better able to support her than I was.

He went to work on 1 February, and she had gone when he returned home. From that day he had neither seen her again nor had any word of her whereabouts. 'I questioned him about her clothes and jewellery,' Dew told the inquest, 'and he said that she had taken some with her, and left some behind. She had often said that she did not want anything he had bought for her. He knew she had taken a basket.' He suggested that she may have gone to Chicago to meet a man called Bruce Miller, with whom she had had an affair when he was appearing in London between 1899 and 1904. This affair, Crippen suggested, had begun while he was out of the country and continued after his return. According to Crippen's statement, it was around this time that 'her manner towards me was entirely changed, and she had cultivated a most ungovernable temper, and seemed to think I was not good enough for her, and boasted of the men of good position travelling on the boat who had made a fuss of her, and, indeed, some of these visited her at South Crescent, but I do not know their names. I never saw the man Bruce Miller, but he used to call when I was out, and used to take her out in the evenings.'

'It is quite four years since she ever went out at all to sing,' Crippen dictated, 'and, although we apparently lived very happily together, as a matter of fact there were very frequent occasions when she got into most violent tempers, and often threatened she would leave me, saying she had a man she could go to, and she would end it all.' (The latter presumably meant that she would end their marriage rather than commit suicide, though the phrasing is perhaps ambiguous.) 'I have seen letters from Bruce to her, which ended "with love and kisses to Brown Eyes",' he then added, firmly cementing the link between Miller and the 'man she could go to' which some later writers have tried to blur.[20] 'About four years, ago, in consequence of these frequent outbursts, I discontinued sleeping with her, and have never cohabited with her since,' Crippen then claimed. 'I never interfered with her movements in any way, she went in and out just as she liked, and did what she liked; it was of no interest to me. As I say, she frequently threatened to leave me, and said that if she did she would go right out of my life, and I should never see or hear from her again.'

Crippen frankly admitted he had made no effort to locate Cora, and that he was now living with Ethel: 'Miss Le Neve has been in my employ, and known to me through being employed by the firms I have worked for, for the past eight years, and she is now living with me as my wife at Hilldrop Crescent. I have been intimate with her during the past three years, and have frequently stayed with her at hotels, but was never from home at nights.' He admitted that he had given Ethel some of Cora's furs and jewellery, which Cora had not taken with her. He also gave a brief account of his childhood, his medical training, his first marriage, which had produced a son he no longer saw and ended with his wife's death, then explained how he met and married Cora.[21] Crippen ended by assuring Dew he would take out advertisements to attempt to locate Cora, concluding: 'I will willingly go to my house with you to see if I can find any letter which may throw any light on the matter, and I invite you to look round the house, and do whatever you like in the house.'

It was a strange statement: disarmingly frank, seemingly open, and yet confessing to a long campaign of deception of which, for all Dew knew, it might have been merely the latest example. He then interviewed Ethel, and found her to be in agreement with Crippen on all the salient points, but credulous to a degree that might have indicated contrivance. He decided to take up Crippen's offer to search Hilldrop Crescent straight away.

As Crippen and Ethel busied themselves around the house, Dew and Mitchell were given free access to the entire property and grounds. As he was when giving his statement, Crippen seemed not the least concerned that Dew might turn up anything incriminating. When time came to look in the cellar, there was no noticeable change in Crippen's demeanour, and he and Ethel, who tended to spend most of their time in the basement kitchen and parlour just as Crippen and Cora had, watched placidly as the two men scratched at the ground. Dew observed that the cellar floor was encrusted with dust and did not appear to have been disturbed for years. Dew confirmed Crippen's relaxed state at the trial:

> At our interview I put a number of questions to him and he answered every one of them quite readily. I suggested going with him to the house and to go over it, and he readily agreed.

> *He did not show the smallest reluctance?*

> None at all. I think it would be between six and seven in the evening when we arrived at the Hilldrop Crescent house.[22] Dr Crippen went with me into every room, and he did not attempt to conceal anything. I said that I should like to go into the cellar, and he came with me.

> *No difficulty whatever about it?*

> No.

> *Did he show the smallest trace of worry or anxiety as to going into the cellar with you?*

> He was perfectly cool.

Later Dew would add a foolish embellishment to account for Crippen's relaxed attitude as he poked and prodded inches away from the mass of human flesh beneath the floor. A revolver was subsequently found in the house[23] and Dew would insist it had not been there when he had first looked. In that case, Dew reasoned, Crippen must have had it in his pocket as they searched the cellar, and he had no doubt that had they uncovered his secret there and then, they would not have lived to tell the tale!

Oh dear. Is Dew really expecting us to believe that, in front of Ethel and with Valentine also in the building, Crippen would cold-bloodedly murder a Scotland Yard chief inspector and his sergeant, who would have notified their colleagues of where they were going, and who would be missed within hours? Yes, it would appear he is, and, shamefully, there have been no shortage of earnest historians willing to take him at his word in the years that followed.

Satisfied that they had seen all that they needed to see and doubtless concluding that they had strayed into some sordid, bed-hopping intrigue of a sort only too commonplace among Bohemian theatre folk, Dew and Mitchell said their goodbyes and left. But, he would later claim when he tidied the events up for public consumption, for some reason Dew couldn't get the case out of his mind. He couldn't rest by day; he lost sleep at night: it was the Ripper all over again. He allowed his doubts to torture him over the weekend, but he returned to the Yale Tooth offices on Monday, 11 July. There, Crippen's partner Dr Rylance told him that he had come into work to find a note from Crippen, saying that he needed to absent himself for some time. In Crippen's office he found his and Le Neve's discarded clothes. At the inquest, Crippen's assistant William Long was cross-examined by the Coroner as to what had gone on there. The information he gave became one of the most defining elements of the whole case. On Saturday, 9 July, he told the court, Crippen had asked him to go to a shop in Tottenham Court Road to buy a suit of clothes for a boy:

You said you would?

Yes.

He gave you a list of the clothes?

Yes.

You got all the clothes there?

Yes. The suit, shirt, and other things, tie, collar, and hat.

You bought a pair of black shoes also?

Yes, I took them back (to Crippen) and went upstairs, and afterwards he came to the work room and I placed the clothes there. I found the suit Mr. Crippen was wearing on Friday in the forceps cupboard on Monday.[24]

Long added that he had then received a letter from Crippen, asking his assistance in winding up his household affairs. He authorised a payment of £12 10s due to the landlord for the last quarter's rent, and asked if Long could take care of Crippen's maid Valentine, who would need to obtain passage back to France. But it was the boy's clothes that would make the headlines. With a sinking feeling, Dew had rushed to Hilldrop Crescent, but it was too late. Valentine ushered them into an empty house. The birds had flown, and unless some extraordinary attempt at misdirection had been made, Ethel was now disguised as a boy.[25]

It is at this moment that Crippen's guilt was sealed, both for the police and prosecution at the time, and for most commentators thereafter. It is, they all tell us, the most obvious sign of guilt imaginable, and a sheer-sided mountain to be overcome by anyone who dares to argue their innocence. But imagine, for the sake of argument, that he *was* innocent. Imagine he had told Dew the truth: Cora had run away, he had no idea where she was and no reason to think she was not alive. In order to put an end to constant interrogation, he had lied to everyone he knew, telling them she was dead. He had moved his lover into their house. They had set themselves up as man and wife. Ethel had told her family and friends that they had been married at a registry office. Over five months had quietly passed. Now, suddenly, a Scotland Yard inspector had appeared. People had been complaining; his story was not believed; the clear and obvious implication being that foul play had occurred.[26] The inspector has as good as ordered him to find out where Cora has gone. Ethel has learned that he had been lying about Cora's death, too: instead of living with a widower, she has been living with a married man. Crippen fears that if Cora is found, his new life with Ethel will be over. And if she is not found, he will be under permanent suspicion, and may no longer be able to leave as he had already intended and begun arranging, while a potentially interminable investigation unfolds, the finger of suspicion pointing at him the whole time, his relationship with Ethel paraded in the press and assumed to be the obvious motive for getting rid of Cora... Why would they *not* flee? What is even *slightly* hard to understand about it? *Ah*, you say, entirely unmoved by my emotive arm-twisting, *but why in disguise?* Perhaps because the police would be looking for an older man and a young woman, and would not be looking for a man and his son? Or is that too rational an answer?

Before leaving on the 11th, Dew and Mitchell had another search in the house and dug over the gardens. Nothing was found. 'That sinister cellar', as Dew was later to describe it, the one that 'seemed to draw me to it', was again very casually examined, and remained unsuspicious. On 12 July they were back again. They again tried the cellar, with its 'loose board near the door' that 'each time it was stepped upon seemed to creak out *stop, stop*' ... and again they stopped, stopped without thinking to lift the bricks. On the 13th they came *again*: Dew would later attribute his return to a spot he had already examined three times and found nothing to 'my sixth sense'.

That famous police photograph, taken from the position of the back door, looking down the corridor towards the open cellar door, is one of the most iconic in all of crime. It hardly looks real; it is as if a set dresser has styled it for some TV or movie recreation. All is in place: the eerie gaslight fitting, the dingy staircase leading down, the heavy, beaded drapery hanging over the cellar entrance. There is a large ornamental plate on the wall, a servants' bell over one of the doorframes.[27] It seems a place expressly designed for mysteries, to be visited but occasionally, and always in half-light... and in that regard the photograph is actually somewhat deceptive. The Crippens did most of their living and even socialising down here. The unseen rooms, roughly where the photographer is standing, are the kitchen and breakfast room where the Crippens and the Martinettis spent their fateful last night together. (Sir Melville Macnaghten, Assistant Commissioner of the CID, marvelled at how 'good digestion could have waited upon appetite' thereafter, with Crippen aware of how close he was to festering remains. It's a good question and well worth asking, given that he had access to an entire three-floor house. I can see no good answer, only an obvious one.) The back door, behind the camera, opens onto the garden, the front door being a level up (the underside of the front door steps are visible in the coal cellar), and when opened for access the back door must have flooded the visible space with light and fresh air. What to us seems so baleful, ominous, pregnant with menace, was in reality an everyday living space, unexceptional, a mirror of every other house in the street and of thousands more in London. The 'Crippen touch' has made something out of almost nothing again.

And actually, there is a much more prosaic reason why investigative minds would have immediately fixated on the cellar, rather than, say, the bathroom or the back yard. Cellars had long been established as the place where dead bodies were most likely to be found. Dark, cool, hidden away, visited only briefly and occasionally, rarely disturbed – they offered the perfect hiding place for the evidence of domestic murder. Corpses were forever turning up in them. (Search 'body found in cellar' in any newspaper archive and you will return literally hundreds of discrete hits.) In fact, another one was found in a cellar at Eagle Street, Holborn, on 19 September 1910, *during* the Crippen inquest.[28] Now, if Crippen had been living *there* rather than in Hilldrop Crescent, we'd be saying *the exact same things* as we do about the Hilldrop remains: *bit of a coincidence, isn't it? He must have had something to do with it…* But of course, had he been living in Eagle Street, Holborn, he would have had nothing to do with it at all. Had there been any doubt in the police's mind as to the age of the Hilldrop Crescent remains, it would have been the easiest suggestion in the world to believe that they were the work of some unknown murderer, at some unknown stage in the house's history. This is why the front line of the Crippen offensive was fought over the decomposition-rate evidence, and the secondary finds from the same location.

The real mystery is why it took Dew so long to actually *dig* there, and his and Mitchell's repeated visits on consecutive days, during which they turned up nothing much, have understandably troubled later conspiracy theorists. Why it took Dew until this visit to consider that the remains might be under the floor of a room he had already searched three times has to remain uncertain. So, too, does any exact account of just how the eventual find was made. According to the official version in Dew's autobiography *I Caught Crippen*, and in the evidence he gave at the trial, the dogged inspector and his sixth sense dug at the ground of the cellar with a poker until one of the bricks yielded to his probing. He levered it out with the poker and then, finding its neighbours similarly loose, tore at the floor until a space big enough for digging was revealed. 'I knew that I was on the eve of a great discovery,' he later wrote. It's one of those classic accounts, akin to Howard Carter's telling of the opening of Tutankhamen's tomb, and it probably owes just as much to later, journalistic spring-cleaning. In one interview at the time of the discovery, sufficiently well detailed to suggest authenticity, he tells a somewhat different story:

> I saw nothing amiss when I first went through the house, and though I searched each room carefully twice, with the same result, I was not satisfied. I thought it would be well to go back and test the walls with an iron bar. So I went back the fourth time, and at first found nothing amiss.
>
> The cellar walls all seemed sound, but striking about with the iron bar I struck a loose brick, and out it fell. Instantly I began to tear away the loose bricks, and underneath I found a mass of human flesh, eaten away with lime. Not a bone was found, and I believe the murderer, with his medical skill, separated them from the flesh and threw them into a canal not far from the house.[29]

Here we see the debuts of some key notions: first that Crippen has surgical skill (he did not), and second that he may have dropped the missing portions of the body in the Regent Canal (in other words, that the fact that most of the body was not to be found anywhere in the house or grounds needed urgently to be accounted for). On the other hand, there is the soon-to-vanish detail that the flesh was 'eaten away with lime': this will do a full reverse-turn and become the assertion that the remains are in excellent condition and may even have been aided in their preservation by the lime. But the most arresting touch here is that uncanonical image of a faintly unhinged Dew walloping the cellar interior with an iron bar, to be swapped for posterity with the much more appropriately Sherlockian one of him testing the floor with a poker, his sixth sense throbbing away.

And there was no question that it was Dew himself doing the poking in his later accounts. But author David James Smith uncovered Sergeant Mitchell's own statement of events from that day, preserved in a box of case papers at the National Archive. 'We dug parts of the garden and then with a small poker probed parts of the floor and basement,' Mitchell affirmed. 'We then went into the coal cellar, and on probing the brick floor, which was covered with coal dust, *I dug the poker between two of the bricks in the centre of the floor. I loosened and removed them,* and Chief Inspector Dew then dug the floor up, and uncovered some pieces of human remains as described.'[30] (Italics mine.) Yet by the time he came to give a further statement the following day he had doubtless been straightened out, because suddenly he was merely 'present', with all glory going to Dew. Poor old Mitchell! To be written out of history by an ambitious superior was probably the sort of thing that happened to ordinary coppers all the time. But this time it's Dew's turn to be caught out doing it.

No matter. Be it by bar or poker, wielded by Dew or Mitchell or both, the pair soon found themselves confronted with a nauseating mess of skin and offal, shallowly buried in the London clay, its exposure filling the small space with air so foul, they recalled, that they were sent gasping to the street, and fortified themselves with brandy before resuming the work.

And so the morning papers all carried excited news of the find, and police handbills appealed for information on Crippen and Le Neve, who were, it proclaimed: WANTED – FOR MURDER AND MUTILATION. This was the moment when the Crippen cult began – and also when it began to lose touch with reality. As Cecil Mercer noted in his autobiographical novel *As Berry and I Were Saying* (written under his *nom de plume* Dornford Yates): 'Who it was that drafted that bill, I never knew: but I need hardly say that the crime of mutilation is quite unknown to the law.'

Chapter 2

The 'Doctor'

Cross-examination of Dr J.H. Burroughs –

Would you describe him as a kind-hearted, well-mannered man?

He always appeared exceedingly kind-hearted and courteous towards his wife.

Cross-examination of Clara Martinetti –

Did you form the opinion from what you saw of him and heard him say and the way he acted that he was a kind-hearted man apparently?

Yes.

Cross-examination of Louise Smythson –

Would you agree that Dr Crippen seemed always a good-tempered, kind-hearted man?

Yes, he always seemed so.

Cross-examination of Emily Jackson –

Do you agree that he was a good-tempered and kind-hearted man?

He always gave me that impression.

Cross-examination of Marion L. Curnow –

Have you always formed the opinion that he was a kind-hearted and amiable man?

Oh, yes.

Cross-examination of William Long –

You, like the other witnesses, remember that he was a kind-hearted and amiable man as far as you could see from his outward manner?

I have always found him so.

Cross-examination of Adeline Harrison –

Do you agree with the other witnesses who spoke to the same effect, that Dr Crippen was always very amiable with his wife?

Very kind, very amiable, and a very good husband.

Hawley Harvey Crippen was, in the words of an article published immediately after his conviction, 'a psychological riddle'. For a case that was (or at least seemed) open and shut, the guilt of the accused established with such insulting ease, why was there so much lingering mystery about the central figure? As the article noted, the crime was one 'which was mysterious, perhaps, in some of its aspects, but not hedged round by half as much mystery as the character of the man who has been convicted of committing it'.

> No more extraordinary man has ever stood in the dock within living memory. Certainly no man in our time ever fought for his life against such tremendous odds with less display of nerve or emotion. His sang froid simply astounded everybody. Nothing seemed able to shake it… He made the most damning admissions in a tone of voice and with gestures for all the world as though he was admitting some slight indiscretion committed in the days of his youth… The terrible impeachment by Mr Muir in his final address for the Crown failed entirely to shake the inflexible composure of the man, and he remained absolutely unmoved throughout the pathetic and eloquent appeal of his own counsel, which moved many in the court to tears…[1]

Could this man, whom literally every single prosecution witness of his acquaintance recalled as warm-hearted and amiable, really be the man that the prosecution somehow convinced the jury he must be: a man who killed his wife, chopped her into oozing scraps and spread her around London? And if not, then what?

Is it too predictable to start at the beginning? We shall risk it. This is a story that needs all the stability it can get. But trying to find Crippen before he was Crippen is not so easy. Any British researcher who dares to think that all they need do is put 'Crippen' into a search engine, very soon makes the same dispiriting discovery. That surname – sounding to us so unusual, so redolent *a priori*, somehow, of the sinister form of fame it now betokens (author Andrew Rose has noted its 'evocations of "ripper", "criminal" and "creepy"'[2]) – is anything but exotic in America. At the end of the nineteenth century and the turn of the twentieth, myriad unrelated and irrelevant members of the species crowd the printed record, obscuring our man's trail, leading us in all directions; the exercise of sorting these Crippens from those Crippens and those Crippens from the Crippens over there evoking images of very small needles and very large haystacks. Even today the name is unexceptional, and across America can be found attached to numerous upstanding men and women in business, local government and law enforcement. Not least, of course, there is Bob Crippen, celebrated astronaut and winner of the Congressional Space Medal of Honor. Nothing sinister about him!

Our Crippens were celebrated and upstanding too, at first. They are from Coldwater, Michigan. Pioneer stock. Grandfather Philo Crippen (whom Crippen would dubiously immortalise when he fled the police under the name John Philo Robinson) was born in a log cabin in 1809, and had built up a successful business from nothing when Coldwater was just a small turning on a dirt road. His son Myron had inherited his successful dry goods store and moved into the most imposing house in town by the time he and his bride, the former Andresse Skinner, welcomed their son Hawley Harvey into the world in 1862. In these innocent years the name 'Dr Crippen' meant Bradley Crippen, Coldwater's much-admired general practitioner. A Civil War veteran, he will die at the age of 73 in 1909, spared by a year the ordeal of seeing both his name and his calling simultaneously disgraced by his headstrong relative.

Biographers have painted the Crippen household as one where prosperity mixed with austerity, a careful, precise environment, solid, and humourless, and characterised by that veneration for the virtues of discipline and honest toil so typically to be found in the homes of the self-made. For those born into its rewards, by contrast, such cautious asceticism can be baffling, and rebellion almost the default mode of acclimatisation. Hawley Harvey Crippen was born into that exact third-generation dichotomy; a roof, a bed and a hot meal never to be doubted, and with far greater reward and more conspicuous pleasure within easy reach. Every Sunday the family would be found in the front pew of the local chapel, and according to Tom Cullen, the biblical instruction would then continue when they returned home, with either Myron or grandfather Philo supplementing the day's lesson with additional Old Testament readings.[3] For Hawley, one suspects, this was always just a waiting game.

Were there any secrets lurking behind the carefully maintained Grandma Moses exterior, any hint of the kind of entanglements that would become indelibly associated with the name thanks to the adult Hawley? Just a tiny suggestion might be sensed in a report that appeared in the California Daily Alta of 12 February 1885. Described by the paper as 'an event of considerable interest to pioneers of Michigan', it concerned the wedding of two local citizens: both of them no fewer than 75 years of age – and both bearing the surname Crippen. The groom was Philo H. Crippen, Hawley's God-fearing grandfather, whose first wife Sophia had died less than a year earlier, in March of 1884. The bride was Ruth Crippen, widow of Philo's brother, Lorenzo D. Crippen, owner of the local saw and grist mill and former Coldwater Village President. A hero of the sinking of the steamer *Atlantic* on Lake Erie in 1854, when he saved two female passengers by breaking into their staterooms as they filled with water, Lorenzo had been carried off in the famously cold New Year of 1864, when it was said the mercury stood at 32 degrees below zero. Had love only blossomed between his widow and his brother in the few months between Philo's bereavement and their subsequent wedding, or had there been extra-marital flirtations, of a sort that would reappear so famously in the family history two generations later, for some time longer? Impossible to say at this distance, and certainly it would be flagrantly irresponsible to suggest the possibility of any helping hand hurrying Sophia or Lorenzo Crippen out of the way... but at least we can be sure the Crippen line was not entirely straight and narrow prior to the arrival of Hawley Harvey. Philo and Ruth would go on to enjoy five years of legal association, dying within two months of each other in early 1890. 'They have been residents of Coldwater for fifty years,' noted the *Alta* at the time of their wedding, adding that despite their advanced years, 'both are youthful in appearance and very fond of society'. If there *had* been anything improper going on behind the lace curtains, young Hawley, 22 at the time of the wedding, newly qualified and just starting out in business for himself, would surely have been aware of it.

After Crippen's arrest, his lugubrious father supplied some melancholy nuggets of biography to the American press:

> This trouble overtaking my boy and me in my old age seems like a dream, an unreality, and I, who cared for him when he was young; who watched him grow from a boy to a man, brilliant in his profession and honoured, cannot believe that even the thought of such a crime could ever enter his mind. When but a child he showed an unusual mind, a disposition to overcome all obstacles, to attain every object he sought. He was always fond of music and though but a child he clamoured for a violin. We thought him too young to care for one and learn to play it, whereupon he set to work and made one out of a wooden box and was soon playing snatches of several popular tunes on the instrument of his own manufacture.
>
> When still in the public schools he fixed his mind on taking up the profession of medicine, and at his first opportunity entered a doctor's office in San Jose, from where he went to Ann Arbor, Michigan. While attending school there he became acquainted with a Dr Phil Porter of Detroit, and studied in his office for a period. Afterward he attended the Cleveland university and graduated with the highest honours.[4]

Let us not be too impressed by those qualifications, by the way. The most persistent myth in the whole Crippen saga is that its protagonist has the right to be considered some sort of doctor. It was and remains useful, even vital, to the prosecution case that this charade be maintained, but the stubborn facts of the matter point in an entirely different direction. In most of the news reports at the time of the discovery and pursuit he is described as 'an American dentist', but the 'Yale Tooth Specialists'[5] was only the latest of many commercial enterprises in which he had feigned medical expertise. Prior to this he had set up his stall as an eye and ear specialist, sold useless preparations by mail order, and worked for Munyon's Homeopathic Remedies, famed for their revolutionary Pile Ointment (soft paraffin), Catarrh Cure (sugar) and Asthma Cure (sugar and alcohol). Munyon's also offered an intriguingly named 'blood cure'. One wonders how many people needed to be cured of blood, but it's likely no harm was done since it was, once again, sugar. A typical 1896 advertisement told how Munyon's 'wonderful little pellets' could be relied upon to cure just about every disease on the books:

Stop Killing Yourself with Dangerous Doses of Poisonous Drugs—Get Munyon's Guide to Health and Cure Yourself With a 25-Cent Remedy! Positive and Permanent Cures for Catarrh, Rheumatism, Dyspepsia, Liver and Kidney Troubles and All Special Blood and Nervous Diseases.

Munyon's Rheumatism Cure never fail to relieve in from one to three hours, and cures in a few days. Price 25c.

Munyon's Dyspepsia Cure positively cures all forms of indigestion and stomach trouble. Price 25c.

Munyon's Cold Cure prevents pneumonia and breaks up a cold in a few hours. Price 25c.

Munyon's Cough Cure stops coughs, night sweats, allays soreness and speedily heals the lungs. Price 25c.

Munyon's Kidney Cure speedily cures pains in the back, loins or groins and all forms of kidney disease. Price 25c.

Munyon's Nerve Cure stops nervousness and builds up the system. 25c.

Munyon's Catarrh Remedies never fail. The Catarrh Cure (price 25c) eradicates the disease from the system, and the Catarrh Tablets (price 25c) cleanse and heal the parts.

Munyon's Asthma Cure and Herbs relieve asthma in three minutes and cure in five days. Price, 50c each.

Munyon's Headache Cure stops headache in three minutes. Price 25c.

Munyon's Pile Ointment positively cures all forms of piles. Price 25c.

Munyon's Blood Cure eradicates all impurities of the blood. Price 25c.

Munyon's Vitalizer restores lost powers to weak men. Price, $1. A separate cure for each disease. At all druggists, 25 cents a bottle.[6]

Other ads, such as an 1895 one that claimed 'careful investigation by the press' had confirmed that '997 people had been cured in one week' by his remedies, relied on compelling testimonials:

Relieved After Ten Years of Torture.

Professor James M. Munyon— Dear Sir:

While residing in Australia several years ago I contracted muscular rheumatism in its most painful form, and although I consumed enough medicine to have destroyed the stomach of an ordinary mortal, I received little or no relief until Tuesday last. It was then that I decided to use the contents of one of your sample bottles, which my son obtained at the *Chronicle* office. I am free to admit that the result astonished me. For several days prior to this I had been unable to use my arms, and the right one in particular; but in less than forty-eight hours I experienced relief to such an extent that I actually made myself useful around my place of business. In addition to the disappearance of all pain in my arms, I found that the pellets had acted beneficially on my kidneys, which had been causing me considerable annoyance. I intend continuing the use of the rheumatic cure.

SALMON MATHEWS, Proprietor of the
Fair Furniture Company, 859 Mission Street.[7]

And by uncanny coincidence, all of the other patients keen to share Munyon's glory with the world were also business owners who just happened to mention the name of their business and where to find it, just like Salmon!

There was big money to be made from this rubbish. As well as his numerous sub-managed mail order outlets, Munyon maintained a huge store on Broadway and 26th Street, New York. Among his properties was 'Munyon Island', in the middle of Lake Worth: 1 mile long and maintained by a staff of forty, on which he built a hotel for the comfort of his richest patients and what was described as the most magnificent mansion in the State of Florida for himself, and around which he would cruise in his private steam launch.[8] Compare this lifestyle to that of Crippen, grubbing around, making up his idiot preparations and trudging off to the post office to mail the packets, and it will be seen just how long this particular food chain was, the scenery at the top where the dolphins played all but unrecognisable to those at the bottom, where the sprats and minnows toiled.

It can be tempting to soft-pedal on the subject of quack medicine, to play it as disreputable but colourful and basically harmless evidence of the American entrepreneurial spirit. Over the decades it has acquired its own patina of romantic, period gloss, charged with imagery of the travelling medicine shows that are so much of a piece with the American pioneer experience, and with which the Crippens of Coldwater would have surely been familiar. But there is a hard truth underlying all the myth-making: the trade was in the exploitation of the vulnerable, the exploiters knew what they were doing, and the cost in human misery was not small. By definition it attracted calculating and callous individuals, the sort of men who, like Orson Welles's Harry Lime, viewed humans as 'dots' for the counting. ('Would you really feel any pity if one of those dots stopped moving forever?' he asks in the film *The Third Man*. 'If I offered you twenty thousand pounds for every dot that stopped, would you really, old man, tell me to keep my money, or would you calculate how many dots you could afford to spare?') Neither may the victims be glibly written off as only gullible adults who should know better, as a somewhat chilling 1895 Munyon's advert reminds us: 'If you are confronted with such evidence as this, and insist upon galloping to the grave by doctoring the old way, have mercy on the little ones who are too young to know right from wrong. Cure them with Munyon's harmless remedies and let them grow up with good healthy constitutions, free from drug poisoning.'[9]

It says nothing good about Crippen at all that he was willing to cajole and defraud the ill, the disabled and the despairing into wasting money on what he knew full well were useless remedies. I am tempted to go so far as to say it is evidence for the prosecution, a sign (mindful though we should be of the truth that the past is a foreign country where they do things differently) of distinctly sociopathic priorities. One wag wrote that Cora Crippen's penchant for tying pink ribbons to the corners of her picture frames was in itself sufficient grounds for murder, and for the reduction of the crime to justifiable homicide. Well, if that's to be the game, I shall counter that Crippen's seemingly untroubled and long-standing commitment to the one industry, other than spiritualism, most dedicated to separating the desperate from their necessary funds is cause for execution.

Most notorious of all Crippen's dubious associations was with the Drouet Insititute, which robbed the deaf and hard of hearing by selling them useless bits of sticking plaster to put behind their ears. Despite the classy sounding name, it was the brainchild of conman J.H. Nicholson, who persuaded an alcoholic French doctor to lend his name to the enterprise to give it a veneer of class. The institute was exposed by a crusading editor named Evan Yellon, himself deaf, who published a magazine for the hard of hearing called *The Albion Review*. Yellon visited the Institute's London offices in the early 1900s and was attended by an uncharacteristically flamboyant Crippen: 'His frock-coat was orthodox enough; but he wore with it a shirt of startling hue, adorning the front of which was a "diamond" as big as a marble; and the jaunty butterfly tie vied in hue with the shirt.' According to Yellon, Crippen evinced complete confidence that Drouet's remedies would be his salvation, after an inept five-minute consultation during which he probed Yellon's ears with 'a filthy spatula'. Yellon wrote of his experiences in a book entitled *Surdus In Search of His Hearing*: in an addenda to the 1910 edition he wrote:

> Just as this book was going to press the police discovered that a ghastly murder had apparently been committed at 39, Hilldrop Crescent, London, N.W., the private residence of 'Dr' Crippen... from what I saw of him he appeared to me about the last man I should expect to be guilty of any great crime. He simply belongs to the tribe of rat-men – the petty swindlers of afflicted people, and the first care of this tribe is to keep their own persons out of danger. Crippen had dissolute rogue written all over his face when I met him, but he did not seem to be the type of man to figure in a crime of passion. Still, no man can accurately forecast the trend of any one human character.

J.H. Nicholson was imprisoned in 1902, and the Institute was disbanded in disgrace after negative publicity it received in 1909, when a locksmith was found to have died as a result of a serious ear abscess exacerbated by the corn plasters the Institute was prescribing. Crippen calmly acquired their assets and continued in business as 'The Aural Remedies Company'.

He had his own remedies, too, including an ear ointment for deafness called 'ohrsorb' – Crippen would find himself pathetically explaining the name, a combination of the German word for 'ear' and a contraction of 'absorb', in court – and 'Amorette', his famous nerve tonic. At the time of his disaster he was working on something new, called 'Sans Peine', in which he had sufficient faith to instruct Ethel to obtain the recipe and go into business with herself. (It says something for his ingenuousness that he thought there might ever be a future market for a medical preparation invented by Dr Crippen.) Many years later, a certain 'C. Sawden', one of his former mail order patients, recalled the kind of treatments he was dispensing: 'At that time I was a Customs House Clerk in the Long Room at Durban, Natal, South Africa. I sought his treatment for progressive deafness and he mailed me a broad adjustable headband with pressure pads fitting over the ears. There was also a bottle of solution for moistening the pads. When clamped over the ears, normal hearing appeared to be restored, but some hours later defective hearing returned. The doctor's arrest put an end to further treatment.'[10]

Understandably, the London *Times*, *Telegraph* and *Daily Mirror* made a habit of referring to him as 'Dr' Crippen, in recognition of the essentially specious nature of *all* his professional claims. That such medical qualification as he did possess would have been insufficient for him to legally present himself as a doctor in Britain is well known: it is worth adding that it barely justified the title in America either, and had anything even resembling the level of checks and standards required today been in place then it never would have. Even by the painfully inadequate standards of his day he was on thin professional ice, and the Medical and Surgical Register of the United States quietly drops him from their records as early as 1900, long before his name became immortal for all the wrong reasons.[11] It is sometimes suggested that he began as a genuine doctor but was tempted or coerced into pursuing quackery instead, to the detriment of his reputation but the benefit of his bank balance. While this is unquestionably his professional path from 1894 onwards, to all intents and purposes he was a quack from the first: the 1882 medical degree on which his use of the prefix Doctor was founded was in *homeopathy*, then, as now, a pure pseudo-science, and certainly not one that qualifies the holder to practise legitimately as dentist, oculist, deafness curer or anything else Crippen claimed to be that requires actual medical expertise. Yet his prosecution would sink so low as to open by telling the jury he 'had a very good degree'. Perhaps they didn't quite know what homeopathy was, though they would be made privy to some of its absurdity in the course of the proceedings.[12] No doubt he took a keen interest in medicine, as he did in many things, and no doubt he really did attend lectures on mental disorders at London's famous Bedlam (where he first saw hyoscine being used as a sedative). He is at all times a dilettante, however, and always a quack, and the key point to remember, as we find our hero happily spreading the disease of alternative medicine, is that an interest in the real thing, running alongside all the hucksterism, may not be alchemised, however keen it may be, into actual medical competence. *That's* homeopathic thinking, right there! Nothing but genuine training and genuine experience can bestow surgical prowess on even the keenest amateur, which is the only reason I can think of why the prosecution at his trial did not begin by savaging his pretentions to be anything other than a layman, the better to paint him as innately fraudulent, especially given the court's careful and correct use of the prefix 'Mister' when addressing him.

They had certainly pulled no punches in 1898, when Crippen had appeared as a witness at the County of London Sessions concerning a colleague who had stolen money from Munyon's Homeopathic Remedies. 'You call him "Doctor",' the judge said, referring to Crippen's description of his colleague. 'What are his qualifications?' Crippen admitted he did not know. 'You are called a doctor,' added the prosecution. 'You are not qualified?' 'I don't pretend to be,' Crippen replied.

You advertise 24 remedies. Aren't they all the same?

No.

Can you tell me any other ingredients than sugar and water in these cures?

I don't think I need answer that question.[13]

Flash forward to Crippen's own trial, and he suddenly has to defend his *in*experience, in the face of what might be felt to be some pretty telling evidence of innocence. Dr Pepper had this to say about the dissection of the remains: 'It has been done by a person skilled in removing viscera… There is no cut or tear in any part except where it was necessary for the removal. It was removed all in one piece.' Bernard Spilsbury was asked if the work had to have been done by a person with considerable anatomical knowledge: 'Certainly someone having considerable anatomical knowledge… one who has done a considerable amount of evisceration.' Crippen, who is not known to have so much as gutted a fish, must have listened to this evidence with a happy heart. Yet somehow the prosecution convinced the jury that his complete absence of anatomical knowledge and surgical competence was evidence of anatomical knowledge and surgical competence. It was essential to their case that Mr Crippen be *perceived* as a doctor, and so a doctor he was, and a doctor he has remained.

But a keen awareness of the bogus nature of Crippen's medical gifts is a good place to start in any consideration of the man, because it points to one of the most paradoxical features of him: that here is an individual who, even before he figures in the most dramatic murder mystery of his age, has lived a life of much incident, in two continents, one who moves on the fringes of a worldwide trade in patent remedies and, separately and simultaneously, of London's theatrical and music hall society, who has a gaudy wife and a compliant mistress, and yet remained to all who recalled him the quintessential suburban nobody. These multiple Crippens suggest a peculiarly advanced ability to compartmentalise his life into discrete and never overlapping parcels: the bland professional, the flamboyant con-man, the academic, the partygoer, the milquetoast, the despised husband, the hero-worshipped lover. Crippen had an enviable ability to be exactly the man he needed to be as circumstances and company demanded: a talent that would eventually baffle his accusers, and sow seeds of doubt in the minds of many as to his true nature. His performance in the witness box, his calmness and implacability in the face of what appeared to be the most damning demolition of his innocence imaginable, impressed all who saw it. If it *was* grandfather Philo's example that helped him to show one face to the world and an entirely different one in private, it was a lesson well learned.

The earliest mark made on history by Hawley Harvey Crippen that I have been able to find was a small announcement in the press on 17 September 1882, informing readers that 'Hawley H. Crippen, graduate of class from High School of 1881, has returned to his native state to enter upon a course of medicine at the Ann Arbor University of Michigan. He has been studying with Dr. E.S. Breyfogle for a year past.'[14] The association with Breyfogle shows that Crippen was starting as he meant to go on. Edwin Solomon Breyfogle was born in Ohio in 1854 and graduated with honours from the Hahnemann Medical College of Philadelphia in March of 1875.

The college was founded in 1848 and named after Samuel Hahnemann, the founder of homeopathy. Breyfogle soon made a name for himself in the field (as did his brother: William Lermantine Breyfogle, president of the Homeopathic Kentucky State Medical Society and the Indiana Homeopathic Medical Institute) and must surely have been the influence that set Crippen towards homeopathy as the best outlet for his medical curiosity. (Breyfogle died at the age of 57 in March 1912, of pernicious anaemia, for which homeopathy is of absolutely no earthly use.[15]) This is important, because prosecution-minded historians like to imagine a transition between Crippen the serious practitioner and Crippen the quack, where none really exists. Nicholas Connell, for instance, claims that 'from early respectability he was drawn to homeopathy, but he soon slipped into the murky world of quackery'.[16] But the truth is that there was no early respectability, and no subsequent slip: homeopathy *is* quackery, and he was a homeopathic quack from the very first.

Over the next ten or so years Crippen would drift from one fly-by-night enterprise to another, impressing all he met with a fastidiousness and hardworking dedication quite at odds with the absurdity of the enterprises upon which he was engaged. All sensed that this was a man who was going somewhere. Along the way he also picked up a wife, Charlotte Bell (for some reason referred to in several later news reports as 'Susan Ball Crippen'), about whom frustratingly little is known other than that she was Irish and seems to have met Crippen while working as a nurse. They appear to have married around 1887, and had a son, Hawley Otto, in August of 1889. Charlotte died, reportedly of 'apoplexy and paralysis',[17] claimed in some reports as a complication of the birth of a second child that did not survive, at the end of January 1892. Crippen and Cora married the following September: a whirlwind courtship, especially for a man one might expect to be preoccupied for at least some of that time with grief. In those robust times, such speedy reattachments were not unusual, and indeed, we already have grandfather Philo's precedent (at the age of 75, what's more!). Nonetheless, given Crippen's future behaviour it is surely worth entertaining the suspicion that Hawley and Cora may have met and fallen for each other while Charlotte was still alive.

Understandably, in the aftermath of the discovery at Hilldrop Crescent, questions began to be raised about the death of the first Mrs Crippen. In fact, a major revelation seems to be brewing in a series of reports that went round the world in mid-July, shortly after news of the fugitives and their flight became public. But for some reason the matter was just as swiftly dropped, to be left dangling, unresolved ever after. It may be that it deserves a second look. Here is the most detailed account:

W.R. Bell, of Winfield, a brother of Charlotte Jane Bell Crippen, first wife of Dr Hawley Harvey Crippen, who is wanted in London for the murder of his second wife, Belle Elmore, says that his sister was also slain.

The first Mrs Crippen died nineteen years ago in Salt Lake City, Utah, under mysterious circumstances. In her last letter to her brother she told of her fear of death at the hands of her husband. Dr Crippen left Salt Lake soon after his wife's death and there was no investigation.

Inquiry by the police into the death of the first Mrs Crippen... shows that Mrs Crippen had a premonition that she was to be killed.

Her brother, W.R. Bell, today told this story:

'My sister, Charlotte, studied to be a professional nurse, and about twenty-five years ago – I think 1885 was the exact date – was graduated from the old Hahnemann Hospital, then at Sixty-Second Street and Ninth Avenue. While she was in training there, a young doctor named Hawley Harvey Crippen was an intern, and they fell in love with each other.

'Soon after Charlotte's graduation they were married. I don't know where or by whom, but I know they started housekeeping in Sixty-Second Street, near Third Avenue, and later went to a house somewhere near the armory at Sixty-Second Street and Columbus Avenue. There Crippen set himself up as a dentist, but he got in some kind of trouble and they moved to Thirtieth Street, near Lexington Avenue.

'Again the authorities got after him and this time he moved – this was about 1890 – to some town in California. I didn't hear from my sister much previous to this time, but I know that they moved once more from California to Salt Lake City.

'Here the mystery begins. Charlotte wrote to me that her husband was taking advantage of his medical and surgical knowledge and was compelling her – because of certain ordinary and to-be-expected circumstances – to undergo operations by the knife. She had undergone, she said, two dangerous cuttings. Her husband, she wrote, was then playing the part of optician as well as dentist, although he was really neither. Meanwhile, I should say, they had a son, born in the first year of their marriage.

'I was furious when I got these letters,' Mr Bell went on, 'and it was in my mind to go West and kill this man who was maltreating my sister. But I restrained myself. Then came the worst letter of all. Charlotte wrote something to this effect:

'"My husband is about to force me to the knife again, and I feel that this will be the last time. I want my relatives to know that if I die it will be his fault."

'She did die under the third operation, and I went to Salt Lake. But when I got there Dr Crippen had vanished, taking with him his boy. I never heard of him from that day until this week, when I learned that his second wife had been slain.

'I sent the letter of Charlotte Jane to my brother, De H. Bell, who lives in Dublin, Ireland, soon after her death, and he probably still has it.'

Cable dispatches from abroad proved this to be true. One message announced that De H. Bell and the Irish police had started an inquiry into the death of Charlotte Jane Bell.

A telegraph message from Salt Lake City also declares that the police there had begun to look into the record of Dr Crippen and his first wife.

According to Mr Bell, Dr Crippen appeared in Dublin a couple of years after his first wife's death – about 1892 – and demanded from her mother, who was still living in Dublin, certain small valuables the wife had left. He was refused these, and the next thing the Bell family heard of him was that he had married, about that same time, Belle Elmore, an actress – whose body has now been dug up.

'I could pick Dr Crippen out of 100 men or 1,000 men,' declared Mr Bell vigorously, 'and I hope he comes to this country and is caught, so I may have the opportunity of doing so.'

A sister – Mrs Daniel Leary of 225 West One Hundred and Twentieth Street – was also found by a reporter, but she did not care to say anything about the slain woman or Dr Crippen, beyond admitting that she knew the doctor well and could identify him. She, too, according to Mr Bell, knew of the fear that the first Mrs Crippen had died through her husband's insistence upon alleged unnecessary operations.[18]

Where do we start here? First, we have to keep in mind that this all came to nothing whatsoever, and in record time at that, so it's fair to assume that no police department found remotely as much to chew on as did the *Brooklyn Daily Star*. Further, alarms should at least gently tinkle at the spectacle of Mr Bell paraphrasing letters that are said to definitely exist, albeit in the possession of someone else, but which seem never to have entered the official record. The combination of these two things would, ordinarily, prompt us to convert this into a paper aeroplane and aim it at the desperation file without a second glance.

And yet… there is something bizarrely compelling about it. In part it's the avalanche of convincing circumstantial detail, the refreshing cynicism as to Crippen's professional attainment, and the intriguing portrait of him going from job to job, always somewhat under a cloud, such as would be his working pattern throughout his life. Intriguing, too, that Bell implies Crippen and Charlotte went off and married without the family's knowledge, and that they only had their word for its having happened at all. Crippen and Cora would do exactly the same thing.[19] And as we know, Ethel told *her* family that she was Mrs Crippen too, married at St Pancras Registry Office – that one, at least, we are told with confidence was sheer fantasy. So now I'm wondering: was Crippen genuinely married to *any* of his wives? Or, alternatively, was he married to them all *including* Ethel, albeit bigamously? (That would certainly help engine their flight when Crippen was forced to confess to Dew that he had invented the stories of Cora's death.) At the very least, this habit of always marrying clandestinely suggests a degree of deviousness, a recognition that he would not be seen as the ideal husband. No question: this is an article that can suck us into deep whirlpools of speculation – and we haven't even mentioned those operations yet.

'Forced operations' – what does that even mean? The euphemistic talk of 'certain ordinary and to-be-expected circumstances' sounds like abortion, but then 'meanwhile they had a son' confuses things mightily.

What it sounds as though Crippen is urging her to have is exactly the operation that Cora is said to have had in the early days of their marriage: removal of the ovaries and/or uterus to make pregnancy impossible. If he *was* enjoining Charlotte to have operations that would prevent her having further children, the tectonic plates of the Crippen legend shift considerably. That he was saddened by his inability to have children with Cora, and his keenness to do so with Ethel, are firm planks in the story, but his callous abandonment of Otto to the care of his own parents immediately after Charlotte's death suggests anything but warm paternal feelings.[20] If the opposite of what we think we know is true, and that Crippen resented Otto (as would certainly be suggested by his later treatment of him) and was trying to ensure such an encumbrance was not repeated, then all sorts of uneasy suggestions present themselves. Might Charlotte have died as a result of just such an operation rather than natural causes, as her brother here suggests? Might Cora have undergone hers at Crippen's own urging at the start of their marriage – or even earlier? One further oddity is that, according to an anonymous letter from 1910 held in the police files on the murder, it was at the Hahnemann Medical College, where Crippen had likely shadowed Dr Breyfogle, and where Charlotte's brother claims that she had graduated, that Cora underwent her operation. Did Crippen ask a friend to perform the procedure both times? And the timeline is all shot, too – who can say when Cora entered the picture in this version of the story? In these days was Charlotte the Cora, and Cora the Ethel?

Might he have insisted Cora had her ovaries removed because, as a Catholic, she would not allow him to use birth control? As a Dublin girl, it's a reasonable possibility Charlotte was Catholic too.

Might Cora's tragic inability to have children, supposedly lamented by them both ever after, have really been her tragedy alone, and his convenience? Might *that* have been the source of her slow simmering resentment of him, a contempt that gnawed and ate at their relationship as the years dragged on, that turned to fury when he began locking his bedroom door anyway, and dared look elsewhere? Was it even standard practice to have this operation performed other than for reasons of medical necessity? Might Crippen have needed to ask a favour of a surgeon he knew, for Charlotte and then again for Cora? Several of the newspaper accounts of the scar on the cellar remains speak specifically of Cora having had 'an illegal operation'.

Later, Ethel will also become pregnant with Crippen's child, and this pregnancy ends in miscarriage in September of 1908. (By this time, Crippen has converted to Catholicism too.) This is vouched for by Ethel's landlady, Mrs Jackson, who told the police that she called a doctor, who asked Ethel what had become of her baby, to which Ethel replied that she had gone to the lavatory and felt it pass. Mrs Jackson, like the doctor, only had Ethel's word for this: it is entirely possible that Ethel had in fact had an abortion, or even that her miscarriage had been induced without her knowledge by Crippen. Given the perfect nature of Ethel and Crippen's love for each other, according to the official version, it is surely relevant indeed that after this experience she began going out with another man, a chemist's assistant called John Stonehouse, also lodging with Mrs Jackson. Had this been a straightforward miscarriage, this sudden redirection of her affections would be very surprising indeed. There is also the small but definite possibility that Ethel became pregnant a second time.[21] In March of 1909 she left Mrs Jackson's, supposedly to stay with her aunt in Brighton, returning again in September. Then, also in September, her sister Nina and her husband registered their second child, a daughter called Ida Ethel. It is to be expected for an aunt to be fond of her niece; nonetheless, there is a hint that Ethel's fondness for her namesake, of whom she was made godmother, was especially strong. After Ethel was found not guilty at her trial for assisting Crippen, Nina brought Ida to see her: 'I had her god-daughter, my little girl, in my arms, and Ethel was overjoyed to see the child, for whom she has a great affection. She took the child in her arms, and kissed it passionately.'[22] Was this Ethel's own child, born during her seven incognito months?[23]

The popular image of Crippen is not of a man who would shrink from the chance to raise a child with Ethel. But it is hard to imagine how he expected to manage fatherhood and his vastly increased responsibilities towards Ethel in his then situation. Even when we can be sure she was pregnant, prior to her miscarriage, he was presumably aware that things would have had to have changed and very decisively, yet he never gives the impression of a man getting ready for the major changes that being the father of a family brings. It is radical to imagine him insisting she abort her child, maybe even forcing her to give away a second one, though given his previous attitude to fatherhood we could darkly suspect him of having a hand in the outcome. A reference to it in one of his letters is ambiguous: 'I would have wished our little one had lived that you might have had what would have been part of both of us.' It might, at a push, be interpreted as Crippen now regretting a selfish earlier decision, but it sounds straightforwardly sincere. Still, the death certainly let him off the hook, and allowed him to continue coasting along, and he must have felt the relief of that. It is feasible that he could have used it as an excuse to tell Ethel she needed to have the operation to ensure it never happened again. If he had urged the same operation on his first two wives, why not on Ethel? Except by now he is in England, with no sympathetic friends willing to perform a risky, non-essential surgery… We will return to this, and speculate further, later on. For now, even if we conclude that this is all much ado about nothing, just a coincidence, and giving us no real grounds for suspicion, we are still left with a coincidence that is worth noting: this strange repetition in Crippen's love life of surprise marriages with no prior announcement, followed by unsuccessful pregnancies, and by vaguely defined operations undergone alongside them.

Chapter 3

The Pursuit

A statement made yesterday by Scotland Yard was in the following terms:

> 'It is believed that "Dr" Crippen and Miss Le Neve are now on board a vessel bound for Canada. Chief Detective-Inspector Dew has left Liverpool for Canada, and hopes to overtake the fugitives and arrest them on arrival.'

Beyond this the authorities declined to go. We are, however, able to give the full facts of this remarkable discovery and pursuit, of the authenticity of which there is no question.

Daily Telegraph (London), 25 July 1910

The news of Inspector Dew's find in the basement of number 39, Hilldrop Crescent did not break – it exploded. And not just in London: from the first it seized the headlines in America, Australia too, and Europe would not be slow to follow. Here was one of those once-in-a-generation cases where all one needed to do was to simply state the facts; and the result was a readymade penny dreadful, and with its climax irresistibly unwritten:

> The discovery on Wednesday evening of a terrible crime enacted at 39, Hilldrop Crescent, Camden Town, created a sensation throughout the district. The body of a woman was found buried beneath the flagstones in the coal-cellar...
>
> Digging operations were commenced in the garden, but the arduous efforts of the officers were not rewarded. Attention was then turned to the house. The removal of some flagstones in the coal cellar, which is beneath the front door steps, revealed a ghastly spectacle. There were found the mutilated remains of the unfortunate victim, the body having been cut up, and large pieces of flesh were lying about in various directions.

The sight, to quote the words of one of the excavators, was absolutely sickening, and enough to knock over the strongest of men.[1]

The power of the press had the predictable effect, and by 17 July, what is being described as a 'morbid throng' – comprising 'thousands of Londoners'[2] – had descended on the crime scene in the hope of being first to learn of some new discovery, or at the very least of seeing a few bits of the previous one being taken out in a bag. What was in fact taken out, shielded from the prying eyes of idling ghouls, was a large, unidentifiable mass of flesh and skin, from which all expected means of identification had been studiously removed: no head, no limbs, no genitals and no bones. Just the trunk of an unknown person, and despite the confidence of reports such as the above that the body was a woman's, in truth, the sex, let alone the identity, looked set to be beyond discovery.

London, July 14 – The nude and battered body of a woman, believed to be that of the American vaudeville actress Belle Elmore, was found in the cellar of the house occupied by Dr Hawley Harvey Crippen and herself at Hilldrop Crescent by the authorities yesterday. As a result, the New York police have been requested to keep a sharp lookout on all inbound steamers for Dr Crippen, who is charged with the murder of his wife.[3]

The 'battered body' of Belle Elmore is a constant refrain in the early reports of the discovery. Why the remains should be so consistently described as 'battered' is something of a puzzle, given that they were not, and that there was no particular reason to think they might be, and when any journalist worth his salt would have known that 'dismembered' or 'mutilated' were much more sensational, and therefore lucrative, adjectives. But 'battered' they remained for some time, at least until their generally unbattered nature became relevant to the police's case against Crippen. Then, not long after they stop being battered, they become 'burned' for a while (presumably by the quicklime rather than by flame),[4] before that too vanishes into the ether, to be replaced by the next useful certainty.[5]

Battered, burned, both or neither, the newspapers of two continents were now abuzz with them. Every literate soul on three continents knew the basic facts, the names of the protagonists, and the fact that the suspects were still at large somewhere – maybe in their very own city, village or town. The world kept one eye open for Crippen, the American dentist, and for Ethel Le Neve, her name frequently misspelled in those early days, and often described as French, seemingly in confusion (exacerbated by her Gallicised surname) with Valentine Lecocq, the French maid who had first answered the door to Inspector Dew.

Valentine leaves the story very shortly after this, to be entirely forgotten by most who have written on the case, at least until the files were reopened and more recent writers found a wealth of new material to draw upon. One might have expected the police to have been exceptionally eager to talk to Valentine, and in some detail, given that she was the only person they could at that point lay their hands on who had actually been in the house for any significant period of time *after* 31 January. And yet she doesn't appear to have interested them much at all. Some money was scraped together to enable her to get back to France and back she went, later giving a press interview but never, it would seem, a police one. At the inquest on Monday, 29 August, Dew explains that she was a young girl of 17 with no friends in England, so she was sent back to France the next day![6] Perhaps they were short of translators at the Yard: her English was said to be less than rudimentary. Or perhaps it was assumed that a mere housemaid, and a foreign one at that, would have little of material value to contribute. If that was indeed the reasoning, I can't help thinking that a considerable mistake was made – and we will have cause to return to her later. Here is the interview she gave on returning to Paris; it is clear her testimony would have been well worth hearing. As well as a vital witness to the private life of Crippen and Ethel, she was the only witness to their activities and state of mind immediately after Dew's departure, and the following day. She also recalled being in the coal cellar with Crippen:

One day Dr Crippen came down to help me to chop some wood. During all the time, he was with me his face did not change, and he was very pleasant and kind to me, as he and Madame always were… It was a nice house, with beautiful furniture, and Monsieur and Madam were always happy and laughing together. I did the house work and Madame did the cooking.

Nothing happened till the day before they disappeared. On that morning, Monsieur Crippen had gone as usual to his office, and Madame was dressing to go out when the detectives called. She was so upset, but she hurried her dressing to come down to see them. Then she went out with them. All returned in the evening about 5 o'clock — Monsieur and Madame and the two detectives. They talked for two hours and then the detectives looked through the house and went away, leaving Madame very much upset. She was very pale, and told me she felt ill. She went to her room, and Monsieur Crippen went after her, and they talked, ever so long. Next morning Madame came down, more pale than ever, and her eyes were red, and she started and said, 'Oh, oh!' at the milkman's knock. She must have been crying a great deal in the night. But the doctor was just as cool and calm as he always was, only he went out without speaking to me. And then, Madame, who seemed in very great fear, got all her jewels—she had beautiful jewels, and wore a lot of them always, and she had such splendid dresses, too many for one wife, I used to think—and she came down dressed to go out in her blue costume and round turban hat, trimmed with roses. She was so nervous, and in such a hurry, and only carried her handbag, but just before she went out she came into the kitchen and gave me five shillings for my week's wages, and a letter for her little brother, who was coming that day, and who came later on. At half-past seven I heard the postman and ran to the door. It was a letter for me from Dr Crippen, written on his office notepaper, half in French and half in English. 'Don't be afraid,' was written in French, and then in English, 'We shall not be back tonight, going to theatre.' I never saw Monsieur or Madame again.[7]

One other soon-to-be-scrubbed-away detail appeared in some reports on 14 July: 'The police today brought in two coffins, and it is believed by this circumstance that a second body has been found.' This obvious inference occurred to the journalists right there at the scene, and they immediately queried it. 'The undertaker says the two coffins brought to the house were to facilitate the handling of the mutilated and decomposed corpse.'[8] Nobody likes to be put on the spot, but you can surely do better than that, Mr Undertaker! The question you were asked was not why were you bringing coffins at all, it was *why did you bring two of them*? One senses a degree of sheepishness here from the first. And sure enough, the two coffins disappear from official accounts even quicker than Valentine Lecocq. In his evidence at the trial, undertaker Albert Leveton says that what he arrived with was 'a shell and a coffin', and that the remains were put in the shell. Fair enough: a shell is a reusable coffin-shaped container that undertakers commonly used to collect bodies from the place of death and transport them back to the funeral parlour. (These days they have been superseded by collapsible stretchers.) But, why the coffin, then? Even allowing for the negligible difference between the two, nobody I consulted could explain why the undertaker would bring a shell *and* a coffin. Pedantry as to terms aside, clearly (if not literally) two coffins *were* brought to the site. And we still don't know why.

Some of the early Cora myths also debut in this report, and it is one of the smaller mysteries where they came from, unless the papers had already been round to the Music Hall Ladies' Guild. They sound like the claims of some phony press release, dating from the time of Cora's original assault on the halls:

> Mrs Crippen was born in Philadelphia, and was the daughter of a Polish nobleman who fled from Russian persecution in Poland. She first sang in London and instantly became popular, having a most wonderful range of voice. Returning to America she married Crippen. Having discovered she was entitled to a Polish estate, both sailed for Poland, not returning to America. They lived until recently in an expensive London establishment, and were apparently rich.[9]

'It is declared the head was crushed with blows, and the corpse hacked with a knife,' suggests the same report, scoring a full off-the-board miss with both guesses. Caution is needed here, though: to dismiss the press as generally unreliable on the strength of such oddities is to throw a very important baby out with some largely irrelevant bathwater. As a rule, the British press did not invent out of whole cloth, push sensational versions of events that it knew to be fallacious, or set out to mislead or exaggerate. It prized what reputation it possessed for reliability, not least because each paper was in competition with the others: sensation may sell in the short term but readers would soon tire of any organ that consistently steered them in the wrong direction, and exposure of shady tactics was still enough to ruin a publication. (Observe, as illustration, the fate of the London *Evening News* when it was caught out publishing a fake Crippen confession, discussed in Chapter 5.) By and large, the reports on the emerging case against Crippen *are* reliable, even if many of them show a clearly *evolving* case, with more than its share of detour, reversal and regrouping. But it is, I think, undeniable that they are generally saying *what the police want them to say*, particularly during the Coroner's hearings. It adds up to a kind of discreet collaboration, with the popular media very deliberately used as a covert means of dissemination by the authorities. The reports are often not fully to be trusted in themselves, but that is their value. Where they are inaccurate they are revealingly so, in ways that march in step with the investigation, reading much more like fellow travelling than catching up from behind. To some degree this was a fact freely acknowledged, even loudly hailed, as the *Daily Mail* made clear:

> Yesterday, Scotland Yard made a new departure of a most interesting character in their method of crime investigation. The authorities for the first time in their history took the press into their confidence…[10]

Inspector Dew's love-hate relationship with the popular press was interesting, and in some respects pioneering. Disenchantment with the police force was fairly widely voiced by the turn of the twentieth century, and reflected in popular literature, where the plodding and unimaginative official investigator – immortalised as Conan Doyle's 'sallow, rat-faced' Inspector Lestrade – frequently served as contrast to the insight and resourcefulness of private or amateur detectives. Above all it was the police's summary failure to catch Jack the Ripper in 1888 that gave voice, familiarity and respectability to this hitherto sublimated, inchoate resentment. On 17 January 1888, a new newspaper, *The Star*, had hit the streets of London. It represented a radical change in attitude from most other newspapers of its time, which were generally mindful of the status quo. This was a crusading organ, edited by an Irish nationalist politician, T.P. O'Connor. That the press might have a role to play in the promotion of social justice was a Victorian innovation – the so-called 'New Journalism': essentially the old sensationalism with a new-found conscience – which first found voice in W.T. Stead's shocking (and shockingly impassioned) exposés of child prostitution in the *Pall Mall Gazette* in 1885. According to more reactionary opinion this was a distortion of the fundamental purpose of newspapers, which was supposedly to print fact without taint of slant or fervour. O'Connor's *Star* turned this dictum on its head: now newsworthiness was in large measure defined by social relevance. The Ripper murders, therefore, were not merely another crime spree that incidentally cast a uniquely clear light on a hitherto ignored scandal, that of the hellish conditions in which the working poor were forced to live at the heart of the most prosperous city in the world: they were the agency, the engine, by which the exposure of that scandal could be made public. Of course, this crusading purpose would not long endure if it did not sell newspapers, thus sensational murders came to serve as both validation and insurance. But there was a snag: the police tended to consider the press to be about as welcome at a crime scene investigation as a swarm of horseflies. 'One thing is absolutely certain,' the *Star* fumed in a blistering editorial published on 10 September 1888, 'and that is that murderers will always escape with the ease that now characterises their escape in London until the police authorities adopt a different attitude towards the Press. They treat the reporters of the newspapers, who are simply news-gatherers for the great mass of the people, with a snobbery that would be beneath contempt were it not senseless to an almost criminal degree.'

Dew, at this time a detective constable, longed to catch the Ripper and certainly recognised the force of the *Star*'s argument. In keeping the newsmen at arm's length, he later reflected, the police had 'deliberately flouted a great potential ally, and indeed might have turned that ally into an enemy'. That line in the *Star* about 'the ease that now characterises (murderers') escape in London' was a rebuke he carried with him from then on, like a photograph in his wallet, and he was determined to disprove it now he was in charge. More than usually, therefore, as we see new ideas appear in otherwise repeated accounts, only to vanish and be replaced by others in turn, we can feel entitled to hypothesise that they are being fed to the papers by the police themselves, discreetly shaping the terms of the enquiry to those that best fit the blueprints of the case they are building. It would also allow them to exercise a measure of control in a case that was spiralling in the other direction: no more twin coffins from here on. For all of these reasons, Dew's olive branch to the yellow press was an essential evil. To the *Daily Mail* it was merely common sense:

> Unfortunately, the formalities necessary have prevented the foreign police from being instantly notified and put on the alert. Astonishing as it may seem, the Paris Criminal Investigation Department yesterday had not been notified that Dr Crippen and Miss Le Neve were wanted. The notice has to go first to the Foreign Office,

whence it is transmitted to the British Embassy in Paris, when again it is communicated to the French government, and by them it is forwarded to the French police. This elaborate process gives the offender every chance.[11]

The message is obvious: if the creaking wheels of bureaucratic diplomacy turn too slowly, for the sake of justice the *Daily Mail* et al will have to take charge. But in opening up these new lines of communication Dew may not have expected quite how much truly useless information would flood in as a consequence. Almost overnight, Crippen was everywhere, and everybody seemed to have seen him. A man and a woman were arrested in Wales on the grounds that they looked a bit like Crippen and Le Neve: they were taken into custody and then released.[12] A café keeper in Belgium served a couple with strong English accents, 'and one of them apparently was a woman dressed as a man. They left for Brussels in a tram car.'[13] In Chicago police arrested 29-year-old Albert C. Rickward, searched him and examined his luggage, 'despite the difference of nearly 20 years in the ages of Rickward and Dr Crippen'. Rickward was said to be 'greatly incensed at his detention'.[14] A hairdresser in Liverpool got in touch with Scotland Yard to say that he had just shaved the moustache off a man who looked a bit like Crippen.[15] Still another lookalike was in New Jersey, shooting himself in a park:

> On notification from the police of Trenton, New Jersey, a New York headquarters detective was despatched to Trenton today to examine the body of an unknown man who shot himself in that city yesterday in a baseball park. The man resembled Dr Crippen in many particulars, being about the doctor's age and stature and wearing a short moustache which appeared to have been recently trimmed.[16]

The fact that Scotland Yard had offered a £250 reward for the fugitives caused its own share of problems too:

> Samuel Woolgar, thirty-one, labourer of Renda Road, Custom House, was charged with being disorderly.
>
> A constable said that the prisoner stopped a man in the street and said, 'You are Dr Crippen, and I want that £250.' He caught him by the arm and threw him to the ground...
>
> As he left the dock, the prisoner said, 'You won't catch me looking for Dr Crippen any more, then.'[17]

Elsewhere there were reports that Crippen was at large disguised as a vicar,[18] while in Paris, 'police believe that Crippen is masquerading as a woman, and the descriptions sent out include this probable disguise'.[19]

Most tantalising were the reports from the police in Vernet-les-Bains, France, who were said to be 'satisfied that a strange man calling himself Henri Talbot... who subsequently took a hurried departure for Spain was none other than Crippen'.[20] This Spanish trail was generally considered the warmest, and Scotland Yard issued 'thousands of descriptive pamphlets in English and French offering a reward for the apprehension of Crippen'.[21] On 21 July, a man answering Crippen's description was seen at Puigcerdà, a Spanish border town.[22] Or was he altogether more cunning? 'The suspect, according to the belief of the authorities here, instead of making for Spain, is headed for Andorra, the little and almost forgotten republic of shepherd inhabitants nestling in the foothills of the Pyrenees. Once in this country, it is said extradition will be difficult if not impossible.'[23] However, a M. Vignier, 'prefect of police of the department of Pyrenees (Orientals)', expressed his confidence that such was not the case, under one of my favourite headlines: 'Crippen Not Among Shepherds'.[24]

While many feared for the safety of Le Neve – will she be the fiend's next victim? – elsewhere, reports were coming in that she may have taken her own life. From France came word that 'a young woman who committed suicide at Bourges on the 13th inst. is believed to be Ethel Le Neve. The deceased is declared to have some striking points of resemblance to Crippen's typist.'[25] Associated Press on 22 July considered the matter as good as settled: 'The woman was a foreigner and gave the name of Jeanne Maze. The police of Paris and London have been notified.' Others were not convinced, however, including M. Sebille, head of the research department of the police, who pointed out that the woman's suicide note was written in French, on the face of it an unusual touch for a woman from Norfolk. 'Furthermore the suicide's features were those of a person of a Slavonic type and Sebille believes she was a Nihilist.'[26]

Dew had another good reason for staying in the good books of the press: doubts were beginning to be raised as to his handling of the case. Within a week of the find the grumblings had even reached Parliament:

> Mr W. THORNE (West Ham, S., Lab.) asked the Secretary of State for the Home Department whether he could state who was responsible for allowing Dr Crippen to get out of the hands of

the police when it was known by the Chief of Police at Scotland Yard that Dr Crippen had made several false statements about the murdered woman which cast suspicion upon the woman's husband that he was responsible for the crime; whether he was aware that the Chief of Police on June 30 began his investigation on the strength of information given by Mrs Crippen's friends, whether he was aware that during the investigation the police kept no close watch upon Dr Crippen, and it was in consequence of the pressing enquiries that caused Dr Crippen to vanish; and that it was not until July 13 that a search of his house was made, which gave Dr Crippen three days to get away before the police acted, which showed that the Chief of Police had Dr Crippen under his observation for nine days and then allowed him to get away; and whether he intended taking any action on the matter.

Mr MASTERMAN – If the hon. Member will repeat his question later the Secretary of State will endeavour to answer it. It is very undesirable to discuss at the present time details of the important enquiry on which the police are currently engaged.

Mr W. THORNE – Can the hon. Member suggest when I ought to put the question down again?

Mr MASTERMAN – I can only suggest that the hon. Member should watch the course of public events.

Mr W. THORNE – Or wait until he is captured. (Laughter)[27]

'The police… explain that they were powerless to detain him prior to the discovery of the corpse in the cellar,' the *Daily Telegraph* helped out.[28] Dew was still smarting from this when he came to pen his memoirs in 1938. 'Certain people with no knowledge of police procedure and less of the law blamed me for allowing Crippen to go,' he wrote. 'Ridiculous!'[29]

By now, detailed reports were being filed on the state of the remains, and those on the preliminary findings of Dr Pepper's autopsy immediately introduce the certainty that 'a skilled hand must have been at work in their mutilation',[30] an idea that was both gift and burden to prosecution and defence alike. 'According to Dr Pepper, whoever dissected the limbs must have had a full knowledge of anatomy.' There was no reason to presume

Crippen fit this bill, as indeed he did not, though thanks to the combined efforts of the Coroner and the press few would be willing to believe that once time came for the trial. He was a doctor, right?

For the police, as big a problem as the identity of the corpse was the fact that there was no actual evidence of homicide. Nothing on the remains gave any indication of how their owner died: it might as easily have been a cadaver from a dissection room, or even a robbed grave, as a murder victim. The dissection and dismemberment were clearly inflicted post-mortem. Unsurprisingly, grounds for supposing the victim died by violence become a priority in the reports. Somewhat inevitably, a neighbour 'whose garden looks on to the back of Hilldrop Crescent' had, on a reassuringly uncertain date in the vicinity of when Cora Crippen had disappeared, 'heard screams at midnight'.[31] The Associated Press picked up the trail: 'A woman shopkeeper today told the police that some time ago – possibly four or five months – she had heard, apparently in the Crippen home, the screams of a woman following a revolver shot':

London, July 15 – The first story of what may have been the actual commission of the crime was told today by a neighbour of Dr Hawley H. Crippen... the proprietress of a small shop at the rear of the Crippen residence told of hearing a woman's screams and pleas for mercy, coming seemingly from the cellar in which the burned and mutilated corpse was later found. Mrs Crippen disappeared in February last. It was five months ago when the screams were heard, the woman said. Her shop overlooks a little garden back of the Crippen home. To the police the shop keeper said: 'I had often heard revolver practice in the garden. One night about four or five months ago I was awakened by a woman's cries. It was midnight. The screams appeared to come from Dr Crippen's house. I listened and heard a woman's voice pleading: "Don't! Oh, don't!" To me it seemed that the cries were from a woman in the basement of the house occupied by Dr and Mrs Crippen. As nothing developed further I soon forgot the occurrence and did not recall it until yesterday when I learned of the tragic discovery.'[32]

You might think that nobody would have given this desperate concoction the time of day, but that would be to overlook the power of expedience. Never mind that this one witness alone heard these screams, nor that she confidently places them at least an hour and a half earlier than they could possibly have happened. And as for where that certain timing of the screams at midnight came from, perhaps the Associated Press report of the day before can give us a hint: 'The Crippens, it is now stated, entertained a few friends on the evening of January 31, and they left at midnight.'[33] Now *there's* a surprise. The paper says they left at midnight, so that's when the screams were heard. Only problem here is that the paper was wrong: they left at 1:30. It reminds us that we need to be on our guard when prowling secondary sources. If so admirable a candidate for oblivion as this tissue of nonsense is allowed to endure, simply because it meets the needs of certain pre-formed opinions, it makes us rightly wonder what else might have been retained on equally spurious grounds – *and* what might have been just as spuriously rejected.

There were two other reports like this, still to this day respectfully cited by willing stooges to consensus, both every bit as worthless. A neighbour, Frederick Evans, just arriving home from a night in the pub, heard a long screech which he thought had come from the street: he went out to see if anything was amiss but could find nothing. But he had checked his watch and was certain it was around 1.20 – a shade too early for it to be Cora even if it had been the correct day, which it wasn't. Evans was sure it had been a Friday – the only night of the week that he went to the pub – so it could not have been 31 January. Then there was Mrs Lena Lyons and her lodger, Mrs May Pole (!), who lived in a property overlooking the back gardens of Hilldrop Crescent. On a date they pinned as from around the end of January to the beginning of February (promising!) they heard two gunshots. Unfortunately, they too were certain of the time: somewhere between 6.30 and 7 in the morning. So this would mean Crippen kept Cora alive all through the night, and then shot her just as he was setting off for work.

Once the word got around that gunshots and cries had been heard emanating from the basement (though they patently hadn't), a new detail appears as if by magic in the updates: 'The victim's body was buried in quicklime and the presence of a revolver in the cellar suggests that she was shot before being cut up.'[34]

Though the police appear to be satisfied that it was Crippen's wife who found a grave in the cellar of his home, so far as known the identity of the victim has not been known to the satisfaction of the law. After death the body was cut to pieces and some of the bones were removed as if by a hand skilled in surgery and the flesh covered with quicklime that destroyed the possibility of easy recognition.

The police consider significant the story of the shop woman who told of hearing the reports from revolver practice in the Crippen garden on different occasions, and later of being aroused during the night by a woman's scream. A revolver was found near by where the body was interred.[35]

But while the dismal lie of 'the revolver near the remains' does not last long, the story of the screams in the night is allowed to persist, simply because it is useful. We even have authors writing books in the twenty-first century still giving it credence! (And as we have seen, Inspector Dew will himself contribute his own daft revolver story later on.) More convincingly: 'The police are digging in the garden for the head and legs of the murdered woman, which were not with the rest of the remains.'[36] No doubt they were, and for some time, too. It must have been with extreme reluctance that they resigned themselves to the fact that no further graves were to be found anywhere at the site, and instead turned their attentions to coming up with convincing explanations of why and how that could possibly be.

The press reports and the official forensic findings are of course not the same thing, but the former, with their relatively high rate of hits and general absence of outright fantasies, are clearly drawing on something more than guesswork. The worst that can be said for most of them is that they seem to be party to a Chinese whispers effect, as if the story is being mediated through a chain of sources before emerging as hot ink. And we clearly see certain priorities and conclusions forming, some of them hardening into orthodoxy, others being shunted aside and replaced by others. We can be forgiven for sensing, in all this, an official account that is itself evolving, and not unreasonably being informed *by* the findings of the criminal investigation on the ground as much as it is the informant *of* them. The most important assertion of all, needless to say, and the one for which corroboration is endlessly being suggested, refined, rejected or passed into conviction, is that the flesh belonged to Cora Crippen. In the light of all that, this Associated Press report certainly intrigues, and even while being rightly confused by it, I nonetheless ask you to keep it in mind:

A three hours' post mortem examination of the body by an expert of the Home Office today proved conclusive as to the cause of death of the woman. Her head, the lower limbs and most of the bones are missing, but there are more indications, such as portions of clothing and a necklace adhering to the flesh of the neck, that the woman might have been strangled in her sleep. The internal organs will be subjected to further analysis.[37]

Crippen's purchase of hyoscine has not yet been discovered, and so neither has the hyoscine in the body. Instead we have an entirely different and soon-to-vanish-utterly cause of death, supported by details of circumstantial evidence that are never heard of again. Now, as noted, what corruption there is in the official case against Crippen is rarely if ever expressed in outright lies. It is far more subtle than that, some of it even unconscious, perhaps; an affair of nuance and emphasis. Far more than invention its weapon is *selection*, choosing what to prioritise and what to brush to one side. But what is most important, and what the press so wholeheartedly collaborated in, is the *establishment of the narrative*. This is why the Coroner's court hearings are so important, for it is there, far more than in the investigation that precedes it or the trial that follows, that the narrative gets to be laid down, *before* it need be rigorously tested. It is a dry run, but it is also a process of acclimatisation, familiarity and acquiescence. If I were really cynical I might suggest that such is its essential function.[38] And in the Crippen hearings we can clearly see the narrative in liquid form, filling its prepared space, being picked clean of the odd impurity, emptied of a spoonful here, refilled with a new spoonful there, and then left to solidify. Once hardened you have not the *tabula rasa* required by impartial justice come trial day so much as a thickly encrusted slab, congealed black and viscous with myth, short cut and assumption. Why, then, do the strangulation and the necklace vanish from the record? I will suggest a possible reason in the final chapter. In the meantime, the following chronological history will give some idea of the shifting narrative, helped along all the way by unseen hands, and quiet words in useful ears.

16 July – *Impossible to identify*

Professor Pepper,[39] of the Home Office, has made an examination of the murdered woman's remains and declares that it will be impossible to identify the body.[40]

If he did indeed say this, you can just hear the wincing at the Yard!

17 July – *Hard to identify*

Just what the detectives have developed in their investigation has not yet been learned, as the Scotland Yard authorities, chagrined at having permitted Dr Crippen to escape, are keeping very quiet on the result of their findings. They realise it will not be easy to prove that the dismembered body found buried in the cellar of the residence is that of Belle Elmore until the inquest is held.[41]

18 July – *Necklace and skilled surgery*

Professor Pepper, who made an autopsy of the remains on behalf of the Home Office, found that the head and limbs had been carefully removed; also every bone from that portion of the body discovered in the cellar. A portion of a woman's undervest and a necklet remained. Whoever dissected the limbs had a full knowledge of anatomy.[42]

Note that the necklace, noted earlier as reported on 16 July, is still hanging on, but the suggestion of strangulation has been dropped. The woman's undervest appears, and will become canonical, but is not yet joined by the pyjamas or hair curlers. The gun in the cellar, also appearing on 16 July, has also now been dropped.

19 July – *Other body parts needed*

At the inquest yesterday the physicians who examined the dismembered body testified that none of the bones had been found and that their analysis showed that the flesh had been skilfully carved from the skeleton. It has been deemed of great importance to discover the missing members, including the head, hands and feet, in order to complete the body and thus establish legally the case of murder.[43]

No doubt at this point they entertained high hopes that additional remains would be found. It was only when that hope faded that their being essential to the establishment of a case against Crippen is forgotten, and the rest of the helpful secondary evidence starts to appear.

19 July – Inquest – *Impossible to determine sex*

The coroner's inquest began today... The testimony today proved of small service in establishing the identity, as the mass of flesh was so mutilated as to make it impossible even for the experts to fix the sex of the victim... Dr Thomas Marshall, one of the surgeons who performed the post mortem, testified he had not been able to find a trace of the bones and could not swear, on anatomical grounds, if the flesh was that of a man or a woman.[44]

Impossible to determine the sex? No, no, no! I think you mean...

23 July – *Possible to determine sex*

The physicians who made the post mortem examination have been successful in establishing that the parts found in the cellar were those of a woman.[45]

They have? This is likely being claimed now because reports of Crippen having been seen abroad are being given greater credence, so as to strengthen probable cause if time comes to request extradition.

13 August – *The scar*

It is agreed that the remains of the female found in the cellar of Hawley Crippen's house indicated a previous operation upon the body. This confirms the report sent to the *Chronicle* from Quebec that Crippen had performed an operation on his wife before he went to America.[46]

An interesting one, this. The scar takes its central place, never to be dislodged, but the supporting information is a bit hazy and there seems to be some Chinese whispers going on again. This is suggestive of the information – of the scar on the flesh and the fact of a scar on Cora – coming as one package. Police points earned for the studiedly casual use of the phrase 'the remains of the female', but one deducted for calling Crippen 'Hawley' instead of 'Doctor'.

16 August – *Poison and Hair Curlers*

> Owing to the death of Coroner Thomas all the evidence that has previously been taken had to be given again… Professor Pepper the famous Home Office criminal analyst, examined the remains and found that the woman had been poisoned and the body buried in quicklime. The only clues which allowed the analyst to place the body as that of a woman were the long hair and the discovery of hairpins.[47]

The problem of determining the sex has been solved by the miraculous find of the hair curlers/pins, the necklace has been forgotten about entirely, and the poison has been discovered (and what do you know – right when it was found that Crippen had bought some!) Most egregious of all may have been the scar. Inspector Dew had been told of such a mark on Cora's stomach by Clara Martinetti. 'Here was something really vital,' he was later to write. 'If that scar could be found on those gruesome remnants of human flesh lying in the Islington Mortuary it might provide the missing link in the chain of evidence of identification.'

As is hoped, so shall it be. All in vain did Crippen's defence try to argue that this evidence devoutly to be wished was merely a fold in the skin, which is almost certainly what it was. We shall temporarily adjourn our inquest on the inquest here, but we will pick up the story of the evolving narrative again when proceedings resume after Crippen's apprehension at the end of August. For now, with the police confident that they have come up with a version of the facts that will stick to their quarry, we can resume the hunt.

Actually, it wasn't too difficult to work out what had happened to the fugitives, and without the avalanche of false sightings, bogus information and downright mischief occasioned by the opening of the case to the media of the world it would have been easier still. Crippen and Le Neve made a pretty obvious spectacle. There is a famous photograph, covertly taken, of the pair on deck. They have just passed obliviously by the photographer who has then captured them from behind. It is pathetically obvious that Le Neve is a woman: her very shape permits no other interpretation. Crippen is promenading alongside her: there is no physical contact; they are not holding hands, and yet, there seems to be an almost tangible bond between them. They seem utterly lost; two people alone together against the fact of existence, each dependent on the other, the world united in opposition against them. Crippen is wearing what looks like a natty straw boater, its lightness, its jauntiness, its triviality all somehow terrible, as if fighting a lost campaign against the pregnancy of its circumstances; as if mutely pleading some forlorn, inaudible case on behalf of the man who is wearing it, and the woman by his side. It is, in its own small way, one of the saddest photographs ever taken. I actually find it difficult to look at.

Its photographer, we are told, is the new superstar who jumps into the story at this point, and the one who is, against much opposition, possibly its least substantial. Captain Henry George Kendall was captain of the steamer *Montrose*, which left Antwerp on 20 July, bound for Canada. Errol Flynn cast as Sherlock Holmes is how we are encouraged to picture him. Kendall, eagle of eye and shrewd of reasoning, spotted that two of his passengers, a Mr Robinson and young Master Robinson, seemed unusually affectionate for father and son. Without arousing suspicion, he studies them further, and sets a few little tests and traps. He makes Mr Robinson laugh, so as to inspect his teeth. He notices the mark of a pair of spectacles on his nose. He snoops around in their cabin and finds that the lad is accustomed to washing his face with a ladies' undergarment. He waits for them to walk past and then shouts out 'Mr Robinson!' to see if they turn around.

Certain that he had found his fugitives, Kendall uses the ship's wireless telegraph to alert Dew back in England. His full message, printed in the *Daily Mail* on 31 July 1910 and reproduced as an appendix in the Crippen edition of *Notable British Trials*, is full of *Boys' Own* touches: 'I discovered them two hours after leaving Antwerp, but did not telegraph to my owners until I had found out good clues.' 'I was well posted as to the crime, so got on the scent at once.' 'You will notice I did not arrest them… as if they smelt a rat, he might do something rash. I have not noticed a revolver in his hip pocket.'

These were the days that set the seal on the case as the sensation of the world. Inspector Dew, like some crime-busting Phileas Fogg, takes the steamer *Laurentic* from Liverpool, bound likewise for Quebec but scheduled to arrive there ahead of the *Montrose*. As the hours and the days tick by, Sherlock Kendall keeps a close eye on his star passengers as he waits for the cavalry to arrive. Will Dew make it in time, or will Crippen even now outfox his pursuers, and escape to a new life with his lady love? Every morning, anxious readers rushed to their papers for the update:

Progress of the Ocean Race

'The *Laurentic* is probably being driven at full speed on her present voyage,' said an expert navigator to the *Daily Mirror* yesterday, 'and it is not improbable that she may be able to communicate with Belle Isle, north of Newfoundland, as early as Wednesday midnight. ...

'At noon tomorrow the *Laurentic* will already be nearer Belle Isle than the *Montrose*, but too far off to communicate direct with the shore. The *Montrose* was last signalled 100 miles distant from Brow Head, near Crookhaven, at 1.39 pm last Friday.'[48]

With extraordinary neatness the same invention that was allowing this serialised account of the story – wireless telegraphy – was helping to throw the net over Crippen and Le Neve. According to the *Daily Mail*, the events caused great excitement among the French police force:

Commenting on the Hilldrop Crescent tragedy, the *Liberté* says: 'Arrest by wireless telegraphy opens a new chapter in criminal history. Thanks to this invisible agent, we are able to follow every move of Dr Crippen and his companion. It is admirable and it is terrible. The story of this sensational capture will rank with the greatest wonders of wireless telegraphy. It has served the police well. It has demonstrated that from one side of the Atlantic to the other a criminal lives in a cage of glass, where he is much more exposed to the eyes of the public than if he had remained on land.'[49]

The enthusiasm was obviously contagious:

This is the first instance of the use of wireless telegraphy to identify persons wanted by the police. 'There is no doubt,' said a senior detective officer yesterday, 'that wireless telegraphy is going to play an important part in the future. It has been used in one or two instances on board ships in connection with crimes, but never before have full descriptions of fugitives been sent by wireless telegraphy. It seems that the one thing overlooked by Crippen was the power of communicating between the ship and the outside world.'[50]

Well, sort of. Actually, like so much about the case, this is largely autoeroticism. Some sober reality is clearly called for. So, first, the descriptions of the fugitives did *not* first reach the *Montrose* by wireless telegraphy. Two old-fashioned flesh and blood coppers boarded the ship in London, before it arrived at Antwerp, to pass on instructions to keep an eye open for the pair, *and* with the information that Ethel was likely disguised as a boy. Neither is it really the case that Crippen and Le Neve would have escaped were it not for the radio. As a ship's captain, especially one with a hankering for the reward money, Kendall was legally entitled to hold the pair on suspicion and hand them over to the authorities when they docked, and surely would have done. All the radio did, ultimately, was facilitate Dew's *coup de théâtre*, allowing him to chase the *Montrose* across the ocean and be ready and waiting for Crippen on the other side. That, and allow readers of the *Daily Mail* to get a fresh cheap thrill every morning with their toast and marmalade.

Kendall dined off the events of the next few days to the end of his life, and the drama grew with the telling. In a series of newspaper reminiscences in 1942, for instance, that revolver he didn't spot in Crippen's hip pocket has been magically transformed into a revolver that he did spot in Crippen's hip pocket:

> Then, on this fifth day, while walking round the deck there came a little puff of wind which blew the tail of his jacket... I perceived that the gentle, reserved Dr Crippen had another side to his character, for now his hip pocket revealed the outline of a revolver. No mistake about it! He meant taking no chances if threatened with arrest. Silently I accepted the challenge. I loaded my own revolver and henceforth always carried it in my pocket. I had resolved to see this business through. If Crippen turned and fired on me, I would shoot him dead.
>
> Why didn't I place the pair under arrest? There were two reasons. First, because of the difficulty in guarding them effectively and ensuring that they would not commit suicide. I had not a big enough staff to keep a thorough watch over them night and day. Secondly, the pair had not yet given me the slightest trouble nor manifested any distrust. So it suited my purpose to continue to play the simpleton. But what a simpleton for a novelist or a playwright![51]

Kendall seems so earnest in his belief that we should swoon at his heroism that the necessity of cutting his florid account down to more reasonable dimensions becomes a positive pleasure. That Ethel is said to be disguised as a boy is routinely mentioned in press reports from as early as 15 July, many of which include the full story of Crippen purchasing the brown suit and bowler. No insight required there. As already noted, two London CID sergeants had boarded the *Montrose* before Crippen and Le Neve, with full and accurate descriptions of the pair. Kendall being otherwise occupied, they passed on this intelligence to Chief Officer Alfred Sergeant. Later, one of those police sergeants, Francis Barclay, applied for the £250 reward for the pair's apprehension, on the not unreasonable grounds that he had pinpointed the correct ship and their likely embarkation point, thus effectively doing all of Captain Kendall's work for him. If he thought he was in with a chance, he had not figured on Captain Kendall. Neither, for that matter, did Chief Officer Sergeant, who was responsible for passing the information on to the captain.

Far from penetrating a masterly disguise through sheer inspiration, Kendall was looking from the first for a man travelling with a woman disguised as his son, because he had been told to. All Kendall had to do was to check out his passengers for the likeliest pair, and that could hardly have been difficult: when Dew finally caught up with Ethel he was staggered that anybody of reasonable intelligence might have thought her a boy for a single minute. But there's some evidence that Kendall had help even with this! Most later reports would claim that only Kendall and the wireless operator, Llewellyn Jones, knew the truth about the Robinsons. But Dominick Keen, one of the stewards responsible for their room, seems to have at the very least been actively involved, only to be entirely written out thereafter: 'I was one of the first to discover, by her neat methods in her room, her way of walking and her effeminate figure that "John Robinson Jr" was a woman. Then we discovered that the labels had been taken from all their clothes, that the lining had been torn from the younger Robinson's hat, and soon Captain Kendall was convinced that he had the much-sought fugitives on board.'[52] Don't let the deference obscure the chronology here: Keen is saying he made the discoveries first and that (in part on account of them) Kendall became certain afterwards. The *Daily Mail* likewise had things this way round: 'One of the stewards in the ship first called the attention of the captain to the fact that they resembled Dr Crippen and Miss Le Neve.'[53]

And do we really think Crippen was fooled by any of this? I find it unlikely. Evidence would follow that Crippen had already taken measures to prevent his apprehension, either a suicide attempt or a complicated plot to have him sneaked off the boat before the police could get to him. Was this merely him covering all angles, or had he sensed the direction of the wind? If Kendall's antics were as crass as Kendall himself paints them, my vote is for the latter. Though Crippen was surprised to see Inspector Dew personally boarding the ship at Father Point, he stressed that it was the sight of Dew himself, whom he would have presumed to be co-ordinating operations from London, that had taken him aback, not the fact of his discovery and apprehension in itself. He had specifically enquired of the wireless operator what the frequent messaging back to shore was all about. Icebergs, he was told. Was Crippen convinced? Given he asked the question in the first place, maybe not. The *New York Times*, frequently a refreshingly cynical voice amidst the generally naïve coverage, certainly doubted it: 'That he is still unconscious of the suspicion he has aroused is hardly possible. "Master Robinson" would know the meaning of the curious glances cast her way by everybody on board the steamer to whom her secret has been revealed, and "Mr Robinson" is well aware of what can be done by wireless telegraph.'[54]

Despite all this, the fight was on to see if Kendall or Dew would get the lion's share of the headlines and emerge hero of the hour. To journalists, Kendall became the ancient mariner who stoppeth one of three, or in his case, vastly more:

'The English papers were full of the case while we were on the other side,' said the captain, 'and I became very much interested in it. I bought all the papers and used to lie in my bunk and read them. Look here,' and opening the drawer of his desk in his cabin, the skipper produced half a dozen papers, each containing pictures of Crippen and Miss Leneve. One of the dentist's pictures had the black moustache blocked out with white chalk.

'I did that,' continued Kendall, 'the first day I saw the man aboard. He was clean shaven then and I wanted to see how this likeness would look without the moustache. I also chalked out the spectacles in the pictures. Crippen wore no spectacles aboard. Here is the result: You can see how closely it resembles the man as he looks today. And here is something else I did.'

The skipper took from his desk a square of white cardboard with a round hole cut in the centre and fitted it over a newspaper cut of

Miss Leneve. Thus superimposed it covered the girl's picture hat and dress leaving only the face showing. 'I did this and compared the pictured face with that of the passenger Crippen said was his son,' said Kendall. 'The resemblance is striking.'[55]

'I am solely responsible for sending the Marconi message and no one whatever called my attention to these people,' he would subsequently lie, 'and it was entirely from my own observations that I suspected them as being the people wanted, and I therefore consider that I am entitled to the reward offered...' The inconvenient steward(s), Chief Officer Sergeant and the two CID boys were all long forgotten. (Shades of Sergeant Mitchell and the poker!) It was just another seedy example of how greed, mendacity and prurience were perverting an essentially tragic murder mystery.

The atmosphere on and around the *Montrose* was like a carnival. 'Every farmhouse about Rimouski, every boarding house, every yacht, sailing and steam is at a premium,' noted the *Daily Mail*.[56] That was just the beginning of it:

> On the shore and on the quay a whole crowd of newspaper men are waiting, with battalions of photographers and forests of cinematograph machines. In the little town accommodation cannot be obtained. Every place is full up, and people are sleeping in bathrooms and on billiard tables.
>
> Every veranda holds whole families, and tents are being let out by enterprising persons at a dollar a night. One man talks about erecting a stand on the wharf to which he will charge admission and from which people will get a sight of the unfortunate pair of absconders before those on shore see them. This move, however, is to be stopped if it is tried.[57]

Dew's supposed introduction to the fugitive – 'Good morning, Dr Crippen' – is worthy of Stanley and Livingstone. Unfortunately, it too appears to be an invention of his later retellings. Though virtually all the contemporary reports are given credence by accurately reporting Crippen's canonical reply – a variation on 'I am glad it is over; the suspense has been too much' – they have Dew greeting his man with the far less laconic 'Crippen, I want you!' But there is no doubt that Dew made a suitably dramatic impression, boarding the *Montrose* disguised as a pilot, before swooping on his prey. There seems little point to this: if there had been any suspicion, Kendall could have had Crippen arrested at a given signal and held him for the few minutes it took for Dew to arrive dressed normally. The whole thing smacks of performance, and the presence of literal boatloads of journalists reinforces the suspicion. There were even reports that Dew 'painted his face, so as to look seamed and weather-worn'.[58] Let us hope these, at least, were hyperbole.

This conscious lubricating of public excitement had inevitable repercussions. As Crippen was led off the ship, 'a tall young fellow dashed at Crippen with uplifted cane, and in a second there was a knot of fighting uniform and plain clothes officers and civilians':

> They just threw themselves upon the rushing crowd of people, battling almost savagely, and driving them back towards the water and along the landing stage. It was an intensely dramatic exhibition on the part of the man – who declares he had no direct personal interest in the parties – of uncontrolled and passionate hatred. No one else joined in, and but for hoarse shouts of, 'Get back there. Away you go out of it' by the police, the silence was almost oppressive.[59]

It was the signal and shaming failure of the authorities that their tactics did nothing to restrain, and everything to encourage, such bestial exhibitionism as this. It is often said that executioners should be recruited only from amongst those who do not want to be one, and that actively desiring the office should count as disqualification. There is a lot of sense in that. Detectives, too, should ward against the temptation of contest and exhibition. The desire to see justice done is of course valid and admirable, but there is also the impersonal love of the puzzle, of solving a mystery, and of matching wits with criminals and winning, and bringing in the quarry, broken and bowed. Such imperatives may run parallel to the pursuit of justice, but they are not synonymous with it. Dew would often say he felt a little sorry for Crippen when he snatched him from the very brink of success, much as trophy hunters sometimes eulogise dead lions and elephants. But there is something sickening about the cat and mouse game played with Crippen, especially with the world's media watching. It seemed sadistic, somehow, and too impersonal: a game of chess played with real lives. And – surprisingly, perhaps; admirably, certainly – there was no shortage of commentators in the press who seemed to feel the same.

> This general exhibition of tiger ferocity on the part of supposed Christian peoples shows what a dreadful hypocrisy our so-called civilisation really is. Here we see two nations, with all their newspaper implements, running down with bloodhound delight a miserable criminal... Even supposing Crippen's crime were the worst in the annals of individual offences, there could be no justification for the terrible barbarity exhibited over the sight of a miserable wretch caught in a trap like a rat. No doubt some account must be taken of the just indignation of people at a crime being committed, and its perpetrator being arrested, but under no circumstances could this be held to justify the Abyssinian-like gloating of two European nations over the prospect of Crippen's position. Here we see millions figuratively jumping on one man-slayer – millions who would lick the feet of an Emperor or other ruler who would slay men in sections. The Crippen murder was bad, but the Crippen 'incidents' are a thousandfold worse.[60]

Those points still resonate, for all the outdated analogies. There was an ugliness to the pursuit of Crippen, and to the braggadocio seemingly underpinning many of Dew's actions and statements. Then there is Kendall, worming his way into the couple's privacy, pretending to be solicitous, making them laugh, encouraging their intimacy, all the while plotting to betray their trust ('we made a lot of them, and kept them smiling'). In an imperfect world, imperfect things must be done. That has to be understood. But that doesn't mean there was anything thrilling about the hounding of Crippen and Le Neve. It would still be a sad thing, even if they were guilty. Necessary evil is no less evil for being necessary.

And while the authorities began the serious work of securing a conviction, the press and public went on their insatiable course, red-eyed and drooling:

BRUSSELS, Friday –
The landlord of the little Hôtel des Ardennes, where Crippen and Miss Le Neve stayed, said to me this evening, 'Since you published an account of your visit here in the *Daily Mail*, English and American

people come every day to take photographs and to ask for details of the room which Crippen took. Everybody wants souvenirs. A rich Englishman offered me £1 for the page in the hotel book where Crippen wrote his name. But a detective had cut out the page the day after you took a tracing of the signature. An American offered me £2 for a copper collar stud which Crippen left behind. An Englishman offered me £2 each for two pamphlets left behind by Crippen – one in German, published at Munich, and the other the catalogue of a nursery-gardener at Saffron Walden.'[61]

Chapter 4

The Marriage

Marriage ought to be a mating, spiritual, mental, physical; but his spirit and Cora's had always rebelled against each other, their minds had clashed at every angle, even the physical part of their union had died an early death. The thought of sexual intercourse with Cora was to Philip as revolting as some bestial act. He could not understand those husbands and wives who go on using each other's bodies when love, respect, understanding are gone and there is nothing left but flesh to hold them together. No matter what the parsons said, married life under those conditions was indecent and beastly and an illegitimate union based on love was beautiful, clean, honest by comparison.

James Ronald, *This Way Out*

For want of a nail the shoe was lost, begins the old proverb, reminding us that sometimes the most momentous events can owe their inception to the most trivial of factors. And indeed, it could be argued that it was for want of a nail that the stage was set for the Crippen tragedy. For it was most definitely the want of nails that brought Joseph Makomarski, a Polish immigrant, to George Schmidt, a German immigrant, in Brooklyn, somewhere around 1870.

Mr Schmidt made nails, and Mr Makomarski sold them. Mr Schmidt also had two daughters, Theresa and Mary. With biblical inevitability, Mary fell for Joseph and Joseph for Mary, and so they were married. In 1873 they had a daughter, her name usually spelled Kunigunde, but in early documents Cungundia. The name, however spelled, had been that of her maternal grandmother. In time, finding it too unwieldy for a first-generation American, she would change it to Corinne Turner, Cora Turner and Belle Elmore, among others. And in 1892 she changed it to Crippen, when she became Hawley's second wife.[1]

Even with the most recent revelations that have so transformed our understanding of the case, it is still plain that it is in the Crippens' marriage that the key to the matter resides. It is one of the many oddities of the case that the account of Crippen's home life relied upon by both prosecution and defence, as well as most of the case's subsequent chroniclers, derives almost entirely from the statement Crippen himself dashed off, in between tooth extractions and over a hearty Italian lunch, during his first interview with Inspector Dew. Since it helps both in offering motive *and* extenuating circumstances, and so pleases all houses, it was allowed to stand for decades, and has only recently come to be treated with due caution by crime historians. There are a very small number of corroborating statements from others, markedly less emphatic in their emphases than Crippen's version, and an equally small but no less certain body of significantly contrary ones. In the main, though, we have the Crippen version, take it or leave it. Most have taken it.

Most uneasily, we have largely Crippen's word alone for the hellishness of his home life. That he was weak tea in the presence of his wife, and that she took charge of his appearance, and spent liberally of his income, is one thing. But what of the rest? Whence the extreme shrewishness bordering on domestic abuse, the wanton promiscuity, the drunken insults, the reduction of poor Crippen to domestic skivvy? Only really from Crippen. The closest we get to back-up on these points is the testimony of Richard Ehrlich, a German lodger at the house, who told *Le Petit Parisien* that domestic life with the Crippens was characterised by 'frequent bickerings and open quarrels'. Cora 'often lost her temper', while Crippen never did, 'though his wife's reproaches were frequently unjustified. He always answered her in a gentle tone and was never rude to her... [Crippen] must have possessed an extraordinary amount of self-control to endure his wife's stinging sarcasms for so long.'[2] And the actor Scott Alexander recalled:

> She sought the company of stage folk, and her behaviour was a trifle 'wild', according to the standards of that day. Dr Crippen, on the other hand, was a strict living man. He was a rigid teetotaller, and this difference in their tastes may have been the first thing that drove the unfortunate man to the arms of his secretary, Miss Le Neve. Those who knew the Crippens never imagined that he was living a

double life for, whenever Belle Elmore was attending a meeting of the Variety Artists' Federation or showing at a music hall, there was the little doctor waiting for her. He seemed to be an ideal husband.[3]

Both of these reminiscences, however, were offered long after the trial, and the firm establishment of the essentials. During the trial itself there was only Dr Burroughs, the honorary physician of the Music Hall Ladies' Guild, who conceded that Cora was 'at times, somewhat hasty' in her manner towards Crippen. Not much to show for so certain a legend.

While most witnesses to Crippen's character, including his accusers, do indeed portray him as a meek and gentle individual, and the least likely man to murder and mutilate, there is equal unanimity as to the good nature and warm, likeable character of Cora. Given the frequency with which they are seen and assessed *together* – irreconcilably alienated couples are rarely visible in tandem with the frequency of the Crippens – it is surprising that there is so little ballast for the standard image of Crippen as Cora's punching bag. They certainly didn't appear to be estranged. He might easily have absented himself entirely from her circle of theatrical friends with no disapprobation, for instance, and he did not. They entertained together, they socialised together, and the friends that knew her also knew him. They came as an item. Crippen explained this in the trial as essentially a sham, an agreement reached between them to present a false image of harmony. But the standard portrait of them from those in the know is of a couple quietly resigned to each other, no longer passionately in love, no doubt, but by no means at loggerheads. Yes, the public and private spheres are often massively at odds, and there is no reason to dismiss Crippen's protestations of domestic injustice out of hand, but just as importantly, let the record show that they find only a very partial echo elsewhere.

By far the most comprehensive account of the pair's life together released to the press was the one given by Adeline Harrison to the *Daily Express*. Harrison, later a journalist herself, and described at the time as a 'dramatic and lyric author', was also a friend of Cora's, who wrote her obituary in the *Music Hall and Theatre Review*. Her reminiscences are notable not only for their detail but also their even-handedness, given that her sympathies tended inevitably to Cora:

I knew Mrs Crippen, or rather Miss Belle Elmore, as she preferred to be called, and Dr H.H. Crippen intimately. She was his second wife, and she came to this country from America to join her husband 12 years ago. He had opened and was managing a palatial branch of Munyon's Cures, facing the Palace Theatre in Shaftesbury Avenue. Mrs. Crippen was a plump, pleasing little woman, with bright brown eyes and dark hair. She was born in America, of Polish parentage;[4] was vivacious, full of joy and life, and very kind-hearted. They seemed – when I first met them – as if the wheel of fortune had suddenly turned, bringing for them the money to acquire the good things of life. They were like a couple of children in their love for excitement. Dinners, supper parties, theatres were the order of the day, and every form of novelty and excitement appealed to them.

Dr Crippen was the typical, quiet, unassuming American who gave his wife all the running socially, and whose one aim and object appeared to be to earn money for her to spend and have a good time. His devotion for her was remarkable. Idolised wife! Why, nothing was too good for her. Her craze for diamonds and the acquisition of gorgeous gowns knew no limit, nor was it restricted by him. She was possessed of a pretty mezzo-soprano voice, and she desired to figure in the music halls in an operetta. I was induced by a mutual friend to write the libretto, and was invited to dine with them at a well-known restaurant to chat over matters. She was vivacious and full of vim, but to him a strange, unaccountable feeling of repulsion – evanescent but recurrent, even after years of intimacy – came over me at that first dinner. The operetta was produced with various songs, and she now and again appeared with varied success at variety theatres. An intimacy sprang up, and we visited each other for years.

During that period they lived at various boardinghouses, then took a flat in Store Street, Bloomsbury. It was through me that they finally rented the house in Hilldrop Crescent. I had a house in Hilldrop Road, and during an evening at my house she was so charmed with the old-world garden and bower of roses that the next day she came up to search for a house in the neighbourhood. They were unable to find a house with a large garden so they rented Hilldrop Crescent, and set to work to transform an ugly back garden into a flowery bower. Meanwhile Dr Crippen's affairs had undergone various changes. Owing to his name figuring in a playbill as manager of one of his wife's enterprises, he had to relinquish his position at Munyon's. Immediately afterwards he embarked on a patent medicine enterprise, and lost capital. Eventually, after a short appointment at the Drouet Institute, he returned to Munyon's, who had given up the premises in Shaftesbury Avenue, and at the same time he dabbled in various other enterprises, including miniature painting and dentistry. The couple always had plenty of money at their command.

Mrs Crippen had two idiosyncrasies – she had a horror of servants or domestic help, and an almost abnormal love of dress and jewellery. Every room in the house at Hilldrop Crescent contained boxes with piles of gowns. Meanwhile she interested herself in the Music Hall Ladies' Guild, and did good work, becoming honorary treasurer. The offices of the guild were ultimately removed to the same building in New Oxford Street where her husband represented Munyon's. She was devoted to the good cause, and the appreciation of her good work by the president and ladies' committee took expression in a handsome bracelet and bouquet presented to her at the annual dinner, which took place a few weeks before her mysterious disappearance.

Just before the dinner I visited her on several occasions in connection with the tickets, etc, and she proudly showed me a new ermine and guipure coat, for which the doctor had paid £85. They were just as affectionate as ever towards each other, and he smiled blandly at her childish delight in her new treasure. She also showed me several new gowns she had purchased, and, a costly silver tea-tray he had given to her. It was an extraordinary sidelight on their home-life that, despite the fact that they always had plenty of money, and a large, well-furnished lounge, they rarely used any room but the kitchen. I have actually seen a twenty-guinea dress thrown carelessly across the dresser side by side with edibles and crockery. One morning she would have for lunch a cup of coffee and a piece of bread and butter, and the same evening, attired in a Parisian gown, she, would be holding a lavish dinner party at the Savoy or the Trocadero. At another time I have seen her go out marketing to buy her own greengroceries with a little cloth bag slung on one of her fingers containing hundreds of pounds worth of diamonds and other jewels.[5]

Crippen's work assistant William Long was another who detected little seriously awry in the marriage: 'He always appeared to be on the best of terms with his wife and was always doing some little service for her, such as sending up a taxicab to the house, buying reels of cotton, matching silk, and would always run to do anything for her.'[6] Neighbours recalled Crippen contentedly gardening; and bricklaying, too: he built a smart brick wall between his garden and the one next door. A cage he erected in the garden allowed the couple's two housecats to exercise without risk of unwanted pregnancies. Nothing seemed to get pregnant around Crippen. Or stay pregnant, at least.

Millicent Gillatt was one of those neighbours; she too was impressed by their compatibility:

> Both Mr and Mrs Crippen used to spend a great part of their time in the garden. He always seemed exceedingly fond of her, and used to follow her round in quite an adoring way… She was much bigger in build than he, and an extremely energetic woman. As an example of her energy, I remember when she first came how the servant, who was there temporarily, was sweeping the carpet in the garden, and she took the broom from her hands and did the work herself. Nothing whatever happened to excite suspicion, and even when Mrs Crippen disappeared in February it was merely presumed that she had left to fulfil an engagement. With the exception that motor cars would sometimes be at the doors at half-past one in the morning, they lived very quietly, and apparently most happily. On Sundays they used to leave the house together in the morning, as though they were going to service,[7] and Mrs Crippen would be dressed very stylishly.[8]

'Professor' Munyon, whose 'Munyon's Homeopathic Remedies' kept Crippen ignominiously employed from 1894, was one of the few to corroborate Crippen's claims in this matter. Cullen quotes him as considering Belle 'a giddy woman who worried her husband a great deal… Some years after he started with me I saw he was distressed. I attributed it to the annoyance of his wife. He had reason to be jealous of her.'[9] Duke Munyon, his son, added: 'He was intensely jealous of her and they often quarrelled. She was pretty and attractive and had lots of men friends.'[10] Again, though, there is that ever-present codicil: 'He and his wife went out constantly together and apparently they were happy.'

In the official version Crippen is almost forced into the consoling arms of Ethel by Cora's rampant infidelity. But the evidence is spotty, at best. Take the story, told in considerable detail by Tom Cullen and stated as fact repeatedly elsewhere, that Crippen came home from work during the day to find Cora in bed with another man. Cullen implies it is Richard Ehrlich, the German lodger, though he offers no source and embroiders the tale with so much detail (Crippen enters to find the kitchen table 'littered with unwashed breakfast dishes, the egg hardened on some of them') that one ends up unable to believe a single word of it. Let us concede that she was perhaps flirty and flighty, as ladies of the music hall might be expected to be, and quite possibly given to intemperance in respect of that silliness in mixed company that often marks the transition from vitality to desuetude (in both sexes), and what then? Open adultery, as the Crippen case reminds us all too clearly, was not taken lightly in middle-class society, and few of her friends would have been forgiving of a woman approaching middle age who incontinently seduces every young man who crosses her path.

The major claim of long-standing dalliance, offered by Crippen in his statement to Dew, got as far as being tested in court, and ended some distance from an unequivocal victory for Crippen. Bruce Miller, a Chicagoan who had toured England with a novelty musical act, had returned to America in 1904, seemingly making him an unlikely candidate for Cora's willing overseas lover, to whose arms she had rushed so impetuously the day after their supper with the Martinettis. In Crippen's telling, the friendship had begun while he was away in America. His assistant William Long, recalling this period, made no mention of Miller but does seem to be hinting at a degree of frostiness between the Crippens: 'Early in 1899 Crippen went to America, Mrs Crippen remaining behind in London. I saw her several times during this period but as far as I know she received no letters from him, and I am not aware that she wrote to him.' Cora, naturally gregarious, alone in a foreign country and rarely in work, must have been extremely lonely, and it would be no surprise if she did take a lover. Nonetheless, in mentioning Miller by name, Crippen must have known that he was taking a risk. This might suggest he is being honest; alternatively, he may simply have anticipated that Miller would have been hard to track down and, even if found, extremely unwilling to return to give evidence. If so, he was proved correct on both counts. But despite meeting a brick wall at his agent, who claimed he had not worked as a performer since returning to America (which was untrue[11]), he was finally found, apparently now working in real estate,[12] and doing a very good imitation of a man who had no idea why he was being bothered. 'I have not seen either of the Crippens in years,' he told the *Chicago Tribune*. 'When I was in London, about seven years ago, I called at their home several times. I was then in the theatrical business and met Mrs Crippen in a professional way. I am not able to account for any reason why Crippen would mention my name. I know nothing of any marital troubles they may have had.'[13] But if Crippen had wagered on his remaining permanently aloof from the proceedings he was to be disappointed: with a little financial inducement, Miller did finally consent to make a guest appearance at the trial.

Modern tellers of the story, keen to redress the balance of an account reckoned too easy on Crippen at the expense of Cora, have likewise gone too easy on Miller. The trial soon uncovered more than a merely professional acquaintance, and there's no question Miller was a liar. When first contacted, presumably unaware that Crippen had generously admitted he had never actually met his supposed rival, he told the *Manchester Guardian*: 'It is true that I toured England with a vaudeville company in 1898 and 1904, and Mrs Crippen was a member of this company. I knew both Crippen and his wife very well.'[14] Only at the trial did he concede that he had never met Crippen, not even when he believed him to be present in the house while he was playing footsie with his wife. Before the cross-examination was over, Miller had made a series of damaging admissions and had prevaricated relentlessly:

Were you fond of her?

Yes.

Did you ever tell her that you loved her?

Well, I do not know that I ever put it in that way.

Did you indicate to her that you did love her?

She always understood it that way, I suppose.

Then you did love her, I presume?

I do not mean to say that. I did not exactly love her; I thought a great deal of her as far as friendship was concerned.

...

Did you ever write love letters to her?

I have written to her very nice letters perhaps.

You know what a love letter is. Did you ever write a love letter to her?

Well I do not know that I ever put it just in that way. I often wrote to her very friendly letters; I might say they were affectionate letters.

Then you wrote affectionate letters to her. Did you write love letters to her?

Affectionate letters.

Ending 'Love and kisses to Brown Eyes'?

I have done so.

Now, sir, do you think those are proper letters to write to a married woman?

Under the circumstances, yes.

...

Have you ever kissed her?

I have.

Never done anything more than kiss her?

That is all.

Why did you stop at that?

Because I always treated her as a gentleman, and never went any further.

Miller also admitted that those innocently affectionate letters numbered several a year, that he had sent her gifts and money, and that they had exchanged 'large' photographs. Two portraits of Miller were still on open display at Hilldrop Crescent after Cora's disappearance: Dew confirmed at the trial that one of them was framed in her bedroom.[15] Still, on the vital points Miller held firm: he swore he had no idea where she was, and he had not been conspiring with her to begin a new life together. In different circumstances the defence might easily have scored with the observation that there was little practical difference between making a clear invitation and blithely giving the impression of doing so – and Miller clearly fell into the latter category. The jury, I suspect, did not like him one little bit, but in the end they believed him, for obvious reasons. If Cora Crippen was butchered and buried in Crippen's cellar then *plainly* she had not gone to Miller. 'Crippen had cast insinuations that I might know the whereabouts of his wife,' he proclaimed to the press, 'and I went to London to prove that I had not seen the woman for over six years. She had two of my pictures in her room, but there was no attempt to conceal her friendship for both me and Mrs Miller.'[16] The casual mention of 'Mrs Miller' is typical of his sophistry: his wife Edith had stayed in America, apparently estranged; certainly there was never even the smallest friendship with Cora. And how many married women keep large framed pictures of another man in their bedroom? One would need to be obsessed with proving Crippen's guilt to deny this was an incredibly relevant piece of evidence.

'See, we met as theatrical people,' Miller wittered on. 'Crippen, in his defence, declared that, instead of being dead, she was in America with me. I went over on the same ship with Theresa Hunn, her sister. With Inspector Dew, I went to the Crippen residence and identified my pictures. I told him everything, the same as I testified. There was nothing to conceal.' *See, we met as theatrical people.* Translation: our rules are not your rules. But Bruce Miller wasn't theatrical people; not really. In fact, he had far more in common with Crippen than the jury, and subsequent crime historians, would ever suspect. We shall have more to say about the real 'Mr' Miller later.

Let us again now raise the issue of children: it may yet prove important. The case is sometimes made that, while the Crippens are both said to love children, and while it was the greatest (perhaps even the defining) tragedy of their marriage that they were unable to conceive, Crippen's decision to abandon his son to the care of his own parents should be read as a vote of no confidence in Cora's maternal potential. But the timeline suggests that Crippen opted to take no further role in the upbringing of Otto more or less immediately after his wife's death. If meaningful at all, the suggestion that Cora was a factor influencing his decision is evidence that she may have been on the scene before his first wife died. Tracked down in America when the murder scandal began, Crippen's father Myron made his son's case, tellingly embellished with error: 'Dr Crippen placed his son, Hawley,[17] in the care of myself and my wife nineteen years ago... The reason for this was that Dr Crippen believed that his boy would be better taken care of by us than by his second wife, whom he married less than two years after the death of his first wife.'[18] Whether deliberate or unconscious, that mutation of a few short months into 'less than two years' speaks volumes. Though painted in the official literature as a pining would-be father, I have seen no evidence anywhere to suggest Crippen regretted his decision not to take charge of Otto again when he remarried. There is something almost inhuman about a father who decides to respond to a 2-year-old child's loss of his mother by depriving him of his father also: many of us, I suspect, could conceive of no action more alien to our natures, unless it was strictly understood by all parties, not least the child, to be a temporary measure until a normal home environment can again be provided. Such assurances, emphatically, Crippen did not make, or ever intend. Instead, he seems to have packed Otto away like unwanted baggage, and maintained only formal and sporadic contact with either child or grandparents from then on. 'The last time Dr Crippen saw his son was twelve years ago, when we met in New York by appointment,' Myron continues. 'When Dr Crippen's mother died in January, 1909, he sent $50 toward the funeral expenses. This was the last we heard from him directly.'

The press located both Myron and Otto and solicited their opinion on the breaking news. Myron was loyal: 'I hesitate to believe that my son could be responsible for his wife's death. I have confidence that the facts when they are disclosed will show that he did not commit the crime.'[19] Otto, who had good reason to be resentful of a father who abandoned him to the upbringing of his grandparents, was notably less sympathetic: 'When I received the letter announcing the death of my stepmother... I immediately became suspicious... It is too bad to think that a man of his age would do such a thing.' Nicholas Connell, who notes the son's misgivings but not the father's convictions in his book *Doctor Crippen*, claims that 'Otto hinted that his father was a sexual predator when interviewed by the *Los Angeles Herald*'.[20] He did nothing of the sort. What he in fact says is: 'I understood he passed most of his time in the company of various women who *accepted his advances*.' (Italics mine.) This is not only materially different from Connell's reading, it also carries an entirely different inference, which is that Crippen spent his leisure time in the company of what used to be called 'fast women'. This is so far from any other account of him as to carry no real weight at all, but Connell is anxious to slip it by so as to shore up an equally orphan assertion from Louise Mills, Belle's sister: 'She wanted me to live there permanently, but I did not stay because Crippen always bothered me as soon as his wife was out of sight – he also molested my other sisters when he came over and visited us in Brooklyn.'[21] She adds that Cora told her she feared Crippen and did not feel safe around him, something none of his other accusers even hint at in their assessments of their marital relations which, though they assuredly paint Cora as a less absurd figure than the popular myth, more or less conform to the general understanding of her as the dominant partner, and Crippen her timid sergeant. Again, Mills had very good reasons indeed to hate Crippen, and her venom here, though readily understood, can only be cited as valid evidence disingenuously. She also swears that he was a drug addict.

Cora's stepfather, Frederick Marsenger, was more inclined than most to point the finger at Ethel, suggesting that the couple were sufficiently contented until Crippen was tempted to stray.[22] Thus we arrive at that element of the story in which so many find the dimension of purity sufficient to lift it from the merely sordid to the genuinely tragic: the love affair of Crippen and Ethel. In the news reports, and to a lesser extent in the evidence at the trial, one senses a narrative straining to write itself in the form of greatest convenience, much as water takes the easiest route from source to outlet. Conventional melodrama should dictate that Ethel is timid, easily led, naïve, and Crippen commanding, magnetic, charismatic; their relationship that of Trilby and Svengali. (Several reports suggested that she was under Crippen's hypnotic control.[23]) And while it was possible to squeeze Ethel – *just* – into the Trilby role (much to her benefit when time came for her trial) there was no way Crippen could be recast as Svengali. The man, for all his professional assurance, daring escape bid, and implacable resilience in the witness box, was, in his everyday persona, the very opposite of the matinee idols to whom Ethel must have looked for representatives of the masculine ideal. One might imagine him, just, diverting her from the path of righteousness, in a shabby London of rented lodgings and stunted opportunities, but it takes *genuine* devotion to cut off one's hair, dress as a boy, and jettison everything one knows – family, soil, convention, moral certainty – in exchange for the unmarried love of a timid, balding, unadventurous flimflam merchant.

They had met in professional circumstances, when she and her sister had come to work as secretaries at the Drouet Institute, that ugliest of the many reprehensible organisations to which Crippen lent spurious medical authority. Sister Nina left the firm in 1903 to get married, leaving quiet, passionate Ethel alone and vulnerable. She would probably have fallen for any male employer who gave her encouragement. It happened to be Crippen. At first it was probably just the very typical, commonplace attraction that develops between deferential secretary and munificent boss. Over time, however, their love undoubtedly became a genuine bond, a need both for each other and for the reassurance that each other's adoration gave them. The affair seemed to have been physically consummated in December of 1906, long after the Bruce Miller years. By the time of their flight I think it is fair to say that neither was able to contemplate a life apart. 'We were like two children in the great unkind world', wrote Crippen to Ethel in one of his last letters, 'who clung to one another and gave each other courage.'

This is not, I feel sure, because of any shared guilty secrets. The idea that she was entirely oblivious to what was supposedly going on under her nose has come in for systematic bombardment in recent years, and one book in particular makes it its mission to demonstrate that she essentially played the press and the jury for suckers, allowing them to mistake guile for naïvety. Of course, even if there was a case to be made along these lines, it presupposes that there was something going on under her nose to be oblivious *of*, which if Crippen's and her version of events were true would not be the case.

During their flight, Ethel's mother gave a detailed interview to the press that shows just how in the dark her family had been with regards the true nature of her association with Crippen:

My daughter Ethel had been associated with Dr Crippen in her capacity as shorthand typist for ten or twelve years. One day, a week or two before Easter, she suddenly announced to me, 'I'm married, mother! I've married Dr Crippen!' I was, as you may be sure, more than surprised at the news, for I had not even heard of her engagement. I hastened to question her further. I understood from her that Dr Crippen had divorced his former wife, and that Ethel and he had been married at a London registry office, which she mentioned. I was more surprised still when she informed me, in answer to my inquiries, that two of Dr Crippen's gentleman friends had acted as witnesses at the marriage ceremony. Dr Crippen and Ethel spent their honeymoon, which fell at Easter time, on the Continent. We received several picture postcards in pencil from her from Dieppe, saying she was well, but no address was given. The pair, on their return, went to live in Hilldrop Crescent, taking with them a French maid, whom I believe they had brought from Boulogne. Since Ethel came back I have told her on four or five occasions when I saw her, either here or at her place of business, that her father would like to look at her marriage lines, but she always somehow managed to evade having to produce them.[24]

The most useful testimony as far as Ethel is concerned was that of Mrs Jackson, her landlady; at the inquest she had given telling indication of Ethel's level of engagement with the events swirling around her. The naïvety was again in evidence, but it seemed more wilful than innate, as if she were consciously insulating herself from reality:

About the middle of February,[25] the witness said, Miss Leneve appeared miserable and depressed. Such was her state that Mrs. Jackson followed the girl to her room to learn, if possible, the source of her trouble. Miss Leneve, the witness said, was in a terrifying state of agitation. Her eyes seemed fairly starting out of her head. The landlady insisted on an explanation, telling the girl she must have something awful on her mind to be in such a condition. The witness said that the other replied: 'Would you be surprised if I told you that it was the doctor and Miss Elmore? He was the cause of my trouble when you first knew.[26] She is his wife and when I see them go away together it makes me realize my position as to what she is and what I am.' Mrs Jackson asked: 'What is the use of you worrying about another woman's husband?' To this Miss Leneve answered: 'Miss Elmore has been threatening to go away with another man. Dr. Crippen has been waiting for her to do so, when he would divorce her.'[27]

As Ethel's defence pointed out, to suppose that she might have gone to Hilldrop Crescent to live as Crippen's wife if she had known that he had murdered the previous incumbent and buried her under the floor is far harder to believe than that she was genuinely innocent, trusting and oblivious of all. Yes, she knew she was taking the place of Cora, and the opportunity for social climbing was likely part of the appeal. Valentine Lecocq spoke revealingly of her love of jewellery and clothes, which she (Valentine) never imagined for a second belonged to somebody else. Her love for Crippen may have been rose-tinted, but she need not have been blind to the various advantages it might bring her. Modern historians have pounced eagerly upon the discovery that she had likely forged Cora's signature in order to empty her Post Office Savings account, but as the new Mrs Crippen, the previous one having absconded shamefully, she would have felt righteously entitled to do this. The same goes for her helping herself to her furs and costumes. Like so much of the supposedly suspicious behaviour the pair engaged in at this time, the sheer recklessness of it to me suggests a terrible ignorance of where the wind was about to blow, to a degree that is inconceivable had it been done culpably.

Ethel seems to have been a willing fantasist, easily recruited to Crippen's Lewis Carroll private world where reality was what he decreed it should be. Thus in their own minds, and in their own private world, they were not merely as good as man and wife but were literally thus, complete with wedding date, solemnised by rings and recorded in anniversaries. Nothing could be more terrifying to those sustained by illusion than the threat of its violation from the unwelcome world without, which is of course exactly what happened when Inspector Dew appeared on their doorstep, their inevitable impetus to flight. An example of the seeming dream world in which Ethel now moved is given in this interesting recollection by her dressmaker, supplied to the press while the couple were still on the run:

> An extraordinary story of her dealings with Ethel Le Neve has been told by a Hampstead dressmaker. 'I knew Ethel Le Neve well,' said the dressmaker. 'She came to me last November 12 months to get some work done. She was a nice-looking, girl, and I was quite taken with her. She did not dress expensively and I did not see her often until early in February. Then she came with a large box, and said: "Oh, I want you to do a lot of work for me, because in six weeks'

time I am going to be married." I expressed my pleasure at the news, and she said: "Don't you think it's very good of Mr Crippen, the gentleman I am going to marry? His aunt has gone to America, and left the house in Hilldrop Crescent for him to dispose of, and also left me all these things. I want you to make some up, so that they shall be ready for my wedding. They were lovely things,' continued the dressmaker. 'There was one dress and quite a number of dress lengths – a vieux rose, which I made into a costume: a glace silk, which I made into a Princess robe, and a mole-coloured shade, with a stripe, which I made for her. She told me afterwards that she was married in the vieux rose. Between February and Easter she was constantly coming to me to be fitted, and she was happy and cheerful. After the wedding I saw her often, and I asked her one day how she liked married life. "I am very happy," she said, and she also told me they were anxious to give up the house at Hilldrop Crescent, and go in to the West End to live. I had a letter from her, enclosing a postal order for £1 for some work, and asking me to deliver a coat on Friday, as they were going to Bournemouth or Eastbourne for a holiday. The letter was signed "Ethel Crippen". I could not finish it on Friday, and when I took it on Saturday they were gone.

'I remember once I thought it funny that the American aunt should go away and leave all these things behind. I mentioned it to her, and she said: "I expect she did not want to pass the Customs with all those goods."'[28]

It is difficult to know what Ethel believed to be the true standing of their relationship, nor how she realistically saw it evolving. I suspect 'true' and 'realistic' were notions rarely if ever entertained at Hilldrop Crescent after January of 1910. Nonetheless, there is an odd specificity to their role play, if role play it was. Ethel's mother recalls her announcing that she had been married 'a week or two before Easter'. A public holiday is a reliable means of pinpointing a date, and Easter of 1910 fell on the weekend of 26 and 27 March, so it would seem likely the wedding supposedly took place on 12 or 19 March. This tallies with similar claims Ethel made in writing to her friend Lydia Rose and her sister Nina. Then consider the dressmaker, told by Ethel in early February that she was to be married in six weeks' time. Not only does this again match exactly the timing in the accounts recalled by others, it means that not only have Ethel and Crippen fixed a date, they appear to have done so *in advance*. That strikes me as unusual if it were all make-believe, and quietly supportive of the suggestion that they did genuinely go through some form of public ceremony, perhaps using false names. (Crippen also told his tooth-pulling partner Dr Rylance that he and Ethel were married.) And whether in clandestine reality or merely their imagination, they appear to have done so significantly prior to 24 March, when Crippen fatefully cabled Clara Martinetti, and the earliest date we have for his claim that Cora was dead. I suspect that much of his prevarication regarding whether Cora had died or merely fled was for Ethel's benefit: only in the former case, obviously, was genuine marriage possible. But this would mean that Ethel would have been told by Crippen of the phony death story significantly prior to his passing the news on to others. The only other alternative, suggested by the evidence of Ethel's landlady, is that Crippen may have implied to Ethel that his marriage to Cora was not fully legal.[29]

We simply do not know what went on when the doors shut on 39, Hilldrop Crescent, and not just when it reached its head on 31 January 1910, but on every date preceding, each one perhaps laying a little more groundwork for what eventually happened. The problem is: why did it – whatever 'it' was – take so long? There were plenty of reasons why Crippen might have wanted to end his marriage, just as there were plenty of reasons why Cora might have wanted to up and leave. But all the likely triggers were pulled long before the chamber appears to have fired. *If* Cora was shrewish and promiscuous, she had been so for years. Crippen and Le Neve had been together for years too, and intimacy had long since been their normal state of affairs. If Crippen's account of their home life was true we might imagine Cora, motivated by one final twist of the emotional knife – learning of Ethel's pregnancy, perhaps – deciding to finally make good on her oft-delivered threat to up and leave him. But was it? Judging by the reports of their friends, what the Crippens seem most like is one of those couples who have decided to rub along from convenience, love extinguished, but mindful of the usefulness of the arrangement, and equally satisfied elsewhere. Whatever did happen in early 1910 it was surely something out of the ordinary that went above and beyond the now routine indignities and inconveniences of their sham life together, and the question every bit as important as 'what?' is 'why?' To this, the Crown did not pretend to have an answer.

Chapter 5

The Trial

MUIR: Sheer hypocrisy?

CRIPPEN: It is already admitted, sir.

MUIR: Sheer hypocrisy?

CRIPPEN: I am not denying any of this.

On 11 October 1910, at 2.45 pm, a most unusual funeral began. Beginning in Camden Road, it made its stately way to St Pancras Roman Catholic Cemetery in Finchley, where a private ceremony organised by the Music Hall Ladies' Guild began. Inside the coffin was not a human body, just a shapeless mass of flesh, without skeleton, head or limbs. The remains unearthed at 39, Hilldrop Crescent were finally being returned to the ground, nearly three months after they had been discovered.

The name on the grave was Belle Elmore. Exactly one week later, the trial of Hawley Harvey Crippen began at the Central Criminal Court. It was somehow not considered outrageous that his defence team had to argue that the remains were not Cora's, when they had already been buried under a stone bearing her name.

The truth is, the case was fatally prejudiced from the first day that Crippen was reported missing. The defence had not merely to combat the prosecution's evidence but also months of sensational and prejudicial news reporting. Could all of *that* – the body in the basement! the devilish doctor! the hypnotised concubine! the disguise! Dew racing to Canada in hot pursuit! the dramatic shipboard arrest! – could it really be the prelude to a not guilty verdict? Even the greatest defence team in the world would be hard-pressed to pull *that* out of the fire.

And in appointing Arthur Newton as his solicitor, Crippen had stumbled yet again. Following his arrest, offers of assistance, both financial and practical, were received by Crippen. Chief among them was a cablegram that read: 'Dear H.H. Crippen: Your friends desire me to defend you and will pay all necessary expenses. Will undertake your defence, but you must promise to keep absolute silence, answer no questions, and do not resist extradition. Reply confirming, as good deal must be done at once. Signed, Arthur Newton, Solicitor.'[1] Crippen was understandably flattered and accepted immediately: alas, Newton would prove to be a blatant opportunist, who single-mindedly steered his client's case in the direction of his own best advantage. This is not to suggest that he was an inept or even an especially negligent counsel, and many of his sallies, derided at the time, can now be seen to have landed remarkable bullseyes. But he was consumed with the hype and the glory, and much of the basic spadework essential to any defence was neglected.

The press were much exercised with speculation as to this mysterious consortium of 'friends' who had come to Crippen's aid, but Newton 'declined to reveal' their names.[2] The primary one appears to have been Horatio Bottomley, editor of *John Bull*, who put up £200, and from motives that were only incidentally philanthropic.[3] The main reason was that he had cut a deal with Newton, clearly starting as he meant to go on, for the exclusive rights to publish any of Crippen's private observations and reflections. This was the reason why Crippen was enjoined to give no statements, and when fallacious reports emerged of a confession, his 'friends' were understandably worried. Crippen rushed to assure them it was a hoax. It would not be the last.

The Crippen case had been the first time that a news story had been consumed exactly as if it were a serial romance, and the final chapter had fully lived up to the preceding ones. The sequel looked to be just as engrossing, as the fiend and his mistress were shipped back to England to face justice. When Crippen and Le Neve arrived at Euston station, authorities cleared the platform and erected a barrier to keep the public back, but at the first sight of the pair disembarking, a jungle chorus of hooting and booing echoed around the station. 'They shrank closer to their custodians, and it was painfully evident that they could not get too speedily away from the station.'[4] The only thing spoiling the fun was that Crippen was not playing his role at all well. He should have said, 'Curse you, Dew! You have foiled me at the last! I shall see you in hell!' and twirled the corners of his moustache for the full dramatic effect. Instead he deflated entirely, like a slashed tyre. The pathetic spectacle he presented soon earned him as much sympathy as it did shivers. ('The female portion of the population here evidently view the tragedy in a queer light,' noted the *Daily Herald*. 'Their sympathies seem to be entirely with Crippen, as many of them are sending flowers to him.'[5]) Mrs Ginnett, who had been on hand for the purposes of identification, noted it immediately: 'The Peter Crippen who was entirely at the beck and call of his whole-souled, energetic, dominating wife was gone. A man who had either sunk into torpidity or had steeled himself to a point of nervelessness was in his place.'[6] From this point on, except when communicating with Ethel, Crippen lapsed into a state of complete negation: this would further compromise him at the trial, when it was constantly revealed just how little effort he had made in his defence. But there is evidence that he had by this time sunk into deep depression. The first indications that the Crippen the world would come to know in detail would be so wildly anti-climactic came at his arraignment. A Quebec attorney had offered his services to Crippen to help him fight extradition[7] and it was widely speculated that he would do so vigorously, on the grounds that he was an American citizen. Instead, he gave no fight at all:

> The judge asked the prisoner if he was Hawley Harvey Crippen.
> 'I am,' said Crippen.
> 'Do you know this man?' indicating Inspector Dew.
> Crippen nodded his head.
> 'Are you ready to go back with him or any qualified officer?'
> 'Yes.'
> 'Do you intend to fight extradition?'
> 'No.'
> As he answered the questions Crippen scarcely raised his head.[8]

There were early suggestions that the press would have needed only small indication of a changing wind to actually side with Crippen. 'Just how much Crippen knows of the case against him is in doubt,' wrote one paper:

> Whether he has learned that the British authorities have been unable to identify the dismembered body found in the cellar of his Hilldrop Crescent home as that of his actress wife, is not known. Without such identification, lawyers say a conviction may be impossible. Inspector Dew said that Crippen was a coward. Dew, however, has been mistaken about Crippen before now. He was mistaken when he accepted Crippen's promise to remain in London.[9]

There was certainly a lot of press resentment against Dew. 'As usual the securing was entirely passive, so far as the police authorities were concerned,' griped the *New York Times*, 'and was the result, not of anything they had done, but of the thing they did their stupid best to prevent – the wide publication of every known fact concerning the murder of which Dr Crippen is suspected.'[10] Had Crippen come out swinging there would likely have been many in the media – the *New York Times* among them, perhaps – prepared to go to bat on his behalf. Instead, he didn't seem to care.

The only person presenting a more pathetic picture than Crippen at this time was his father. The American papers had obviously hoped to have their own on-the-spot star witness to draw upon, but Myron proved aged and melancholic. 'I have not the money to go to Hawley, but if I had I would gladly go and be of whatever consolation I might be to him,' he told reporters. 'I have not received any word from him and do not expect to. It is hard to have to be alone and suffer, but I do not think it will last long. I am not long for this world now, and since this trial has come to me I have not had a single day of good health. They can't prove anything on Hawley. They can't even prove that Belle Elmore is dead. Why should I believe him guilty?'[11] He was still puzzled by Crippen's lack of communication: 'I think it is strange he does not write me, as I have written him many letters, and the last time that I heard directly he had received my letters was when he wrote to (Otto) Hawley the second last time, a year ago last June.'[12]

Ethel, glad to be back in female attire and supplied, at her request, with a wig to cover her short hair,[13] remained as mysterious as ever: 'It seems that under Crippen's hypnotic influence she apparently does not experience the same degree of terror as the man.'[14] Indeed, Ethel was, if anything, even more enigmatic than Crippen, less expertly composed perhaps, but even more impenetrable, given that nobody seemed able to decide if she was a true innocent or playing them all for fools. Nonetheless, she had the sympathy of the world's press, probably because they misinterpreted the leniency with which she seemed to be being treated by the authorities. This was not because of any belief in her innocence so much as in the hope that she would provide evidence against Crippen – evidence that, for all their show of confidence to the press, they knew was badly needed. (And which it is possible she gave.)

With Crippen and Le Neve back in London and safely under lock and key, the Coroner's inquest resumed on 15 August. Back in July, Coroner Dr Danford Thomas had seemed notably pessimistic, telling the court: 'I do not know whether we shall be able to identify the remains. We shall have to adjourn as an analysis is being made of certain parts to see if poison was used. The police are doing their work ably.' But now, in the euphoria following Crippen's apprehension, the picture was looking altogether rosier.

6 September – *Poison found*

The prosecutor definitely stated that the physicians who made the post-mortem examination of the mutilated parts unearthed in the cellar of the Crippen home had discovered the presence of hyoscine, a colourless liquid poison, and also detected evidences that an operation had been performed. It had been known that the authorities had been working on the theory that Belle Elmore had been in the hands of one having at least a rude knowledge of surgery, and, further that she had been poisoned.[15]

8 September – *Secondary evidence announced*

Public Prosecutor Humphreys introduced evidence to establish the claim of the Crown that the parts of the mutilated body found in the Crippen home once formed a part of the person of Belle Elmore, the missing wife, and to strengthen what has been popularly regarded as the missing link in the chain of circumstantial evidence against the accused. Mrs. Adelaide Harrison, whose acquaintance with Belle Elmore had extended over a period of twelve years, examined strands of hair found when the dismembered body was uncovered and swore that she recognised the exhibit as similar to that worn by Belle Elmore. A torn bit of feminine underwear, also discovered by the searchers in the cellar, was introduced, and the witness declared that she had seen Belle Elmore clothed in undergarments of a like texture. Testimony had been offered before showing that the lower part of the body bore a scar, the result of an operation. Mrs. Harrison testified that she had seen a similar scar upon the body of her friend.[16]

14 September – *Edging towards identification*

Professor Pepper was the first witness called by the prosecution. At considerable length he described the examination which he made of the parts and set forth his conclusions. He could say that the members found were undoubtedly from a human being. Professor Pepper said that the hair discovered included a short strand of fair texture wrapped up in a handkerchief of the size commonly used by men. The witness identified particularly a piece of flesh six by seven inches in size as coming from the abdominal wall. It bore a scar which, in his opinion, was undoubtedly left by a wound from an operation. He said that the scar was in a vertical direction and more than four inches in length. It was old and might have been on the body for many years. The condition of the organs recovered were healthy, and in the judgment of the witness indicated a stoutish person in middle life.[17]

The verdict of the Coroner's jury was as follows:

We are agreed that the human remains found in the cellar of the house in Hilldrop Crescent were those of Mrs Cora Crippen, otherwise Belle Elmore, and that death was due to the effects of poison, and that the poison was hyoscine administered by her husband, Dr H.H. Crippen. We are unanimously of opinion that a verdict of 'Wilful Murder' should be returned against Dr Crippen.

You have to wonder why they even bothered with a trial. The above summation, probably in error on every point, demonstrably in error on the great majority, confirmed the popular perception of Crippen as a man already hanged, waiting only on the date and time. But for the sake of appearances the date was set: Crippen would be tried for his life on Tuesday, 18 October.

That the defence was a study in desperation is one of the most established features of the trial. What is less understood, simply because history is written by the winners, was that exactly the same applied to the prosecution. Because it won, and was therefore assumed to be correct, posterity has been generous to its own catalogue of illogicality, wild guesses and irrationally plugged gaps. This was a case that had very little evidence of any sort, for or against. The only thing the prosecution had going for it that even approached objective empirical value was the medical evidence – and that, ironically, is the one part of it that we can now say with absolute certainty was wrong. The rest was largely a tissue of naïve character assassination, coasting on the invaluable work of denigration already done by the world's media. In this, the case found an ideal prosecuting counsel in Richard Muir, not yet Sir Richard but already with a fearsome reputation for being 'thorough and dangerous' and 'with an unpleasant way of pressing his case a bit too hard against the accused'.[18]

Most glaring was the lack of coherent motive. True, in our pop-Freudian, post-Norman Bates, Hannibal Lecterphile age, motive has become terribly unfashionable, almost jejune. None of the *best* murderers have one. But Crippen is different. It would be the easiest thing in the world, if the remains in the basement were one of a series of murders of which we suspected him, to say that it doesn't matter why he did it: he was just a sicko psycho who killed for kicks. (One writer wondered rhetorically if he might not have been some unidentified Edwardian serial killer!) But most of us would agree that to do so would be mere evasion. The Crippen case *demands* motive, yet at the trial, when the evidence seemed a lot more straightforward than we now know it to be, nothing terribly convincing was advanced.

The best the prosecution could manage was that getting Cora out of the way would leave the field clear for Crippen and Ethel, while Cora's money would enable them to start their new life on a sound financial footing. It must have sounded anti-climactic even to them. It also makes no sense. In the hope of distracting them, prosecuting council Richard Muir reminded the jury – as if they needed reminding – of the multiple occasions on which Crippen had behaved inexplicably. Not just fleeing with his mistress in disguise, but his seemingly not having lifted a finger to help his defence after his arrest. The catalogue seemed so damning it obscured an equally important point: if this is plainly not how we would expect an innocent man to behave, then how much less is it how a guilty man would? A murderer, certainly one who bothered to mutilate a corpse so as to obscure its identity, would have had all these angles covered. It's impossible to imagine him not doing so. He might give himself away, of course, or his defence might crumble under the weight of the evidence or of cross-examination, but Crippen didn't even *have* a defence, other than 'it wasn't me and I don't know anything about any of it'. That is not a guilty man's defence. The judge asked, of his unposted advertisement to ascertain Cora's whereabouts: 'If he believed that his wife could be found, why should he not have sent it?' But that is *exactly* the wrong question. Several good answers might be given to that question. The *real* puzzler, on the other hand, is: If he believed that his wife could *not* be found, because she was dead and he had killed her, why *then* should he not have sent it?

So what story did the Crown have that was so much better than Crippen's? Cecil Mercer, who prepared the prosecution's reconstruction of events, revealed the shockingly juvenile level of their reasoning when he recalled the case in his autobiographical novel *As Berry and I Were Saying*:

> That certain things happened we know: exactly how they happened, we cannot be sure. Though much of what I tell you must be assumed, every conclusion was most carefully drawn, and myself I have no doubt that the very gruesome picture which I shall present differs hardly at all from the tale which would have been told, had someone been there to see. ...
>
> Belle Elmore drank [poisoned] stout, and Crippen undressed. By the time the coma had supervened, Crippen was in his pyjamas. He seized his wife's hair and dragged her out of the room and down the stairs. She was still in her underclothes. ...
>
> Well, he dragged the body downstairs and into the kitchen. He got it on to the table, above which was a burning lamp. This must have meant a great effort for the body was a dead weight and Belle Elmore was not a small woman by any means. That done, he stripped the body, in which, as like as not, there was still some life. His knives and scalpels were ready and so he cut her throat. That blood he caught in a bucket and poured away. When the veins had been drained he cut off her head.

This reads more like a sadistic sex fantasy than anything even remotely rooted in the facts of the case. The idea that Crippen might slit his wife's throat while she was still alive and watch her bleed to death on a kitchen table is beyond grotesque, and the suggestion that doing so would result in a discreet flow of blood that could manageably be 'caught in a bucket' is extraordinary. Both man and kitchen would of course be awash with gore. At the Coroner's inquest the police surgeon, Dr Thomas Mitchell, had confirmed that he and Pepper had examined the house for bloodstains, and the police had also made a most thorough examination, but found none.

> How he disposed of her head, no-one will ever know. And a human head is a difficult thing to destroy. And nobody had any theories. The head was gone.
>
> He then dissected his wife from A to Z. Only a man who had some surgical training could have done this… By now the monster was working stripped to the waist, for the labour was heavy, and he was up against time. …
>
> For hours the work went on. At six in the morning, he'd very nearly done. And then something – no one will ever know what – something happened to make Crippen lose his nerves. I always think it likely that it was some sound – a milkman's cry, perhaps… which showed that the world was stirring… that people were waking up. Be that as it may, panic was Crippen's portion for half an hour. And his one idea was to get what was left away and out of sight. Almost all the flesh was gone, except the slab which was bearing the tell-tale scar. In his frenzy, he snatched this up and thrust it into the grave. It was, in fact, the very last piece of flesh which he put in. In went his pyjama top, too, and Belle Elmore's underclothes, and tufts of hair, some false as well as real. But never a bone. …
>
> Then he smeared the coal dust over the top of the grave. Where he hid the bones for the moment, I've no idea.[19]

Then he went to work, on no sleep, and visited the Martinettis to check on Paul, all without seeming anything other than his usual self, despite having spent the entire night butchering his wife, and despite the fact that her head, limbs and groin were still in the house, seeping evidence. Then after a hard day's work he went back home, and got rid of all the rest of the body, nobody knows where, and removed all physical evidence from a kitchen that must have looked like a medieval slaughterhouse, in time to invite his mistress to come and live there the next day. Still, historians who have puzzled for decades over the question of just why Crippen would leave seemingly incriminating evidence in the cellar after successfully disposing of the remainder elsewhere will no doubt be gratified to learn that it was probably because he was startled by a milkman.

Let's be honest, apart from the kinky stuff about him stripping to the waist and slitting Cora's throat, this reads like it was written by a child.[20] It is a disgrace. Yet it is, essentially, the account of the crime that was put before, and accepted by, the jury, and that was deemed cogent enough to override the multiple accounts attesting to Crippen's good character, affectionate nature, and calm and untroubled manner during the time he was supposedly hacking and slashing away at home.[21] Here is William Long:

Take the critical time, which is early in February of this year; used he during that time to come daily to his work just the same as usual? Did he ever omit a single day as far as you remember?

No.

Did he come at the regular times?

Yes.

Did he ever show any trace of uneasiness?

No.

Any worried appearance about him?

No.

No hunted or worried appearance or anything of that kind nothing unusual about his manner?

Nothing whatever.

And diligent in his work as before?

Yes.

No trace of abruptness as if he had got anything on his mind?

Not the slightest. He was just as kind as ever.

And talking as freely and in the same way as he always did, without constraint or restraint?

Yes.

As Alfred Tobin put it in his opening speech for the defence:

His manner at the time of the alleged murder, and for months afterwards, could not be wiped aside. Just before his wife's disappearance and for months afterwards, he showed no sign of agitation, no sign of fright, no seeking to avoid his friends and his wife's friends… The next day (after the supposed murder) he went to work as usual having, it was suggested by the crown, murdered his wife and left her body in the house alone. He could not have got rid of the bones, the head, the hands, and the feet, and buried the flesh in the few short hours between 1.30 a.m. and his going to work the next morning. What murderer would run the risk of leaving the body behind like that?

Even the secondary evidence – had they not struck lucky with the dating of the pyjama jacket – was only circumstantial. Back at the inquest, Newton had somewhat taken the wind out of Adeline Harrison's sails after she identified the hair curlers as belonging to Cora. In reply to Newton's objections, she admitted that they 'resembled thousands of others'.[22] The trial pressed on as if this had not been conceded. In fact, there was even a vital challenge to the *primary* evidence buried in the medical testimony. It was revealed that the corpse's stomach was empty, while it was a fixed element of the prosecution's case that Cora had been murdered immediately after a dinner party. Crippen's team apparently did not spot this, or bring it out, but it should have been devastating defence evidence. If it was Cora, she could not have been killed when the prosecution alleged. Yet it was impossible for her to have died earlier, and impossible for her to have died later. This simple fact alone was enough to prove the remains are not hers, without the letters D, N and A ever needing to be mentioned. Yet it floated past the jury, the defence and the judge like pixie dust. Neither was sufficient made of the fact that, if the scar were in the position on the remains that the prosecution affirmed, it didn't appear to have a navel. Yet all witnesses who claimed to have seen the scar on Cora also testified to her navel being present. In his final letters, when Crippen knew he was past all hope of reprieve, he is still raising the point, and quite rightly.

Perhaps the weirdest claim of all concerned the clay that must have been removed from the cellar to make room for the remains. Dew told the jury: 'In the garden I found a raised heap of earth covered with garden litter and empty flower pots. I caused that to be dug, and I found on the top there was a small quantity of loam or garden mould, and underneath six to eight inches of clay, and below that again all loam.' 'You saw the amount of clay that had been dug from the hole in the cellar?' asked the prosecution lasciviously, at which point even the judge was forced to call time: 'Is not that going a little too far? It is quite sufficient that somebody did find clay there.' But for that interjection, presumably, the Crown would have suggested that Crippen may have lifted the bricks from the floor of the cellar (of a rented house he would soon be leaving), removed some of the clay, inserted the remains, and then buried the excess clay in the garden – when he could have buried the *remains* in the garden, saved 90 per cent of the work, and achieved his desired aims with 100 per cent more effectiveness and hope of success.

Clearly, everything hinged on the medical evidence, and the expert testimony. If there was even a small chance the jury might not be convinced by sick horror stories and lunatic conjecture, then it was vital that they be blinded with science. In this they were more than aided by their choice of experts. Augustus Pepper had a formidable reputation, but it was Bernard Spilsbury, the rising superstar of the path labs, who made the strongest impression. Spilsbury's name and reputation squat like some malevolent toad over the history of British murder trials in the early twentieth century. He was a man who knew not the meaning of doubt, and who regarded contrary opinions as so many flies, to be swatted and disposed of, a man whose mere 'attendance at a mortuary', noted Dr Robert Brontë, was 'enough to condemn an accused to death even before the committal proceedings have begun'.[23] The ruinous effect of this can well be imagined, and only now is the full human cost of his arrogance being counted.[24] Professor Keith Simpson, one of his vastly more likeable successors, noted in his book *Forty Years of Murder*: 'It is in teaching, training pupils, writings, the media and in lecture travelling that a lasting repute lies. Spilsbury did none of these things.'[25] His refusal to work with collaborators or students or to allow his findings to be peer reviewed, his arrogance and flamboyance, and the fact that his very presence in court came increasingly to be seen as an automatic and *a priori* sign of the prosecution's credibility all, it has been shown, did lasting harm. Crippen was far from the only casualty of his egomania. 'It will be a sorry day for the administration of criminal justice in this land', complained J.D. Cassels, QC during the

Sidney Fox trial, 'if we are to be thrust into such a position that, because Sir Bernard Spilsbury expressed an opinion, it is of such weight that it is impossible to question it.'[26] And that sorry day had dawned, according to Andrew Rose in a recent biography of Spilsbury, who plausibly argues that Fox was executed not merely for a crime he had not committed, but for a crime that *nobody* committed. The victim, Fox's mother, had almost certainly died of a heart attack. Spilsbury conjured up a strangulation where none existed; he was unhesitatingly believed; Fox died.[27] 'Perjury consists of wilfully giving material evidence that a witness knows to be false or does not believe to be true,' notes Rose. 'Spilsbury's evidence in the Fox case enters this dangerous territory.'[28] Rose forensically catalogues numerous cases in which Spilsbury vainly clung to opinions he knew to be unsound, made fundamental errors of fact, presented evidence grounded in flawed methodology, embellished evidence, and withheld important facts. Among this profusion, his 'dogmatically expressed opinions' in the Crippen trial 'can no longer be sustained'.[29]

Look in vain for any such uncertainty in the standard Crippen literature, however, even in present-day accounts such as those of Nicholas Connell or David James Smith, where Spilsbury and his manifestly flawed assertions are still placed on pedestals and venerated. It's like the rest of the twentieth century never happened and you're right back in the courtroom, where Spilsbury could even contradict his own side's evidence with impunity. Doctor Willcox, appearing for the prosecution, had testified that he had been forced to put the alleged scarred tissue in a fluid 'designed to prevent further putrefaction' on 8 August. But Spilsbury, who had not examined it until 9 September, glibly asserted that 'no putrefactive changes were present'. Once again, the defence failed to point out this anomaly.

The single most under-discussed element of the trial – then and ever since – is the medical evidence for the defence. The defence's experts have been much lampooned, in fact, for even *attempting* to refute Pepper and Spilsbury. When Crippen dared to respond to a point by saying 'I refute that', Muir railed on him and exclaimed: 'You refute *expert forensic evidence?*' – stressing the adjectives to allow the full absurdity of Crippen's position to anchor itself to the jury. And the expert medical testimony for the defence – what of that? That sort of expert testimony, it seems, we *are* at liberty to dispute – and, indeed, to discredit. And as for the experts who proffered it – well, they were mere phonies, buffoons, or else they were tricked into giving evidence (though not, surely, into giving evidence of the nature desired of them?)[30], or they had an axe to grind against Pepper, or Spilsbury, or his hospital, or something or other. Perhaps they just wanted to come in out of the rain and make trouble. Anything, clearly, other than that they had a validly different opinion and a duty to air it, because that would make Spilsbury and Pepper less than infallible, and what little evidence of Crippen's guilt as existed less than watertight.

It is perhaps the biggest surprise of the court transcripts that the defence were able to obtain experts of at least equal calibre to those of the prosecution, but who held, explained and stuck to entirely different views. First was Dr Gilbert Turnbull:

> I am director of the Pathological Institute at the London Hospital. The conducting of post-mortem examinations falls to my department. I am Master of Arts, a Doctor of Medicine, a Bachelor of Surgery of the University of Oxford, a member of the Royal College of Surgeons, London, a licentiate of the Royal College of Physicians, and I am also a member of the Pathological Society of Great Britain, which is the largest pathological institute in the United Kingdom. In 1907, 1908 and 1909 the average number of post-mortem examinations made under my supervision was 1251 each year. Complete microscopic investigations are carried out under my supervision. I devote the whole of my time to that and to the microscopic examination of similar material that is sent down by the surgeons. I have on three occasions – 9th September, 15th and 17th October – seen the piece of skin and flesh that is now shown to me. On 9th September a slice about four inches long was made across that piece of skin by Mr. Pepper. That slice goes across the right hand of what has been called the horse-shoe depression as the skin lies on the tray. The cut does not go across the folded side of the so-called horse-shoe which Mr. Pepper thinks is a scar; it goes, across and beyond on each side of the so-called scar. There is another cut through this other limb of the depression which was made by Dr Spilsbury; I think it is said that Dr Spilsbury made it the same day. That cut goes beyond the fold on either side, and goes outside it on each side. I have examined the portions removed by this cut and a third cut that was made. First of all, one single long cut was made at our request. There was a piece

removed, up by the fold, and then a second piece from the so-called scar, and then a third piece from the edge, completely outside the scar. I have examined those three bits with the microscope.

Does your microscopical examination enable you to say whether that, is a scar in fact, or which one of those bits was cut?

It enables me to say that it cannot possibly be a scar. I have formed that opinion because of certain structures which are found in this area which is described as a scar, and which have never been found in a scar before. First of all, there are two groups of hair follicles. In one group there are three hair follicles, and in the other there are two hair follicles. A hair follicle is the sheath round the hair. In these follicles or sheaths the hairs are also to be seen, cut in cross-sections. In addition to that, one finds in two of the sections in relation to these hairs, as one would expect, a large piece of sebaceous gland, and then another large piece in another section of the same sebaceous, or fatty gland.

One of the reasons that Spilsbury had forwarded to *prove* it was a scar, rather than a blemish, was that there would be no hair follicles growing in scar tissue: 'If it should be established that there is in the scar a sebaceous gland or a hair and a hair follicle, that would be conclusive that it is not a scar.' So Turnbull is not merely forming a different conclusion here, he is saying the whole underlying basis of the prosecution's position is in error.

Next came Dr Reginald Wall:

I am a Master of Arts, a Doctor of Medicine of the University of Oxford, a Fellow of the Royal College of Physicians, London, and a member of the Royal College of Surgeons. I obtained the Fitzgerald Exhibition at Queen's College, Oxford. The examination for that is in classical subjects, and has nothing to do with medicine. I obtained the Andrew Clark Exhibition in medicine and pathology at the London Hospital. I am assistant physician to the London Hospital, and also to the hospital for consumptives at Brompton. Until the beginning of this year I was one of the pathologists to the London Hospital. I am an examiner in *materia medica* at the Apothecaries Hall. I am a Fellow of the Medical Society of London, and also of the Royal Society of Medicine. I am the author of various medical works. I was demonstrator of physiology for two years at the London Hospital College. I have seen the piece of skin and flesh which was before the last witness. I saw it first on 9th September, second on 15th October, and third on 17th October. I was present when Mr. Pepper made one transverse cut across the piece of skin, including the site of what he said was a scar. I was not present when Dr. Spilsbury made the subsequent cuts for the removal of pieces of skin for microscopical examination. On 15th October my examination of the piece of skin commenced at 11.30 and finished at 4.15. It was an examination with the eye and with a hand lens, not a microscopical examination. At the second examination on 17th October we saw the piece of skin for a third time to identify certain points that we wanted to confirm, and the remainder of the time we were present we were examining the microscopic sections which had been prepared by Dr. Spilsbury. The time spent over that examination was a little over two hours, mainly on the microscopical examination.

As the result of those examinations is that one groove – one limb of the so-called horse shoe – in your opinion a scar or not?

In my opinion, it is not a scar. I could not see on inspection by the naked eye or with the hand lens such an appearance as I should have expected to find if there had been a scar in that situation. I found appearances which I could explain much more easily on the supposition that the skin had been folded in that region. Secondly, after the incision which had been made by Mr. Pepper very kindly, I did not, on examining the cut surfaces of the edges of the skin, find such an alteration in structure as I should have expected had there been originally a scar, and on comparing the cut surface at the site where the scar was alleged to be I did not find that the appearance of the cut surface differed from the appearance of the cut surface of the other part of the groove where it is admitted there is no scar.

The prosecution's tactic in both cases was to tie the experts in knots of trivia, in the hope that the resulting tedium would encourage the jury to forget all about the substantive points. This took the form of an endless toss-up about the presence or absence of the abdominal muscle, which certainly affected whether the flesh sample was from the stomach or not, but in no way altered either man's certainty regarding the scar, which, when the cross-examination finally returned to the matter in hand, Turnbull was happy to reiterate:

I put it, as Mr. Pepper has shown it, that the skin has finally healed showing a mark which is seven-eighths of an inch at the lower part, an inch and three-quarters higher up, and a quarter of an inch another inch and three-quarters higher up. Would that affect your judgment at all as to its being a scar or not?

I think that is against it being a scar.

Do you say that a mark of that kind could be caused by folding, that is to say, a mark which is wider at the bottom and narrows up?

Yes.

Turnbull is routinely presented in the standard accounts as a shallow dissembler, who rashly endorsed a view he did not really agree with from petty resentment of the official experts, and was tricked into standing by it in court. This can already be seen to be absurd, purely on the trial evidence, but it is undermined yet further by the fact that he was *still* asserting the point as late as 1917. Spilsbury's biographer Andrew Rose discovered his notes in the Royal London Hospital archives, showing that he made another detailed 'diagrammatic reconstruction of Dr Spilsbury's sections... said to contain no sebaceous glands or hair follicles', and again set out his arguments for believing absolutely that Spilsbury was wrong. Finally, in 2002 the slides were examined by Professor Bernard Knight. Despite Spilsbury's claims of complete certainty in court, Knight was able to find no definite indications whatsoever of scar tissue.[31]

On the matter of how long the remains might have been under the cellar floor, the prosecution had to tread especially cautiously, because they knew that even though the medical team was certain they could not have been in the cellar longer than the period of the Crippens' tenancy, there was no actual objective timescale by which a body invariably decomposes, and the defence might easily use that fact to sow unwarranted seeds of doubt in the minds of the jury. Cleverly, they decided to be upfront about it, before then proceeding to the expert opinion. If the defence then went back to the original ambiguous statements it would look as though they were clutching at straws. Thus Pepper answered with a clear 'yes' to the suggestions that 'it is quite beyond the reach of science to determine with accuracy the period of death from the process of putrefaction' and that 'two different bodies buried in the same soil and under apparently similar conditions frequently present such differences as to baffle all attempts at generalisation'. That should have introduced an unacceptable degree of uncertainty, but it did not, because the prosecution had a trump card, a universal acid that ate away all reasonable doubt: the pyjama jacket.

Inspector Dew claimed to have found, in a box in Crippen's bedroom, three pairs of pyjama trousers and two pyjama jackets. To his *very* good fortune, a portion of what seemed to be the missing third jacket just happened to be in the pit with the remains: better still, it was the portion with the maker's label! It was presumably first assumed that this merely tied the fragment to Crippen, given the incomplete state of one of his three sets of pyjamas. But they were to be even luckier (and this I believe really was unanticipated luck) when it was discovered that the material the pyjamas were made from did not exist before 1908, and the vendor, Jones Brothers Ltd., still had a record of all three sets being sold to Mrs Crippen early in 1909. This stroke of good fortune essentially made any scientific speculation about the rate of decomposition irrelevant.

Then there was the hyoscine. This was the one there was no getting away from: there was the fact of the hyoscine in the remains, the fact of Crippen's purchase of the drug, and the fact of his inability to satisfactorily account for the quantity he had obtained. But again, things are not so simple as we think, and when the court transcripts are read in full, we find the expert testimony of Dr Alexander Blyth. The Crown's witness, Dr Willcox, had said that of the three potential alkaloids detected in the remains – hyoscine, hyoscyamine and atropine – he could be sure that it was hyoscine, even though they were so similar as to have only recently been separately classified, and on very specific grounds:

> From a careful examination of the alkaloid I found it to be gummy, which is a characteristic of hyoscine. Gumminess is not characteristic of hyoscyamine and atropine; they are crystalline.

Willcox had also dismissed the suggestion that the traces might have been of an animal alkaloid occurring naturally in the body during putrefaction, rather than, as he maintained was the case, a vegetable alkaloid that would have had to have been introduced artificially. But Blyth rejected both claims:

> I am a member of the Royal College of Physicians, a Fellow of the Institute of Chemistry, a Fellow of the Chemical Society, and I have various other qualifications. I am the author of a medical work entitled *Poisons: Their Effects and Detection.*

> *Dr Willcox told us yesterday that going through the ordinary processes, he at last extracted a gummy substance. Now is a gummy substance characteristic of hyoscine and not of hyoscyamine, atropine, or any animal alkaloid?*

> Certainly not. You can have a gummy substance in extracting various alkaloids. Often the slightest impurity, especially with regard to hyoscyamine, causes it not to crystallise. ...

> *Further, Dr Willcox said that small round spheres were produced. Are those round spheres characteristic of hyoscine alone, or are they also, found with hyoscyamine and atropine?*

> I have not been able to get them. I have attempted to get what Dr Willcox has stated according to the depositions that have been forwarded to me, but I must confess that I have not been able to distinguish between the atropine, hyoscyamine and hyoscine by hydrochloric acid, as Dr Willcox has done. No one knows whether those round spheres might be produced at last in the case of animal alkaloids.

> *Dr Willcox told us that in the lungs, which were most decomposed, he found only a trace of any alkaloid. If this was an animal alkaloid, in fact, would you expect that he should have found most of the animal alkaloid in the most decomposed part, the lungs?*

> I should not have expected so, because animal alkaloids arise, it is well known, at a particular stage of putrefaction, and when that stage is passed any animal alkaloid that has been produced becomes more or less destroyed, so that in the same decomposing tissue at different times of its putrefaction you would never expect to find the same amount of putrefaction alkaloid. ...

In your opinion, is it possible to make a mistake between animal mydriatic alkaloids and vegetable mydriatic alkaloids?

I think the evidence points that they are the same thing.

But is it possible to make a mistake between the two?

You would like me to answer yes or no, but that would not be fair. In my opinion some of them are identical, and therefore it is possible to make a mistake between the two.

Why did the jury reject such absolute certainty so confidently? Clearly, something had gone wrong with the Crippen trial, and a big part of the problem lay in its contamination by the media. Today, when it is understood that a sensational crime will receive saturation coverage, the inconveniences and pitfalls it brings are more clearly understood, and can be anticipated and to some degree diluted. Juries are clearly instructed to disregard information gleaned from outside the court (however difficult that may be in practice); defence counsel are alert to the potential for adulteration and quick to have impure inferences pointed up or stricken from the record. But with the Crippen case this unwelcome phenomenon was playing out for pretty much the first time; nobody would have even been much aware of the threat it represented. One clearly intuits from the transcripts of the trial that the prosecution are not so much opening and developing a case as picking up an ongoing story from where the papers left off. It feels almost like a formality, as if Crippen had pleaded guilty, or been seen by a hundred witnesses with his wife's corpse. One senses strongly the presumption of guilt.

The battleground in which the prosecution set out to claim their victory once and for all was in cross-examination. 'The English system places the burden of proof upon the prosecution,' writes Thomas Grant in the popular bestseller *Court No.1 The Old Bailey*. 'The prosecutor sets out to prove the defendant's guilt, the defence to controvert that proof. The result is a contest, two sides struggling against each other, albeit in accordance with strict rules. And at the heart of that struggle is perhaps the greatest contribution of the common law to justice, as well as to the aesthetics of a trial: the cross-examination.' But there is a giant paradox here. If the burden of proof is on the prosecution, cross-examination should be unnecessary. The case should be able to stand without any additional persuasion, grandstanding or showboating. It shouldn't be necessary to present the jury with a theatrical sketch of the accused in performance in order for them to reach their verdict. 'A well-constructed cross-examination can capsize a seemingly impregnable case,' Grant continues, seemingly with approval. 'It can destroy an attractive defence.' What could be more inimical, in that case, to the dispassionate pursuit of justice he has just been trumpeting?

It is worth remembering that in being cross-examined at all Crippen was enjoying the dubious benefit of an innovation scarcely a decade old. Until 1898, English law made no provision for such tactics: the accused was legally barred from giving evidence at their own trial. What sounds today like a handicap was originally enshrined in law for the prisoner's own benefit, so that the prosecution might not score advantage in court above and beyond the reach of their evidence. Whether one wilts or flourishes under cross-examination is purely a matter of temperament and personality: it sorts the hams from the Hamlets, but has the most tangential connection imaginable with the impartial establishment of guilt or innocence. The idea that it might aid the pursuit of justice over and above the clear dissemination of the evidence is, to say the least, a curious one. The truly wicked probably have least to fear from it, those most deserving of a fair hearing the most. And in the Crippen trial we can clearly see its effects at their most baneful, with Muir repeatedly belabouring Crippen with the same questions, then ignoring his answers and asking them again, not because anything further is to be gleaned but simply to grind him down and establish him in the minds of the jury as weak and incapable of making a case for himself. For instance, when Muir asks Crippen if he went to a nearby cabstand to enquire if Cora had left by that means, and Crippen replies 'I made no inquiries whatever' (i.e. not at the cabstand nor anywhere else), Crippen is not only clearly answering the question posed, he is also providing additional evidence of value to Muir's case. Yet Muir absurdly snaps back: 'Please listen to the question!' and asks it again. He could be in no doubt that Crippen had answered him correctly, but he is not interested in obtaining information, he wants to stage a performance, in which he constantly asks the same question, over and over again (did Crippen enquire of this person? Or of this? Or this?), and to secure the same defeated answer each time. Crippen's response pre-empted his flourish. And, indeed, on and on he then goes. By the time he gets to asking about Crippen's *milkman*, even the judge (generally hostile to Crippen) is forced to bring down the curtain:

MUIR:
Have you enquired of the milkman whether he saw your wife alive after you had left the house on that morning of the 1st February?

CRIPPEN:
I have already said that I have made no enquiries.

JUDGE:
That answer covers everything; you can make any comment on it you like, Mr Muir… He has said definitely that never at any time has he made or caused to be made any inquiries whatever.

Whereupon Muir carries straight on, obliviously. He repeated this 'same question a hundred ways' tactic when grilling Crippen as to the lies he told regarding Cora's disappearance. 'I do not see why you keep on with these questions, because I am willing to admit and tell you they were all lies right through,' Crippen replies dismally. Yet to Grant, 'the frisson that must have rippled through Court Number One' at these ugly exchanges 'is still detectable on the page'. Indeed it is, and entirely to justice's detriment.

Perhaps the most famous, and unpleasant, exchange of the entire trial came when Muir tried to goad Crippen into saying he feared being arrested for murder when he and Le Neve fled. For some reason it is routinely held up as a masterpiece of cross-examination (and in the negative sense described above, I suppose it is):

When did you make up your mind to go away from London?

The morning after Inspector Dew was there, the 8th or 9th.

Are you sure about that?

Yes.

Had you the day before been contemplating the possibility of your going away?

I would not like to say that I had made up my mind. When Inspector Dew came to me and laid out all the facts that he told me, I might have thought, well, if there is all this suspicion, and I am likely to have to stay in jail for months and months, perhaps, until this woman is found, I had better be out of it. …

Upon what charge?

Suspicion.

Suspicion of what?

Suspicion of… Inspector Dew said, 'This woman, has disappeared, she must be found.'

Suspicion of what?

Suspicion of being concerned in her disappearance.

What crime did you understand you might be kept in gaol upon suspicion of?

I do not understand the law enough to say. From what I have read it seems to me I have heard of people being arrested on suspicion of being concerned in the disappearance of other people.

The disappearance of other people?

Well, I am doing the best I can, to explain it to you. … I could not define the charge, except that if I could not find the woman I was very likely to be held until she was found, that was my idea.

Because of what?

I cannot say why. I can only say that no other idea than that entered my head. If I could not produce the woman…

Yes, what would be the inference?

Mr. Dew told me that I should, be in serious trouble. Well, I could not make out what the inference would be.

And that was why you contemplated on the afternoon of 8th July, flying from the country?

Quite so. That, and the idea that I had said, that Miss Le Neve was living with me, and she had told her people she was married to me, and it would put her in a terrible position. The only thing I could think of was to take her away out of the country where she would not have this scandal thrown upon her.

Now, to me it seems obvious that Crippen knew full well that Muir was trying to get him to say 'murder', and that he instead withstood the barrage without doing so, giving perfectly coherent answers to each question. Far from being tricked into some rash or psychologically revealing admission or evasion, Crippen is simply playing the game by Muir's rules – and winning it, to boot. Try as he might, Muir could not shake him. ('If you tell the truth,' said Mark Twain, 'you don't have to remember anything.') His story held up, along with his confidence in it. He did not need to rationally fear apprehension for murder in order to decide to flee. He did not fear being held for murder but, exactly as he says, for being in some way materially responsible for Cora's disappearance. (How many times in detective stories is a suspect, with no charge forthcoming but merely a burden of suspicion, ordered: 'Don't change your lodgings without telling us,' and told they may not leave the country?) Though he doesn't say it, it would have been obvious that any outcome from this point on would be bad news for him: the worst case scenario that he would end up in exactly the position he now found himself, the best that Cora would be located and bang would go all chance of the new life he was planning with Ethel. No, he had to go away. The cross-examination obscured rather than illuminated this point, which was of course its purpose.

Another occasion on which Crippen was grossly misrepresented in cross-examination came when the prosecution questioned him on the occasion he was visited after his arrest in Canada by Cora's friend Mrs Ginnett:

Was Mrs. Ginnett a great friend of your wife's

Yes.

She is well known in the theatrical profession the music hall profession, especially in America?

No, not to my knowledge. She is well known on this side, I do not know about the other side.

Did you see her in Quebec?

I saw her in Quebec, that is, she came to the room where I was, but I did not speak to her.

Do you mean you could not speak to her, or that you could have spoken, and did not?

I think she asked if she could speak to me, and she was told she could not.

She was in the same room with you?

Yes.

As near to you as I am now?

More near than that.

For how long?

A few minutes.

At that time you knew you were charged with the murder of your wife?

Yes.

Did you ask Mrs. Ginnett to try and find your wife?

I could not speak to Mrs. Ginnett.

Just answer the question first, did you, ask Mrs. Ginnett?

I did not, because I supposed that I should not be allowed to speak to her.

Never mind about supposing, you did not speak to her. Why did, you not speak to her?

Because I supposed I would not be allowed to speak to her.

Did Mrs. Ginnett come into this room and ask to speak to you?

I do not know what she came into the room for. She came into the room and sat down, and I heard her speak, I think it was to Inspector M'Carthy, I am not sure, but I understood her to ask could she speak to me, and I thought he said no, but I know she did not speak to me, and consequently I did not speak to her.

Now, if your wife was alive and in America, there was her friend, Mrs. Ginnett, who is an American, is she not?

She was in America then.

Her headquarters are New York?

Yes.

Could she not have found your wife for you?

I do not know.

Or try?

She could have tried, but I did not speak to her, because I supposed I could not.

This is desperate, nasty stuff, successfully conveying to the jury, through smear and provocation rather than anything approaching legal argument, that Crippen must have known his wife to be dead (or else why not enlist Mrs Ginnett's aid in finding her?). But how many times can a man say that he was not permitted to speak? It is incredible that the judge did not step in here (instead, he took an active part: two of the questions in the extract above came from him rather than counsel) and appalling that the defence did not have the rebuttal at its fingertips. For earlier in the trial, Crippen had clearly said:

> While Inspector Dew went down to see Miss Le Neve, the chief inspector, or the man who was with him, told me, 'We deal very differently with people in Canada when we arrest them to what they do in England; we tell them that they must not say anything.' He added, 'Now don't you say a word on anything – cut your tongue out – have nothing to say.'

And the application Crippen had received from Arthur Newton offering representation had specifically decreed:

> You must promise to keep absolute silence, answer no questions…

And in an interview with Mrs Ginnett published at the start of August, she too made it clear that neither of them was free to speak to the other:

> I had known Inspector Dew in London and through my friends there I had communicated with him several times of late. He expressed his pleasure at my being here, spoke of the assistance I could be to him

and then said, with some restraint: 'Mrs Ginnett, I am sorry, but the law will not permit you to speak with Crippen.' Then he walked through a door which he opened. 'Come this way,' he said.

I stepped through the door and found myself face to face with Peter Crippen. Seated in a chair, his hands in irons, huddled on his lap, he was staring directly at me and I was staring at him. His eyes distended and I knew then that he recognised me. He braced himself and it seemed as if he were about to speak, but evidently he, too, had been warned in advance and he sank back in his chair again.[32]

That had been in the public record since it was published on 22 August. The mind yet again boggles – at the sleaziness of one side, and the shoddiness of the other.

As the bleak pantomime drew towards its close, demand for seats at the Old Bailey surpassed all records. Hundreds of written applications were received. One woman wrote that she and her sister should be given seats because of the large amounts her aunt had given to charity. Another, indignant after four unsuccessful attempts, asked for a refund on the stamps.[33] Policemen, actors, churchmen and county magistrates all joined the clamour. W.S. Gilbert was spotted in the public gallery, as was Gus Elen, the great coster comedian of the halls. The seventy seats reserved for the public were ticketed, with morning and afternoon sessions separately attended.

On 22 October, the jury took less than half an hour to find Crippen guilty. After reading out the verdict, the foreman handed the judge a note, which he read and to which he responded: 'That shall be forwarded to the proper quarter.'[34] It was presumed at the time that it was a recommendation for mercy, to be handed to the Home Secretary, but if so nothing more was heard of it, and mercy in all its forms was to be in conspicuously short supply. The judge told Crippen he had been convicted on evidence that 'can leave no doubt in the mind of any reasonable man' and that he should 'entertain no hope' of reprieve. Crippen was asked if he had anything to say why sentence should not be passed, and replied: 'I am innocent. I still protest my innocence.'

Over in America, Myron Crippen reacted to the news with quiet despair. 'My son is innocent, even though he stands convicted,' he told the press, 'and I firmly believe that his wife, Belle Elmore, is alive and

Hawley Harvey Crippen – the photograph that circumnavigated the globe.

Cora Crippen in professional attire.

Cora as The Major.

Ethel Le Neve – her mask never slipped.

39 Hilldrop Crescent, with its subsequent owner, music hall comedian and convicted child sex offender Sandy McNab, December 1910.

The basement.

Typical advertisements for quack dentists, 1900. Crippen's Yale Tooth Specialists company was of this type.

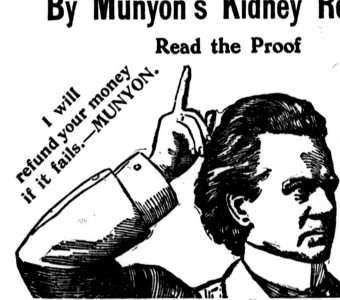
Professor Munyon, Crippen's employer and supporter, in characteristic pose offers to cure all known diseases with sugar and paraffin.

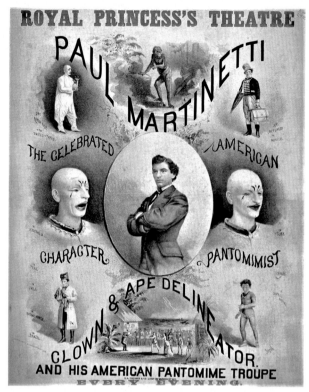

Munyon does it for free.

Paul Martinetti – he alerted the police to Cora's disappearance.

Bruce Miller – had Cora run away to join him in America? *(Saint Paul* Globe, *19 Feb 1899)*

Chief Inspector Walter Dew – at first he thought the case was just a sordid theatrical intrigue.

Dew in 1887 – the Ripper is just around the corner; Crippen a long way off.

The cellar – Dew's perseverance pays off.

The world learns the news.
(Collection of John Trestrail)

THE
LONDON MURDER
MYSTERY.

Mutilated Body
found in a Cellar

Arrest of Crippen & Le Neve
On board S.S. Montrose

THE NAUGHTY DOCTOR
The Crippen Diary.

THE VICTIM.

Mrs. Cora Crippen, professionally known as Belle Elmore.
(Photographed by Hana.)

WELL-KNOWN MOTORIST KILLED.

THE CAMDEN TOWN MYSTERY.

OUTSIDE THE SCENE OF THE TRAGEDY YESTERDAY. *(See page 7.)*

"WANTED."

The portrait of Hawley Harvey Crippen, alias Peter Crippen, alias Franckel, the missing husband, issued by the police.

DAYLIGHT SAVING IN WHITEHALL.

Mr. Churchill states in Parliamentary Papers that arrangements have been made in most of the departments and sub-departments of the Home Office by which the majority of the junior staff, second division clerks and boy clerks, work during the summer months from nine to four, instead of from ten to five.

Mr. Burns states that, at the Local Government Board, it was experimentally arranged last summer that those of the clerical staff who desired

Crippen's father Myron – he went to his grave convinced of his son's innocence.

HAWLEY CRIPPEN.

Crippen on the run – a glamourised newspaper portrait.

Crippen and Ethel on board the *Montrose* – together alone.

Captain Kendall on the verge of shouting 'Robinson!' and running away.

Dew leads Crippen off the *Montrose*. The picture was reprinted hundreds of times in newspapers the world over.

Myron Crippen hears of his son's arrest.

1910 slide show.

Crippen and Le Neve appear at Bow Street. Why is Crippen not wearing his spectacles?

The wolf pack outside the Old Bailey during Crippen's trial.

Augustus Pepper – his medical evidence was
ambiguous, but there was no disputing the
pyjamas and hairpins he helped find.

The pyjamas that were
produced in evidence – from
the Jones Brothers catalogue.

Sir BERNARD SPILSBURY.

When arsenic has closed your eyes,
This certain hope your corpse may rest in:—
Sir B. will kindly analyse
The contents of your large intestine.

MR. PUNCH'S PERSONALITIES.—LXIV.

Sir Bernard Spilsbury – his implacable certainty ensured Crippen's conviction.

EXÉCUTION DU Dʳ CRIPPEN DANS LA PRISON DE PENTONVILLE

Crippen is executed. *(Collection of John Trestrail)*

The Crippen Horror – an early penny dreadful-style account. Note 'doctor' in quotes.

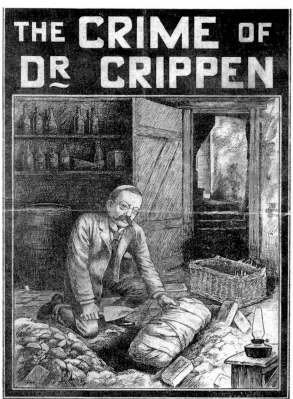

Book cover from the 1940s. *(Collection of John Trestrail)*

The Execution of Crippen
– a penny slot machine
now in the collection of
the Museu d'Autòmats del
Tibidabo, Barcelona.

Chester Stevens, the first actor to portray Crippen,
took the lead in the play *Trapped by Wireless*, staged
while the leading character was still awaiting trial.

Donald Pleasence and Coral Browne in *Dr Crippen* (1962).

Dr Crippen Lives! – undoubtedly the strangest of all the Crippen movies.

John Trestrail with Madam Tussaud's
waxwork Crippen.

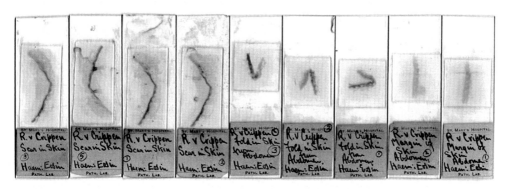

Evidence slides.
*(Courtesy of David
Foran)*

DR. BRUCE MILLER AND THE CONDUCTRESS.

Bruce Miller and one of his automata, both avoiding the camera. *The Strand* magazine, March 1900.

AUTOMATON DRUMMER.

Saint Paul *Globe*, 19 Feb 1899.

Bruce Miller's orchestra, *The Strand* magazine, March 1900.

living somewhere in the United States.' Myron was by this time said to be too feeble to work, broken in health and living in a small, one-room apartment: 'I have no means and cannot work. I have written to him, sending the letter in care of the officials who were conducting his trial but I have received no reply, not even a word. If he would only send a line it would make me feel so much better, but when I get no word, only the news in the papers, it makes me feel awfully blue. I might as well be dead. There is nothing to live for.'[35]

On 5 November, Crippen learned that his appeal had been rejected on every point. In one of his last letters to Ethel, he wrote: 'Today at the appeal I realised more and more that the medical evidence for my defence was so mismanaged that it told against me rather than for me. This I saw at the Old Bailey in the judge's summing up and again today in the summing up of the appeal. I am powerless now, and can do nothing more, but bow to the inevitable.'

Most accounts of the crime banish to the wildest fringes of hoaxers and publicity seekers any suggestions at the time that Crippen might genuinely have been innocent, or that Cora might still have been alive. In truth, a small but concerted body of respectable opinion soon emerged dedicated to just those propositions. 'Professor' Munyon, whose relationship with Crippen had certainly had its valleys as well as hills over the years, emerged staunchly in his corner, offering $50,000 to anyone who could provide evidence of Cora's movements after 31 January. 'I will even pay it to the woman herself, if she will come forward in time to save her husband,' he told the press the day the appeal verdict was handed down. 'I believe that either the woman is hiding to carry out one of the most consummate revenges in the annals of jealousy, or else she has carried an advertising game too far. I never could be persuaded that Crippen killed his wife. He was too gentle a man.'[36] Munyon claimed he had received several letters from people who had seen her alive. We can be cynical of almost everything here, including Munyon's motives (all publicity is good publicity after all), but there's still no getting around his conviction. Who would cynically wager $50,000 – a sizeable sum even today, a vast one then? Rightly or wrongly, Munyon was willing to stake a small fortune on his certainty that the Crippen being sold to the media was not the man he knew. He had nothing to gain from doing so, and with his business going from strength to strength as it was at this time, Crippen might have been felt to be a past association he had every interest in playing down. Yet for some reason he felt compelled to make this gesture.

A conman of a different sort, and one evidently bristling at the minimal returns he had so far received on his investment of £200, was Horatio Bottomley. With his man at his lowest ebb, Bottomley decided to press his advantage, and published an open letter to Crippen in the pages of *John Bull* on 19 November. In it he suggested that the condemned man should unburden himself ('relieve your burning brain', was how he put it) making a full account of what had really happened, lightening his soul and, merely incidentally of course, stuffing the coffers of Horatio Bottomley. At the prison it was decided not to show the piece to Crippen, and he was in complete ignorance of it when Arthur Newton visited him on the 21st and, under pressure from Bottomley, suggested that it might be a good idea to respond. Crippen refused, but an entirely spurious reply, thanking *John Bull* for its interest and claiming to have been touched by its sincerity, appeared regardless, almost certainly emanating from the same source as the initial entreaty. Ethel's legal team issued a firm retraction, embarrassing both Bottomley and Newton, and landing the latter in hot water with the Law Society. This was but the prelude, however, to an even more outrageous hoax that appeared in the pages of the London newspaper the *Evening News* on the day of Crippen's execution. This took the form of a full and complete confession to the crime, which Newton assured the paper was genuine. Needless to say it was not: merely a fiction Newton had concocted and which he sold to the paper via a go-between for £500 – an almost unbelievably shabby and venal thing for the legal representative of a condemned man to do. The already fraudulent confession was further embellished by crime writer Edgar Wallace (whose *The Four Just Men* Crippen had been reading on the *Montrose*[37]) before it saw publication. Its appearance caused instant denials,[38] and the *Evening News*, which had its printers working non-stop to meet demand for the edition, never recovered from its very public loss of integrity, closing for good a few months later. Newton attempted to deny all knowledge of it, but ruination would before long make a scarf for his deserving shoulders also:

> Mr Arthur Newton, K. C., the counsel who defended Dr Hawley Harvey Crippen... has been suspended for twelve months, and ordered to pay the costs, for professional misconduct.

Mr Justice Darling, in passing sentence, said that he was satisfied that Crippen had not been defended as he should have been. The case had been conducted largely for the purpose of making newspaper 'copy'. Others besides Mr Newton, added his Honour, deserved punishment.[39]

For an English judge to opine on the record that 'Crippen had not been defended as he should have been' might have been felt to have sent shockwaves through the media and legal establishment: instead, it seems to have been largely ignored.

On 17 November, a petition calling for Crippen's reprieve was handed to the Home Office, bearing over 1,500 signatures. One man even requested that he be executed in Crippen's place, on the grounds that 'his [own] life was useless, whilst Crippen's scientific knowledge would be of benefit to humanity'.[40] Then, five days before his son's execution, Myron Crippen died. According to his physician, Dr Lee W. Burt:

While the old man was sick with rheumatism and near pneumonia, death was really due to a broken heart. He had one of the most loving natures that a man can have, and the accusation against and conviction of his son were more than he could withstand at his age... He had a grandson, Hawley O. Crippen, a son of the convicted man, living here, but he is poor, has a family and did nothing for his grandfather. He seldom called on the old man. He was there a few minutes last night before his grandfather died, but had gone when death came.[41]

The day before his execution, Ethel visited him for the last time: 'Crippen made no effort to suppress his emotions when the time arrived for the final parting. For the rest of the day he remained in a state of complete nervous prostration.'[42] The same day, executioner Ellis arrived at Pentonville. He had taken the train from Liverpool, where he had executed a wife murderer that morning. Also in attendance was a Catholic priest, Father Carney, who spent the night with Crippen.[43] The *Dundee Courier* noted that 'many hundreds of morbid spectators waited outside the grim walls of Pentonville in the gloom and bitter cold'.[44] While they loitered, a canvas covering was placed over the gallows so that the execution could not be witnessed from the windows of the tenement buildings overlooking the prison yard.[45] According to some reports, 'Crippen managed sufficient strength to walk to the scaffold, but the strain was so intense that he was on the point of collapse when the bolt was drawn.'[46]

Hawley Harvey Crippen was hanged at two minutes past nine on the morning of 23 November 1910.

Chapter 6

The Legend

The White Star Company have been forced to utilise the state room in the steamer *Gigantic* which was occupied by the murderer Hawley Crippen on his return to England, as a gigantic storeroom, as no passenger will occupy it.

The Worker (Brisbane), 4 February 1911

He has outlasted them all.

Would we easily remember Inspector Walter Dew today, were it not for him? What of the supposedly Sherlockian Captain Kendall of the *Montrose*? Both men would later pen memoirs entitled *I Caught Crippen*, and each would be the subject of biographies entitled *The Man Who Caught Crippen*: there, I think, is our answer. Kendall's vainglorious claims of bringing about the apprehension of the fugitives earned him his £250 reward, but weren't enough to save his reputation when, years later, and at the very same location where Dew boarded his ship and arrested Crippen and Ethel, his steamer *Empress of India* collided with a Norwegian ship in dense fog. It sank in ten minutes, leaving about 300 survivors, including Kendall, and over 1,300 dead, in what the press described as the worst maritime disaster since the *Titanic*.

Likewise, 'Professor' James M. Munyon, Crippen's most famous employer, is today little more than a footnote in the story of his former employee. In the aftermath of Crippen's death he seemed to be going from strength to strength, launching perhaps his most elaborate scam of all in 1911. 'Munyon's Hope Cult' was a combination of positive thinking, guru worship and patent pill-popping, the aim of which was to show that anyone could live to the age of 100 or beyond, provided they adhered to the revolutionary creeds of Munyon, the 'Apostle of Hope'. Boasting of thousands of followers, he toured America giving cornball pep talks on the general level of: 'There is more curative power in an ounce of hope than in tons of dope.'[1] He told the *San Francisco Call* on 24 August: 'I confidently expect to enrol at least 50,000 converts to my cult before September 1.' But battered by lawsuits over his phony remedies and weakened by marital setbacks, his winning streak was already coming to an end. He seemed to have been especially unlucky with fires. His medicines factory burned to the ground in 1913 as the result of an electrical fault: some seventy-five employees leaped for their lives from the building's windows and $500,000 worth of damage was done. Hotel Hygeia, the exclusive hotel he built for wealthy patients on his private island, also burned to the ground in 1917. A coincidence? One for the insurers, I think. 'Death before a hundred years of age has been reached is nothing more or less than slow suicide,' the 'apostle of hope' had once claimed; 'a man or woman who dies at an earlier age is simply ignorant of the laws of health.'[2] He died in 1918 at the age of 69.

Few falls from grace were as swift as that of Crippen's huckster solicitor, Arthur Newton: we left him in the previous chapter being struck off for twelve months for his role in the dissemination of the phony confession. Now we must add that he was kicked out permanently in 1913. This time he had obtained money by fraud, and was sentenced to three years' imprisonment. His collaborator in the confession hoax, the odious Horatio Bottomley, had his own brush with fraud, earning him a sentence of seven years in 1922. The once-lauded press baron and politician ended up appearing in music halls, and died in poverty in 1933.

If anyone can be said to take the greatest credit for tying the noose around Crippen's neck it was Sir Bernard Spilsbury, whose expert medical testimony, and the absolute and implacable certainty with which he offered it, was the prosecution's most devastating weapon. Spilsbury became the most famous pathologist in the country, a man whose opinion was rarely doubted and never overruled. He died by his own hand, allowing his laboratory at London's University College to fill with gas from an unlit Bunsen burner in 1947. He was, notes Professor Keith Simpson, 'unloved and unmourned',[3] and it was perhaps a telling illustration of the man's essential wretchedness that he chose to take his life by a means that could so easily have also led to the senseless deaths of huge numbers of innocent people.

The man who literally killed Crippen was hangman John Ellis. Increasingly haunted by his job (and in particular by the execution of Edith Thompson, who sustained disgusting injury on the gallows), he resigned in March of 1924. He then attempted to make his living as a publican and a hairdresser (his father's profession), but his celebrity followed him on both occasions. 'Conversation ceases when I'm about,' he reflected ruefully. 'Socially it's a bad business being a hangman.' In 1927 he took to the stage, re-enacting the execution of Charley Peace. He attempted suicide a few months after his retirement, in August of 1924. Ironically for a man who had executed over 200 people by hanging, he chose to shoot himself, missed, and ended with a bullet in his jaw. Attempted suicide being a crime in England, he was forced to suffer a trial as well as his injuries, eventually being bound over for twelve months. In 1932, wielding a razor, he chased his wife and daughter from the house, then calmly cut his throat twice.

In the immediate aftermath of Crippen's death, it looked, briefly, as though a permanent cost was to be exacted for the irresponsible myth-making that had characterised the media's response to the story. In addition to the newspapers personally sued by Inspector Dew, a more general fake news crackdown claimed a number of unattractive scalps:

> Quite a crop of prosecutions against journalists for contempt of court have followed the Crippen murder trial. The editor and associate editor of the *Daily Chronicle* have been fined £300 for having published, while Crippen was in Canada, a cablegram stating that he had confessed to having poisoned his wife. The managing director of the *Sheffield Weekly Telegraph* and one of the sub-editors of that paper have been 'jointly and severally' fined £100 for publishing the following paragraph before Crippen's case had been decided: – 'Flying from justice, Dr Crippen forgot all about wireless telegraphy. It brought about his capture. In the murder itself, despite the diabolical skill and cunning with which the remains were mutilated, who knows what little, insignificant particle of evidence he may have omitted to obliterate, and which may perhaps be the very thing to fix his fate?' The sub-editor who passed this paragraph has lost his situation in addition to being fined.
>
> In giving judgment, Mr. Justice Darling remarked that the defence had said that the article was not inserted with the intention of influencing public opinion, but for the purpose of edifying and amusing readers. He (his lordship) could not see that such an article

could edify anyone, nor could he see that it amused, although some people were amused at the tales of murderers and the mistakes they might make. There was no doubt that this was contempt of court.[4]

But the truth was, the case had already entered into folklore. Morbid curiosity seekers had made Hilldrop Crescent a place of pilgrimage,[5] and before long the relics were put on sale for the purposes of private worship. 'Fabulous prices' were said to have been realised when the furniture and effects from Hilldrop Crescent were sold in September 1910. 'Large crowds assembled at the auction room prior to the sale and many were unable to gain admission.'[6] But other accounts told of more idle curiosity than big spending. An unexpected addition to the items for sale made the biggest impression, according to some reports:

Dr Crippen's furniture–described in the catalogue as '92 lots, removed from 39, Hilldrop Crescent'–came under the hammer at the rooms of Messrs Tooth and Tooth, Oxford Street, yesterday. This sale realised £135. The auction room was crowded. Curio dealers from various parts of the country were present, and also many members of the general public, obviously inspired by feelings of idle curiosity. So great was the press that the auctioneers' men had some difficulty in displaying the various lots. It was readily apparent that the 'house of mystery' was most comfortably furnished. The furniture was chiefly Old English mahogany, with plenty of easy chairs, and there was quite an imposing collection of small pictures in oils and watercolours. There were, too, a goodly number of knick-knacks of the kind one would expect an actress to gather about her. On the whole, there were no 'fancy' prices; in fact, all the lots went quite cheaply. Sixty-nine small pictures fetched only a sovereign. A violin and a mandolin went for £1 6s. A brass 300-day clock under a glass shade was knocked down for £2 15s. The highest sum bid was £14 14s, the price of an ebonised cottage piano. A curious incident happened when a number of miscellaneous articles were deposited on the table. Opening a small box, a woman pulled out a tuft of dark brown hair. 'This must be Mrs. Crippen's hair!' she exclaimed. Immediately several hands were thrust forward to secure a few strands. There was something approaching a scrimmage, but the auctioneer's man managed to recover the greater part of the hair. Thirty-five popular novels and books, one of which was called *The Fever of Life*, together with a quantity of magazines, were sold for £1 4s. The bidding was especially brisk when the gramophone with which Dr Crippen was wont to entertain his guests was put up. It was sold for £2 12s 6d.[7]

Most of Cora's personal effects, willed to Ethel by Crippen, were instead awarded to Theresa Hunn, Cora's sister, who successfully challenged Ethel for them in court. Hunn then wasted little time in putting them up for auction too. The lots included the notorious 'flaming sun' brooch that Ethel had worn to a Ladies' Guild dinner that had done so much to attach suspicion to the couple. It only raised £20, and some reports again claimed that the majority of the attendees came to gawp rather than spend.[8]

As the one surviving member of the three main protagonists, Ethel came in for more than her fair share of unwanted attention in the affair's immediate aftermath. Her trial, for being an accessory after the fact in the murder of Belle Elmore, had opened and closed on 26 October. The jury took even less time to free her than it had to condemn Crippen. Her counsel argued that she was under the influence of Crippen, whom he called one of the most dangerous criminals of recent times. Lord Chief Justice Alverstone, who had summed up so devastatingly in Crippen's trial, told the jury that he saw no reason to think Crippen had told her anything more of his crime than he had anybody else. The verdict was rarely in doubt:

> As upon the occasion of Crippen's trial, the courtroom was today crowded with members of the legal profession and as many others as could obtain places by right or influence. There was, however, this difference: if Crippen had any well-wishers, they kept in the background, while there was a noticeable sentiment of sympathy for the girl who, for love of a man nearly twice her age, had sacrificed her reputation, deserted home and friends, and remained true to him even when their association made her liable as an accessory to a brutal murder.[9]

But ever since, a question mark has hung over Ethel and the extent of her involvement in the affair. As early as in Filson Young's introduction to the Crippen edition of *Notable British Trials*, after outlining the various suggestions for what actually happened, he adds: 'The only other theory with which the facts may be brought into accordance is one which would involve the collusion of an accomplice, and for obvious reasons cannot be discussed.' This can only be Ethel, then still alive, and of whom such speculation would therefore have been libellous. And then, in *The Mild Murderer*, Tom Cullen quotes the son of Major H.E. Mytton-Davies, governor of Pentonville Prison: 'Father thought that Crippen was an unlikely type to commit a murder. He believed that Crippen was covering up for the real culprit, and was going to his death on that person's behalf. Only the strongest personal loyalty could inspire such a sacrifice.' This, too, could surely only have meant Ethel. But if so, what was he covering? Awareness, complicity, inspiration, *participation*? I *am* somewhat drawn to the idea that he thought she, rather than he, was the one who needed to run away. He was asked at the trial what he said to her to convince her to flee so elaborately: maybe we should have been asking what she said to convince him?

Actually, there is one very strong and very obvious reason for doubting that Crippen was taking the rap for someone else: quite simply, because he *wasn't* taking the rap. With the benefit of hindsight his conviction may seem a fait accompli, the apathetic attitude he took to his defence virtually suicidal. But for all he knew the defence team *might* still have swung things his way; he would then have been freed and the police case would still be worryingly wide open, with Ethel's trial still to come. No, someone who is intent on taking the rap for a crime pleads guilty.

None of which is to deny that Ethel is in many ways the most mysterious of the three key players in the tragedy, and enigmatic in a manner supportive of multiple scenarios and favouring none, in contrast with the more cleanly dichotomous ambiguity of Crippen himself. Indeed, there are two puzzles, nestling in the thickets of the saga, that remain *truly* baffling even in such company, and it may be no coincidence that Ethel is either seen or presumed to be at the heart of both of them. First, and this is the *really* puzzling one, from Dornford Yates's *As Berry and I Were Saying*, in the section where Yates (Cecil Mercer) is describing Crippen and Le Neve's hearing on their return to England:

> As the prisoners left the dock, Arthur Newton rose. 'I ask your permission, sir, for me to receive a copy of the sworn information upon which the Warrant was issued for the prisoners' arrest.' This

request was also quite usual. Before [Chief Magistrate] Sir Albert [de Rutzen] could reply, Travers Humphreys rose. 'The Crown, sir,' he said, 'opposes this application.' Sir Albert looked at him. 'Not without reason, sir. But I give the court my word that by your refusal the defence shall be in no way embarrassed. At next Monday's hearing I will open the case in full, and I will consent to any adjournment which you, sir, may see fit to allow.' Arthur Newton protested with all his might. Such opposition, he said, was unheard of. (So it was.) For years such a privilege had always been accorded the defence. (So it had.) And what were the Crown's reasons? 'I am not prepared,' said Humphreys, 'to disclose the reasons which the Crown has for opposing this request. I have said that it has good reason – and I leave it there.' Arthur Newton replied with some heat. Then he sat down. Sir Albert was very wise. He knew that, without good reason, the Crown would never have dreamed of opposing so usual a request. And, of course, he knew Arthur Newton. And since he had Counsel's word that the defence should in no way suffer if the request was refused, he refused the request. To do so required considerable moral courage, and I can think of no other magistrate who would have done so. So Newton went empty away.'

'And the reason?' said Berry.

'I'm sorry,' I said. 'It was a very good reason, but I have no right to divulge it.'

'Not after forty years?'

'No. I should like to – more than I can say. But that information was secret, and I cannot give it away.'

The 'sworn information' refers to the document that was put before the magistrates, who then issued the warrant for Crippen's arrest. So what could the point of sensitivity possibly be? Was there more going on behind the scenes between Ethel and the authorities than we have ever been made privy to? I put the matter to barrister Matthew Scott, and his response was instructive. 'I don't understand it at all,' he told me. 'I wonder whether the reason for refusing to divulge the information might be that there was what we would now call "public interest immunity" in relation to the document. Typically, public interest immunity attaches to information from informers or confidential information about police techniques, for example surveillance methods. If, for example, and I speculate wildly, there was an informer involved – someone who was suspicious and had spoken to the police, but not prepared to give their name publicly, it is possible, I suppose, that there was a reference to that in the information which Travers Humphries would not want to reveal.' Cue the scanning of our mental libraries to decide who is being left in the shadows here – and why. Our thoughts turn irresistibly to Ethel. It has been a major prop of the story that she stood nobly by Crippen and refused to aid the case against him: might that be untrue?[10]

Then, two enigmatic references, in one of Crippen's final letters to Ethel, to a 'Mrs H'. First he says:

> I know you will be the only one to mourn for me, which I know will please you; but do not, dearest. Think I expect you to put on mourning; that, dearest I leave you to decide on. It may not be well for you to do it in going to Mrs H, and I know that not even the deepest of mourning will be more than a faint indication of your grief.

At first I almost thought he was speaking poetically, and that 'Mrs H' was Ethel herself, 'going to', and indivisible from, the new life she must make for herself. ('H' because Crippen had earlier sentimentally requested that she might change her name to either Mrs Hawley or Mrs Harvey after her acquittal.) But a second reference spoils that reading, and shows that he is definitely talking about concrete plans with a very real person:

> I hope so greatly that you have heard favourably from Mrs H, and that you will be comfortable, and made more cheerful, by the bright sunshine…

It may have been that Mrs H was some newcomer to the story, a philanthropist who wrote to Ethel out of the blue and offered her an escape somewhere until the dust settled. If it were someone already known to us, the list is short indeed, and none makes immediate sense. Not Adeline Harrison, surely? Even if she had somehow come forward to offer Ethel succour, her Brixton abode would surely not offer 'bright sunshine'. *That* sounds unmistakably like a journey abroad (unless Crippen is simply contrasting, with understandable romanticism, the world outside with the confines of a condemned cell). Besides, Crippen does not indulge in this habit of referring to people by their initials on any other occasion in the letters, so I think it is safe to conclude that the purpose of somewhat obscuring the name was to somewhat obscure the whole business. (It was always understood that the letters might be published.) And that hints at someone whose name would be recognisable but for some reason is better left covert. I'm starting to think, absurdly perhaps, of Theresa Hunn, Belle's sister in America, referred to routinely as 'Mrs Hunn'. Ethel would have had no need to keep such a development from Crippen out of any fear of seeming disloyal. He would have been easy to convince that it was just Hunn showing her sensitive side: the self-described 'reader of romances' would have bought the cheap sentiment with ease. And due sensitivity to Mrs Hunn would certainly demand that Ethel should not be in conspicuous mourning.[11] But why on earth *would* Hunn offer refuge to Ethel? Perhaps if she had known that Ethel had collaborated with the police?

We know that Ethel did leave the country for a short while after the trial: in her various memoirs she describes this as on-spec return to Canada, where she attempted to start a new life but soon tired and returned. So far as I know there is no hard proof of this beyond her own word, though her children vaguely recalled her talking of having been in Orlando. On the face of it, it seems peculiar for her to return to so emotionally charged a location. (But then, she often depicts herself in her published recollections as morbidly drawn to the scenes of her various tragedies, accounts that sit oddly with her claims elsewhere in the same pages of being tormented by the fear of recognition. In Canada she claimed she revisited the prison in which she was held, and was greeted affectionately by the staff. On a return to London she spoke of visiting Hilldrop Crescent, Holloway and the Old Bailey.)

But if the idea of Hunn welcoming Ethel to America wasn't unlikely enough to start with, their acrimonious wrangling over Cora's jewellery is surely enough to rule it out of contention entirely. Unless that whole will business, so unnecessary, and seemingly so petty on Ethel's part, reflects a deeper rift between two former conspirators, rather than a senselessly entered-into squabble, with no more to it than meets the eye, between two people who did not know each other at all? A falling-out between Hunn and Ethel, as was only likely, might account for why Ethel seems never to have run to the sunshine with this *or any* 'Mrs H'.

And how troubled was Ethel, really, by Crippen's conviction? Whether she believed him innocent or guilty, it would have been obvious that she was a large part of what had led him to his fate: a sobering thought for anyone, even if they had not just lost the presumed love of their life. One might expect quiet and profound despair, lasting weeks, months, even years. We can perhaps excuse the selling of her story to the papers, and her glibly posing in boys' clothes for a series of photographs, as simply her doing what she must to raise much-needed funds – certainly Crippen himself chose to see it that way – but still one wonders where she would have drawn the line, if not at that. By her own account she spent the day of Crippen's execution in her flat, in bed, stupefied with grief. But Philip Gibbs, one of the journalists preparing her first round of autobiography, said she was with him, and though dressed in black, she was often 'so gay that it was impossible to believe that she had escaped the hangman's rope by no great distance'.[12]

There *is* a way of tying all these threads, but it would leave us with a whole new Ethel: one who might just have been in alliance with Hunn (and who knows where that would take us?) and one who might very conceivably have secretly agreed to assist the authorities after her arrest in Canada, or even earlier, so that the information regarding the warrant could not be revealed at the Bow Street hearing, and so that she would by necessity need to be tried separately, in a sham trial designed solely to have her officially declared innocent in law and thus safe from any future duplicity.

There is no question that she would have legitimately felt the need to escape her celebrity status. Even before she left Quebec the unwanted offers began pouring in: advertising offers from soap manufacturers and beauty specialists requested that she model for them, or give testimonials, wedding proposals ('many of them being from men in positions of prominence both in England and America'[13]), and several offers to appear on the stage.[14] The most notable of the latter came from Isadore Bernstein, then the proprietor of a New York music hall.[15] Bernstein offered Miss Le Neve $1,000 a week to appear in a series of male impersonations. Crippen himself had got to hear of the vaudeville offers and urged her to turn them down ('I decidedly object to anything on the stage for you, darling'): a measure, presumably, of the low esteem in which he now held the profession, for he would certainly have not wanted to deny her the income, and was supportive of her posing in her boy disguise. According to *Variety*, 'talk of having her appear in a London hall as an exhibit under an assumed name nearly precipitated a riot among the artists on the other side.'[16]

The real vaudeville draw, of course, would have been Cora, alive after all, and there were some papers who speculated even as the investigation was unfolding that the crime scene may have been a giant hoax, the aim being to reactivate her dormant stage career. 'Should she reappear,' suggested one, 'she could be booked for music hall vaudeville appearances at almost any price.'[17] So it was no surprise that there should be a plethora of Cora sightings and hoaxes as the case drew to a close. In November she was said to have been under surveillance for five days somewhere in the middle-west, staying at a sanitarium.[18] In Indiana it was said that an attorney had strong proof that she was living there as the wife of a local millionaire.[19] In Chicago, plans were afoot to reveal her alive and well 'from a platform in the Coliseum building, and it is intimated that she will show signs of suffering from mental aberration'. Though many suspected it was connected with 'a story circulated in sporting circles a couple of weeks ago to the effect that an English woman had been engaged to impersonate the slain actress and that the promoters argued "there would be millions in it"'.[20] In Alberta, a woman who resembled Belle arrived in town and was seen to faint when she overheard a farmer say, 'I guess they will make old Doc Crippen squawk over in London.' The police had her under surveillance.[21] Strangest of all was the claim of one Astro Conlin, 'seer and handcuff king', who promised audiences in 1911 that Cora would reappear on stage at London's Lyric Theatre during his show. 'Of course, Mrs Crippen failed to materialise, but there were local papers which fell for this yarn, and Astro is brilliant at getting a munificent salary. He is a very pleasant and brilliant young man, and he gives the kind of a show that keeps everyone guessing.'[22]

In time Ethel would also find herself impersonated, in a mysterious hoax that dragged on for some twenty years in Perth, Australia. As we have seen, she did briefly leave England in the immediate aftermath of the trial, but she was definitely back, and permanently, by 1914, married and starting a family. Even though, as Nicholas Connell has demonstrated, she made her whereabouts known to the press at least twice in the 1920s, and had sold her story on several occasions prior to her celebrated rediscovery by novelist Ursula Bloom in the early 1950s, on the other side of the world an entirely fantastic alternative history was being constructed.

'His wife had threatened to shoot me and Dr Crippen, in a rage, gave her a glass of poisoned champagne to drink,' said 'Ethel', interviewed for the first time (!) and now 'in Perth incognito, in squalid circumstances'.[23] This was June of 1932, and Ethel had been living quietly, but not squalidly, in England for nearly twenty years. So who was the mysterious Perth Ethel, and what was the game? Was it something the press had cooked up themselves, or were they themselves being taken for a ride by a hoaxer? Not a very successful one, if so, if reports of her circumstances are to be believed: more like a genuine fantasist, or else someone who had hit upon an incredibly eccentric way of earning a little much-needed cash. It did, however, appear to be somebody who had been doing some homework: though Ethel had never actually settled in Australia, she frequently claimed to have done in her various exercises in newspaper autobiography over the years. The Australian press, seemingly in the honest belief that Ethel had 'never before been interviewed by a newspaperman', fell overboard for the story, and especially by the possibility that they would at last learn the truth of what had gone on in Hilldrop Crescent over twenty years before. Yet almost nothing in her story conformed to the known facts. She told reporters she had run away from her family home in Wolverhampton to take up her job as Crippen's typist. 'Occasionally he beat her,' proclaimed one lurid sub-heading, 'yet she still loved him.' She had fled to Australia with the assistance of Mrs Booth, the wife of General Booth, head of the Salvation Army.[24] And though she stressed her own innocence, it seems she had become reconciled to Crippen's guilt: 'Little did I know in my distress that under that very floor lay the body of his wife... By almighty God I did not know what we were charged with until I was back in England. Then I was horrified.'[25]

'Is Theory of Crippen Murder Exploded?' asked the *Adelaide News*.[26] 'Crippen Verdict At Last Proved Justified' confirmed the *Sydney Arrow*.[27] The 'different name' the woman had been using – presumably her real one – was never disclosed and was said to be faithfully guarded by the circle of friends keeping her 'true' identity secret, until she died in 1949.

All who knew her agree that Ethel Le Neve was a likeable and highly respected person. When the *Mirror* was speaking to City Coroner

R.P. Rodriguez this week about another matter, topic of Ethel Le Neve cropped up, and he mentioned that she consulted him about 11 years ago when he was practising as a lawyer.

She was seeking guidance on a minor legal matter and was using the name by which she was known in Perth, but Mr Rodriguez, who had an idea about her real identity, asked her straight out if she were Ethel Le Neve. With some reluctance she admitted she was, and added she did not want her identity known.

She then discussed the Crippen case and affirmed her complete innocence of any part in the murder. Mr Rodriguez added that from memory Ethel Le Neve, when she visited him, was a stoutish lady of about 5 ft. 6 in height, and it could be seen she had been very nice looking.[28]

In 1951, when the above was published, the story for some reason flared up again. 'Only a few people know that a grave at Karrakatta is the last resting place of a woman who figured in one of the most famous murder cases of the century,' declared the *Perth Mirror*: 'Only recently have there been whispers of the real identity of the occupant of the grave. Those who knew her under another name are reluctant to volunteer information about how she came to Perth but they say she did her best to hide her identity and would never refer to the famous murder case. A few weeks ago friends visited the grave on the second anniversary of her death.'[29] Were these friends in on the hoax, or more victims of it?

Then it then got stranger:

Here she lived for many years under an assumed name. She sank into obscurity and eventually was befriended by an elderly Chinese laundryman. She remained at his premises until her death 2 years ago.

He too was a mystery man and is not known widely among the Chinese community of Perth. Some Perth Chinese say he died about 12 months ago – others say that with advancing years he returned to his homeland so that he could be buried with his ancestors according to the old Chinese custom.[30]

But no – he was still alive, and either intent on keeping the sting going or else had been unwittingly stung himself:

MELBOURNE, Sat. – A penniless Chinese has asked the Titles Office to help him in a search for a fortune. He says that Ethel Le Neve, mistress of famous British murderer Dr Hawley Harvey Crippen, left this fortune. Le Neve died in Perth on March 7, 1949, The Chinese, Wong Yee Hing, a cook, of Railway Parade, East Perth, who was the only mourner at her Karrakatta (Perth) graveside, is paying for her funeral in weekly instalments. Her personal property, at, probate, was assessed at about £78 in furniture and personal effects. But she owned valuable properties, and, Hing believes, left thousands of pounds in safe deposit boxes. Hing hopes that the Titles Office checks will disclose property under various aliases which Le Neve used. ...

She came to Australia to escape publicity, became a bookkeeper at South Perth, and in 1915, at Fremantle, married a man who died, several years later. An elderly Chinese then befriended her in Perth, where she became the owner of a boarding-house. Friends claim that she began using more than eight different names. As regular remittances reached her from her family in England, she accumulated considerable wealth, which she put in safe deposit boxes. Her will named Hing as executor and beneficiary.[31]

Though he never got his millions, Hing did manage to make something out of the story:

Since publication by the *Mirror* last week of the life – and death – in Perth of the girl in the Crippen case, financial assistance has been offered by readers to Chinese cook Wong Yee Hing, who is still paying off Le Neve's funeral expenses in weekly instalments.

It is known that Le Neve – who was mistress of the notorious Dr Hawley Harvey Crippen – left a considerable sum of money, But it can't be found. Hing, her beneficiary, is almost penniless, and has been making payments on her death expenses for 2 years now.

One reader who offered to assist Hing lived alongside the gaol where Crippen was hanged. Another was one of Dr Crippen's patients.[32]

Meanwhile, number 39, Hilldrop Crescent, hit by a bomb in 1940, lingered on among the rubble until it was redeveloped in the 1950s. Until

then it had been variously used as a lodging house and the home of a
Scottish comedian, Sandy McNab. Unsurprisingly, stories of the property
being haunted were legion. According to one 1912 report, 'those who
have recently lived in the place' have confirmed 'it is now haunted by
particularly lively "spooks"':

> Stories that the house occupied by the Crippens is haunted have
> been circulated ever since Crippen's death. Mysterious noises have
> been heard and lights have been seen that cannot be traced to any
> natural agency. Many men have searched for the source of the 'spooky'
> manifestations, but without success. It goes without saying that the
> 'Belle Elmore ghost' is only the phantom of superheated imaginations.
> Given a house in which a murder has been committed and there are
> always to be found credulous folk who will manufacture occult and
> supernatural manifestations out of the most trivial circumstances.[33]

McNab, whose real name was Adam Arthur, had purchased the house as
early as December of 1910, when *Variety* published a strange announcement
saying that it will be 'his address for 99 years to come'.[34] McNab elsewhere
claimed that he obtained it for half its market value, such a deterrent to
purchase were its unsavoury associations: clearly Frederick Lown wanted
to make a quick sale and have it off his hands as soon as possible. (Lown
had also billed the police for unpaid rent and damage caused by their
investigation.) Varying accounts claim that McNab attempted to turn it
into theatrical lodgings, which foundered because of the sensitivity of
stage folk to uncanny vibrations, and then into a Crippen museum, which
ran aground on the objections of the neighbours. I've not found any hard
evidence for either, though McNab had his own ghost story to add to the
collection:

> Just three days before Christmas I sat typing in the very room in
> which Belle Elmore is supposed to have been murdered. It was close
> on midnight, out of doors the rain was coming down in torrents,
> and the wind shook every window in the house. On my desk was a
> heap of letters and telegrams which required answering, and it was
> my intention to get these off my hands before I retired. My desk was
> facing the window, looking out on the main road, deserted at this
> time of the night.

Suddenly, there was a sound on the panes as though someone had thrown a handful of gravel, and simultaneously came a heavy thud at my room door as though a mattress had been thrown against it. I stopped and listened. I can't say that I was frightened, but I felt a little uneasy. After a minute or so I resumed my work, or at least I tried to do so.

It was no use. My fingers refused to touch the proper keys. 'Bang' went the door again. Mechanically I raised my hand to my forehead, only to find that I was bathed in cold perspiration. I thought I heard muffled footsteps going downstairs, yet I seemed glued to my seat.

I felt myself fainting, and with one mighty effort I sprang to my feet and made for the passage. I gave a glance up the stairs. It was perfectly dark, but looking down on me were two eyes resembling electric lights. With all my strength I rushed to the front door, pulled back the latch, closed the door behind me and sprang down the top steps onto the garden walk. In doing this I sprained my ankle. Somehow I struggled to the gate, then out into the street and searched for a policeman.

In a few minutes I found one and together we returned to the house. He laughed at my story as I inserted the latch key in the door. We entered, closing the door behind us, and then we listened. At first we could neither hear nor see anything. I began to think myself a fool when suddenly a slight noise came from one of the bedrooms. The constable mounted the stairs and I followed. It was not until we reached the very top of the house that we found the room from which the noise appeared to originate. We entered it, lit the gas, but there was nothing to be seen.

We were about to retire when we heard a piercing cry from a cupboard, the door of which was closed and securely fastened with a catch. The constable opened it and out flew a big black cat which immediately commenced to rush around the room. Although the door of the room was wide open, that cat refused to leave. It rushed round and round, flew up the walls, and dashed into the window. It was only when the constable made a dash for it with his cape that the beast made a bolt for the door. We put out the light, closed the door and systematically searched every nook and corner of the house for the cat, but to this day it has never been seen again.

I should say that not a single door or window in the house was open, and how the cat escaped is a mystery. It is also a mystery how it got in the cupboard, assuming that it was the cat which was looking down the staircase on me when I saw the eyes. I am by no means superstitious but I had heard it said that spirits of the departed sometimes enter the bodies of animals, and this incident has set me thinking.[35]

Zoological trouble continued for McNab when he went down to the fatal basement one morning in 1912 to find broken crockery scattered around the kitchen. The cause of the trouble was not Cora's poltergeist but a python that he had supposedly brought back from a tour of Africa: the animal had, understandably, broken free of its cage and made a bid for the hot water pipes, stopping off on the way to eat McNab's pet kitten.[36]

Then, in 1914, an echo of the Crippen case resurfaced in an unpleasant court case involving McNab's son, William Arthur. He had lived and had a child with a woman from Bath named Lily Orlando; she also gave him all the money she had been saving for her marriage when he told her he was hard up. He then jilted her for another girl, and when she complained he suggested she commit suicide, going so far as to offer her an automatic pistol with which to do it. According to Orlando, he said, 'I would like to push you under a train if I only dared, but I suppose if I did they would scrag me like they did Crippen.' The jury ordered him to pay her £500 in damages. As for McNab himself, he was sentenced to two years' hard labour in 1914 for unlawful knowledge of a 13-year-old girl, Margaret Mary Hemmingway. Said to have been stage-struck, she had gone with McNab from Glasgow to London, apparently with her mother's consent. In passing sentence, the judge added that if he could have given a heavier punishment he would have done so.[37] According to the actor Scott Alexander, McNab ended up as the proprietor of a matrimonial agency in Sydney.[38]

As the years passed by, and the case settled into legend, any echo of the name Crippen was good enough to give a news story a lift. Most obituaries of Paul Martinetti, who died in 1925, rehearsed the story of his involvement in the case in detail, and mentioned his professional accomplishments only in passing. (Several papers headlined the reports 'Crippen Case Recalled' in large lettering, then underneath and considerably smaller: 'by pantomimist's death'.[39]) When a Paddington shopkeeper called Lewis Salmon was killed by thieves in 1918, an entirely spurious connection, and an entirely false history, were mobilised in order to make the killing a 'curious echo of the Crippen case':

> Linked up in a curious way with the Crippen crime is a tragedy now being investigated by the London police, the victim being Mr Lewis Henry Salmon, 60, wardrobe and antique furniture dealer, who was found dead in his shop at Bishop's Road, Paddington. He was the man from whom Crippen bought a sack in order to dispose of his wife's remains after he had cut them up. It will be remembered that only a few portions of Mrs Crippen's flesh were discovered in the cellar of Crippen's house at Hilldrop Crescent, but they were sufficient to hang Crippen. A sack was also found at the house with signs that left the police in no doubt that Crippen had used it for disposing of the body. Enquiries showed that he had bought it, together with odds and ends of wearing apparel, from Salmon, with whom he had had various dealings. Salmon also sold to Crippen the male attire which his companion, Miss Ethel Le Neve, donned when she accompanied him on his voyage to Canada.[40]

Not one word of this account is true, and if Salmon was, as it goes on to describe him, 'a care-worn old man with a deeply wrinkled face and forehead and heavy beard (who) had few friends, and kept very much to himself', one wonders how it could ever have got started. Perhaps Salmon had spun the yarn to get himself a free drink or two, and it grew into local legend.

Another well-ploughed field was the 'dubious reminiscence', by those who claimed a personal experience of Crippen. Noted thespian Sir Seymour Hicks – who it would be practically unpatriotic to suggest might be spinning not very much into rather a lot[41] – recalled, 'I knew him personally but not well,' before going on to discuss him in meticulous detail and at considerable length. Confessing to 'a sneaking feeling of sympathy' for him, he noted his resemblance to 'a bream or mullet or some other open-eyed and equally intelligent deep sea fish' and rounded off by claiming to have also been present in Bow Street police station when Ethel Le Neve showed up to try to get her boy's suit back. As a result of cosmic irony deciding it might as well be hung for a sheep as a lamb, it transpired that it was at this exact moment that word was received of Crippen's appeal having failed, and this news was duly passed on to Ethel while Hicks watched. According to Sir Seymour, she said: 'Oh.'[42]

Then there was the criminal ('Peter Braham, to give him one of his many aliases') who tucked into Crippen's last meal:

> It used to be my job to clean out his cell. While the other prisoners were at breakfast the condemned man used to take his daily exercise, and, many's the time I saw him striding up and down in the exercise yard. It was my job to make his bed, clean his tinware, and so on. I'm not ashamed to own up that on more than one occasion I ate the scraps that he left after his meals. The morning he was hanged, as I entered his cell I saw at a glance that he had not touched his breakfast of poached eggs on toast. I was hungry. Crippen was out of his cell. Poached eggs on toast? Lumme, there was a titbit if yer like![43]

Best of all, perhaps, was Mrs Etta Bledsoe, the 'famous American medium':

> Her name became known in England some years ago by reason of her warning to the notorious murderer Dr Crippen. 'I see a wedding,' she said, 'with the bride all radiant in orange blossom. Years are passing, marked by domestic wrangles, and then I see a man on trial for his life for murdering his once happy bride. Finally I see the scaffold on which the man ends his days.' This was the dramatic message that Mrs. Bledsoe claimed to have been the medium of delivering from the other world. Her claim was that the Spirit sending the message was that of the mother of Dr Hawley Harvey Crippen, and the man to whom the message was transmitted was, Crippen himself, then contemplating marriage with Belle Elmore— a union that ended in tragedy years after. 'I was then in my infancy as a medium,' Mrs. Bledsoe says. 'I had met Crippen more than once, and he was very much interested, in psychic phenomena. In particular he wanted to communicate with his mother who had died some months before, because there had been an understanding between them that if there were a means of communicating with the living from the other side she would employ it to keep in touch with him, and apprise him of anything that, was necessary for his guidance in the serious affairs of life.

'Crippen then told me that he was about to marry a woman to whom he was greatly attached, and he wanted to get into communication with his mother in the hope that she might warn him of any pitfalls that might be ahead. I told him I could not guarantee to get into direct contact for him because the influences might not be sympathetic enough but he persisted, and a séance was arranged for his benefit at the house of a friend in Brooklyn, where Crippen was then practising as a dentist. The first séance failed, but the second one was more successful, and I gave the man the message, cited above. It made a big impression on him, but like so many other sceptics confronted with realities, he pretended to think it all bluff and said I had invented the message. I had forgotten all about the matter when he came back to me, about five years later, and told me that, after some hesitation he had married, in spite of the warning, and was then finding that part of the prediction was coming true, that the marriage had resulted in unhappiness, and that he lived in dread lest the latter part of the prediction might be fulfilled. He wanted me to try to establish contact with the spirit of his mother again. I tried, but I was not able to do it.'[44]

Crippen, for the remainder of the century following his death, became a cultural icon, a byword for that very English kind of murder that George Orwell defined as the product of its 'golden age'. Books, movies, songs; all would emerge at regular intervals, a veritable Crippen industry in which the key ingredients – the little man with the round glasses, the intolerable wife, the poison, the cellar, the shipboard pursuit – would be reassembled and made to dance again, just as they had for the news-hungry public of 1910. Over the years, he lost the very real sense of repulsion that the crime had originally attached to him and, to a new world with vastly fewer certainties, became almost comforting. His extended afterlife in popular culture was inevitable.

In fact, like so much else about the affair, indecent haste had governed this development too. Quickest off the mark was a play called *Trapped by Wireless*. Written by Ira Tichenor and staged at the Grand Opera House, Los Angeles, it was in production in August 1910.[45] It looks to have been a curious mix, part sophisticated (the first act was presented as an English music hall show, seemingly anticipating the innovations of the later musical *Belle*) and part naïve (there was a fictitious romance between Ethel and the arresting officer from Scotland Yard, undetectably obscured by the pseudonyms 'Ethelaire Ganeve' and 'Inspector New'[46]). Unsurprisingly, relatives of the real-life dramatis personae were not best pleased, and it looked for a time as though legal measures might be taken to stop it being staged, despite the changed character names. (Actor Chester Stevens played Dr Harley H. Grippen, and the final act was set on the deck and wireless room of the steamer *Santrose*.[47]) But in spite of the threats it went ahead, and played to sell-out audiences.[48] Meanwhile, a slide show, *The Capture of Dr Crippen by Wireless* (1910), was doing a brisk trade in cinemas.

The first full-length movie treatment of the case came, surprisingly enough, from Nazi Germany. Numerous films with British themes were produced in Germany during the war years, all of them intended to show the enemy nation as hypocritical, untrustworthy, decadent, effete or brutal. Two of the better-known examples are *Titanic* (1943), a technically highly commendable account of the doomed ship which lays the blame for the sinking at the feet of the uncaring British ruling classes (a German steward on board is depicted as the one heroic character), and *Ohm Kruger* (1941), which depicts Winston Churchill as the heartless commandant of a concentration camp, feeding rich food to his bulldog while allowing female inmates to starve. Directed by Erich Engels, *Dr Crippen an Bord* (*Dr Crippen on Board*, 1942) retells the story in contemporary dress and settings, and reimagines Crippen entirely: as played by Rudolf Fernau he is tall and romantically attractive, with a full head of hair and a very stylish beard in place of his moustache. But for all its eccentricities and wartime cynicism, the film is recognisably based on the authentic story. The same cannot be said for the same director's weird and rather wonderful follow-up *Dr Crippen Lebt!* (*Dr Crippen Lives!*, 1958). We begin with the revelation that Crippen was not executed as the world believed: his assistant had gallantly taken his place on the gallows. Changing his appearance, the real Crippen flees to the Malay jungle where he encounters a pair of married French scientists who are developing a unique serum against snake venom. His mind doubtless reeling at its potential in homeopathic remedies, Crippen murders the couple to claim the cure for himself. But only after their deaths does he realise that they were not in possession of the actual formula for the serum. Instead, it has been entrusted to their daughter Fleur, living in Paris. Intent on getting his hands on it, Crippen travels to France to track her down, himself hotly pursued by Interpol and Scotland Yard.

The Suspect (1944) was the first English-speaking variation, based upon the novel *This Way Out* by James Ronald. The book is a compellingly sour thriller, summed up by its author's dedication: 'to my creditors, whose increasing impatience has made this book necessary'. Obviously inspired by Crippen, the book's hero Philip Marshall is a put-upon husband who murders his wife – her name is Cora – for the love of a sweet young woman. Cora is a disgusting virago, with legs 'like two pork sausages', and the book revels in its descriptions of their horrendous home life, repulsive dinners and unhygienic living spaces. It is as if all the misogyny latent in the standard version of the case, discreetly coursing through Filson Young's introduction to *Notable British Trials*, had trickled into one book and congealed on its pages like a gravy stain. It does, however, come up with what seems to me the only believable reason why Crippen might have murdered Cora: the book's Cora decides to make trouble on discovery of the affair, and tells her husband that she is going to publicly embarrass them, and have his mistress drummed out of her job and shamed in front of all her friends and colleagues. This, unlike all of the officially offered alternatives, strikes me as something that might genuinely have inspired Crippen to turn murderer:

> Before him lay long years of impotent misery which only the death of one or the other of them would end. Cora was only forty-five and there was nothing wrong with her except a disordered liver, the result of too many sweets, too little exercise. She was so lazy that her tissues would never wear out. Unless she fell under a train or stepped in front of a bus she would go on for another twenty years.
>
> To be married to Cora for twenty more years was unthinkable. Suddenly he knew what he must do. At first the thought was repellent but the more he considered it the more inevitable a solution it seemed. Cora had asked for it, she had only herself to blame if she got it.

The film, with Charles Laughton customarily excellent as Marshall, greatly simplifies the plot, and also makes some intriguing changes, nearly all of them designed to push it further in the direction of the authentic Crippen. Most obviously, the period is changed from the book's present day to the turn of the century. The mistress is made a typist, and the location to which they plan to flee becomes Canada.

It is no coincidence that the most important examples of the case in popular culture all occurred within a few years of each other in the 1960s. The sixties saw an Edwardian revival in culture, décor and men's and women's fashion, and much of what we now think of as distinctively sixties in style – for instance the iconography of the TV series *The Avengers* and the personal styling of Patrick Macnee's John Steed – owed its inspiration to the renewed interest in Edwardian style and themes. To the sixties' cultural sensibility, the Crippen case was an irresistible mix of high style, melodrama and camp, and its three major incursions into the popular sphere reflect this revivalist spirit. First came a stage musical, debuting at London's Strand Theatre in May 1961. *Belle, or the Ballad of Dr Crippen* was the work of Wolf Mankowitz and Monty Norman (key sixties' creative figures who had previously collaborated on the epoch-making *Expresso Bongo*) and featured a fine variety bill cast, headed by Davy Kaye, Jerry Desmonde and George Benson (as Crippen). It portrayed the story as music hall pastiche, anticipating the similar melding of narrative and performance in such as *Chicago* and *Cabaret*, and had it come along six or seven years later it may have been a smash. Instead, its macabre irreverence (Crippen, on the verge of sawing up Cora, stops to play the saw as a musical instrument) horrified some critics. Songs included 'Coldwater, Michigan', 'I Wonder What's Happened to Belle' and 'You Can't Beat a British Crime'. The London *Daily Mail* called it 'a sick joke with music', and Monty Norman later lamented to Tom Cullen that 'clearly the British public were not ready for a musical based on a murder'.[49] The show closed after just forty-four performances, but a cast recording was made, and is now available on CD. It would be interesting to see how it might be received if revived today.

Then, in 1962, came a full-scale movie adaptation: *Dr Crippen*, directed by Robert Lynn and atmospherically photographed by Nicolas Roeg, whose sister Nicolette had just played the title role in the ill-fated *Belle*. The film cemented the revisionist view of Crippen as more sinned against than sinning, and even incorporates the 'Marshall Hall defence' (see Chapter 8) in having him kill Cora unintentionally, with an accidental overdose of the hyoscine he has been slipping in her coffee to reduce her sexual demands upon him. The problem with this, however, is that it makes no sense: Marshall Hall's claim was not necessarily that this is what Crippen did, but rather that if he had been defending him, he could have pursued that line of argument and lessened his sentence. The problem with actually showing it happen that way is that it then becomes inconceivable that it wasn't his defence: Crippen is in effect presenting a fraudulent account of what happened, one that is entirely and irrationally to his detriment.

Donald Pleasence is the Crippen of popular legend, sneaking soundlessly about the house while Cora holds court, his voice rarely rising above a whisper: entirely forgotten, by now, is the confident, even flamboyant man recalled by contemporary witnesses, moving as freely in Cora's world as in his own. It's hard to imagine what Le Neve would have seen in this man: accordingly her relationship to him is portrayed as almost maternal, more motivated by sympathy for his insignificance than the near-hero worship that seems to have been the case in reality. Samantha Eggar's Ethel is overwhelmingly innocent in essence as well as in fact,[50] and the true villain is Coral Browne's Cora, a grotesque harridan, given to repellent episodes of self-pity and grossly physical sexual desire.

Most interesting of all is a real oddity from 1968: *Negatives*. The film uses all the elements of the case that so endeared it to 1960s' sensibilities in its elliptical, meandering story of Theo (Peter McEnery), a man who sells antique furniture and curios, and his lover Vivien (Glenda Jackson), who spice up their lovemaking by pretending to be Crippen and Cora, a game which then spills over into their fractious real-life relationship. The cleverness of the film lies in its isolating of those elements of the Crippen story that already seem to lend themselves to an atmosphere of role play and sex fantasy: Crippen and Le Neve hiding in their imaginary world at Hilldrop Crescent, pretending to be man and wife, his masochistic debasement with Cora, the disguise, the cross-dressing, Crippen's eroticised draping of Ethel in Cora's jewellery and furs. The film even features a scene in which Theo visits Crippen's likeness at Madame Tussaud's, underlining the significance of the waxwork as the supreme fetish object of the Crippen cult.

The whole point of *Negatives*, as far as its relationship to the Crippen story goes, is that this is a history which had now surrendered itself entirely to myth, to fantasy, to a kind of cultural shorthand, very much alive as a set of symbols and icons, but entirely dead as the kind of meaningful historical event that still commands moral or intellectual engagement, its central figure as secure in his nation's folklore, and fully as remote from any sense of living history, as Robin Hood or King Arthur.

And so it remained for the rest of his century. But then, early in the next, an amazing discovery was made in a laboratory at the University of Michigan, and everything changed forever.

Chapter 7

The Bombshell

Were the remains found at 39, Hilldrop Crescent the remains of Cora Crippen? If they were not, there is an end of this case. ...

Of course if it was a man, again the defendant is entitled to walk out of that dock.

Judge's summing up at Crippen's trial

To the British, Crippen is a crime superstar; he is also something of a joke, like Dylan Thomas's Mr Pugh in *Under Milk Wood*, who sports a 'nicotine eggyellow weeping walrus Victorian moustache, grown thick and long in memory of Doctor Crippen', and who spends his evenings fantasising about serving his wife 'a fricassee of deadly nightshade, nicotine, hot frog, cyanide and bat-spit'. But while the Crippen case seems utterly remote from reality for most of us, both campy and antique, from the viewpoint of many on the other side of the Atlantic, divorced from such irreverence and with a century's distance from the grandstanding and hoopla of what many now view as basically a show trial, the affair is turning into a literal and metaphorical custody battle. (The cry of 'He was a Yankee!' by a character in the musical *Belle* is met with the response: 'Criminally speaking, sir, he was as English as you are!' Not for much longer, I fancy.) At stake, as well as the essentially symbolic status of Crippen's mortal remains, is the question of cultural identity, of who has the right to *define* who this man was and what happened to him. The British have made a pantomime figure of him, but to many in America the case evokes not some delicious gaslit yarn but merely a century of injustice. Those Crippens of Coldwater are not an extinct race, and neither are they going to go gentle into that good night.

Retired marketing executive James Patrick Crippen of Dayton, Ohio, is 82 at time of writing, and the dying of the light against which he is raging is the light of justice. He is petitioning British Prime Minister

Boris Johnson and Secretary of State for Justice Robert Buckland to have Crippen's remains exhumed from the grounds of Pentonville Prison and transported to the Crippen family grave in America, where one of three empty plots is already awaiting his overdue return. Despite the deaf ear British justice has turned to all such enquiries so far, the reason for the request is simple, its logic inarguable, its moral force compelling. There is no question that by modern standards of evidence the conviction is blatantly unsafe. And as John Trestrail, one of the key players in this new twist to the old story, points out: 'Justice doesn't have a time limit.'

Trestrail is a forensic and clinical toxicologist and director of the Centre for the Study of Criminal Poisoning. One thing about the Crippen case in particular had always bothered him: why, if he had poisoned Cora, did Crippen then dismember her and hide the pieces? Or, to put it the other way, if he was going to dismember her and hide the pieces, why bother poisoning her first? 'A poisoner wants the death to appear natural so he can get a death certificate,'Trestrail explained. 'It doesn't make sense.' Inspired by this curious anomaly, he decided to see how far modern science might go towards clearing up some of the imponderable mysteries on which the original trial had hinged. In particular, DNA analysis would in theory be able to confirm if the body was or was not Cora's. But that would mean locating two essential samples: the DNA of Cora's living descendants and a viable sample of the original evidence. The former might not have even existed. The latter, even if it could be secured, may not have been surrendered for analysis, or may have proved inadequate as a source. The only thing, on both counts, was to try.

Mitochondrial DNA remains unaltered through the generations in the female line of descent. This means that any direct female descendant would be able to provide a match to Cora's DNA, so Trestrail tasked genealogist Beth Wills with the mission of finding Cora's extant maternal relatives. Cora herself, of course, had no children, and of her sisters, the only one found to have definitely had a daughter was Bertha. Born in 1912, this daughter died in 1973 but had four children of her own, two of whom were located by Wills. These were Marie Hamel, then 64 and living in Los Angeles, and her sister Louise, along with Marie's daughter Anna. They all provided samples for testing, giving the team the DNA of Cora's half-grandnieces and half-great-grandniece. The nieces remembered hearing talk of their aunt's murder during their childhood, but also recalled that discussion of it was generally frowned upon.

Commentators with a vested interest in Crippen's guilt have tried to suggest there are gaps in the genealogical record, or causes to mistrust the accuracy of the research: there are none. It seemed they were on to something when it was found that on Cora's marriage certificate her mother's maiden name was given as Mary Wolff, while on Bertha's it was Mary Smith. This could have meant they had different mothers, rendering all that genealogical research and the DNA evidence worthless, since Bertha and Cora would then not share the same maternal lineage. But this was nonsense. Names on such documents are often misheard and misrecorded, and there is no doubt whatsoever that Cora and Bertha have the same mother. Her name was Mary Schmidt (sometimes anglicised as Smith).[1]

Finding a sample of the original evidence that could be used looked for a time to be a greater challenge. There were three options: the St Pancras Cemetery in Finchley, where the remains are buried, Scotland Yard's 'Black Museum', which has the (evidentially highly unsafe) hair samples, and the Royal London Hospital, where the tissue samples taken for analysis by the prosecution's experts still reside. It is questionable of how much value the buried remains would be by this time, even if exhumation were to be permitted, and the famously inflexible Scotland Yard played true to form by requesting £17,500 before surrendering the hair for tests. Fortunately, the Royal London Hospital proved more amenable and, since they had the actual material from which the original forensic conclusions were drawn, this was the better of the three options in any case. (The hair probably was Cora's, but there is no proof it came from the same body as the remains.) 'This is the slide which Spilsbury used to identify the body as Cora Crippen's,' noted Trestrail. 'And this was the evidence on which Crippen was convicted.'

The slide was obtained by Dr David Foran, a highly respected forensic biologist at Michigan State University, who then performed the DNA analysis. Foran found the supposed scar was stained red in colour, while the cover slip on the slide was held on with a yellowish adhesive that resisted efforts to loosen it with xylene, invariably effective with the mounting media used today. It was eventually decided that pine resin had been used: research showed that this was common practice at the time. As a result, the cover slip had to be chipped away. This done, the exposed tissue was sliced off the mount with a scalpel and DNA isolation was initiated. Two separate methods of DNA purification were then applied (organic and Chelex extraction) so as to maximise the likelihood of gaining viable results. The research has since been published in full detail (scuppering the hopes of sceptics who tried to claim the methodology might have been sloppy and the findings not peer-reviewed). Those of a scientific (or sceptical) turn of mind are recommended to peruse it:

> Given the historical and thus unknown nature of how the cellar tissues were dealt with at the time, how might one be assured that the DNA results obtained in this study resulted from the slide tissue, and not, for instance, from Dr. Spilsbury, who obviously handled the remains (whether he wore gloves of some kind and took other precautions is not mentioned in the records)? Here, the clearly different results obtained from the two DNA extraction procedures are key, in that the standard organic extraction generated no PCR results at all, even though it yields far cleaner and more concentrated DNA than does a Chelex extraction. The amplification success from only the Chelex preparation, which is consistent with fixed tissue and not touch DNA (the latter being routinely obtained through organic extraction, as is standard in our laboratory for instance), indicates a fixed tissue origin of the DNA. Further, the slide afforded a relatively large amount of tissue, certainly many orders of magnitude more than would be present in a touch sample, particularly one dating to 1910. And there is no doubt about the integrity of the slide tissue since that time, as the cover slip, as noted earlier, was extremely secure. These, along with the copious controls incorporated and repetition of experiments, show that the mtDNA and sexing results originated from the slide tissue.[2]

Dr Foran carried out the procedure twice to guard against error or contamination. The mtDNA obtained from the Spilsbury slide was shown to be not the same as that of Cora's grandnieces, differing at five nucleotides at a minimum. The three maternal relatives of Cora Crippen produced identical mtDNA haplotypes, each differing from the reference sequence at seven positions. Likewise, the slide DNA sexing results were clear and replicable, repeatedly producing both autosome and

Y chromosome products. The conclusion was inarguable: the remains obtained from the Crippen cellar were not those of Cora Crippen, and further, the tissue originated from a man. 'We tested and tested and tested,' Foran explained, 'and if I had any doubts whatsoever I would never have come out with it. The body is not Cora Crippen's.'

Several writers have tried to question the integrity of the work, so it is important to understand what can and cannot go wrong in a test such as this, especially since the desire to keep Crippen guilty as charged remains strong in many quarters (as, for that matter, does the desire to exonerate him in others). Dr Foran had no strong feelings in either direction. He explained, 'I don't really care one way or the other whether the body was Cora Crippen's, I have no interest in clearing Crippen's name. What I care about is being right.' The most obvious grounds for attack was the purity of the sample – might it have become hopelessly contaminated over the decades, effectively nixing any attempt to gain viable information of any sort from it today? Nicholas Connell hopefully devotes some four pages of his book *Doctor Crippen* to the various ways in which the material had come into contact with other people in 1910. But this is simply to misunderstand (and at a pretty basic level) how the test works. DNA is not overlaid on a sample like sweat or bloodstains, easily mixed with other people's to create a kind of garbled composite. 'The testing I did clearly indicates the DNA came from fixed tissue, which would not be the case with contamination,' Dr Foran told me. 'I also got a clean, single mtDNA profile, which contamination would not give.'[3]

In the London *Times*, columnist David Aaronovitch contributed a passionate screed of defiance under the headline I'LL EAT MY HAT IF DR CRIPPEN WAS INNOCENT, OK?[4] Like Connell, he took somewhat Luddite aim at the DNA tests and, more reasonably, at the suggestion (in a TV documentary that first broke the news of the results) that the remains might have been a police plant and frame-up. 'And all I have to go on, in the first instance, to justify why I am sure that all this is nonsense and will one day be proved to be nonsense,' he wrote, 'is what you might call – after the 20th-century British historian – Namier's Intuition. "The enduring achievement of historical study," said Namier, "is a historical sense – and intuitive understanding – of how things do not work." The murdered wife works, the planted body just doesn't.' Which is all very well, but makes two errors: first, in presuming that those two options exhaust the list of plausible possibilities (which, as Chapter 8 will show, is very far from the case) and thus making accepting the former an essential corollary of discounting the latter, and second, in its weighing of a likelihood (or even a hunch) against a fact. It does not matter how well the murdered wife theory 'works'. We've all seen how well it works, thank you very much: Crippen ended up dancing on the end of a rope, it works so well. What matters is scientific fact. And if scientific fact showed that the remains in the cellar were of a three-legged elephant then that is what they would be. (I set myself the challenge of writing this book without trotting out Sherlock Holmes's dictum about eliminating the impossible, but I am most tempted here.)

Other parts of Aaronovitch's article defy strictly rational analysis. I don't believe the remains were planted by the police either, but it would not follow if they had that Spilsbury would therefore have perjured himself in the trial, as he seems to believe.[5] Spilsbury was only working with the material he was handed. To the extent that he signed up to unproved conclusions as to the identity of the remains: that would be the case regardless of whether it had been planted or not. And it is vainglory of this sort that is eminently typical of Spilsbury and exactly what we should now be expecting of him: being arrogant is not the same as committing perjury. But either way, who cares? It wasn't Cora. Neither is Aaronovitch's attempt to discredit the genealogical research a success: 'We know (again from the archive) that Cora/Belle had a step-family in Brooklyn, so such lack of consanguinity is not restricted to the modern era.' Yes, she had a step-family, but that was because her *mother* remarried, not her father. Mitochondrial DNA is passed down the maternal line. So this, too, is completely irrelevant.

His conclusion is worth quoting in full:

As to the body being male, well the American team was using a 'special technique' that is 'very new' and 'done only by this team' and working on a single, century-old slide, described by the team leader as a 'less than optimal sample'. Have they, possibly, gone beyond their technique's competence? That, in the end, becomes the test for the time being – the supposed scientific *deus ex machina* versus Namier's Intuition. It will have to do until the [TV documentary's] evidence is debunked. As I absolutely predict it will be.

Aaronovitch wrote his article twelve years ago, and we're still waiting. The technique used, on the other hand, has been repeatedly duplicated, and the results extensively peer-reviewed. For those with a taste for the science, it is actually rather fascinating (others may feel free to skip):

> Sex determination is a critical component of forensic identification, the standard genetic method for which is detection of the single copy amelogenin gene that has differing homologues on the X and Y chromosomes. However, this assay may not be sensitive enough when DNA samples are minute or highly compromised, thus other strategies for sex determination are needed. In the current research, two ultrasensitive sexing assays, based on real-time PCR and pyrosequencing, were developed targeting the highly repetitive elements DYZ1 on the Y chromosome and Alu on the autosomes. The DYZ1/Alu strategy was compared to amelogenin for overall sensitivity based on high molecular weight and degraded DNA, followed by assaying the sex of 34 touch DNA samples and DNA from 30 hair shafts. The real-time DYZ1/Alu assay proved to be approximately 1500 times more sensitive than its amelogenin counterpart based on high molecular weight DNA, and even more sensitive when sexing degraded DNA. The pyrosequencing DYZ1/Alu assay correctly sexed 26 of the touch DNAs, compared to six using amelogenin. Hair shaft DNAs showed equally improved sexing results using the DYZ1/Alu assays. Overall, both DYZ1/Alu assays were far more sensitive and accurate than was the amelogenin assay, and thus show great utility for sexing poor quality and low quantity DNA evidence.[6]

Let us be absolutely clear: Foran's tests show beyond any reasonable doubt that the remains in the cellar were that of an unknown male. We no longer have the smallest idea of what happened to Cora Crippen, and no evidence of any sort linking Crippen to her murder; indeed, we no longer have any reason to believe she was murdered at all. The most we can say is that she disappeared, and no indication of what became of her has ever been found.

For Crippen, the implications are profound. It has been proved that he was not guilty of the crime of which he was convicted and executed. The circumstantial evidence seemingly linking him to his wife's murder instead now links him only to a body – not necessarily even a murder, and linked more ambiguously than ever – belonging to someone with no known connection to him. The range of possibilities this opens will be discussed in full in the next chapter.

But whatever the new findings mean for Crippen, they surely sound the death knell for any effort to co-opt Ethel into his supposed circle of villainy. Hard as it may have been to imagine her willingly co-habiting with a man who had just murdered his wife for the love of her, it is beyond fantasy to imagine she would do so knowingly with somebody who had just murdered someone else, for some other reason. We can speculate as to whether Crippen had murdered the man in the cellar and we can speculate as to whether he had killed and disposed of Cora somewhere else. But remove the Hilldrop Crescent grave site from the latter and any valid link to Ethel from the former and her complete innocence seems not only easy to justify but very hard indeed to negotiate a course away from. As the judge summed up at her trial, Crippen surely lied to her in exactly the way he lied to the world: by telling her Cora had died, and then admitting she had not. His reluctantly conceding that she was still alive makes perfect sense as their impetus to run away together, rather than live openly and sinfully as man and wife in England. It might even have been she who urged it; certainly it was done for her sake. But any and all speculation as to her guilt can be confidently put to bed.[7]

Ironically, however, that's where our confidence ends. That and the invalidity of the prosecution's scar evidence are about the only certainties these new findings bequeath us. The mystery itself, far from cleared away, is only made deeper and more baffling. It is to that mystery, but this time faced squarely, that we now must finally turn.

Chapter 8

The Mystery

'In a bout with the law, Inspector, there is no better armour than a knowledge of one's innocence."

James Ronald, *This Way Out*

L et us not pussyfoot around the evidence presented by David Foran. There can be no doubt as to the conclusions he reached. Any attempt to account for them on grounds of sloppy methodology, mutability of materials, antique or modern contamination of the sample or basic human error are plain and simple gestures of desperation, the last resorts of bad losers, to be dismissed as blithely as they are offered. The results are accurate to an infinitely greater degree than the prosecution's medical evidence. If you discount the former you have no right whatsoever to trust the latter, about anything. One last time: *the remains found in Crippen's cellar were not those of Cora Crippen.* For that reason, Crippen was innocent in law of the case made against him, and he deserved to walk from the court a free man. That he did not constitutes a demonstrable miscarriage of justice for which he should be pardoned without the smallest further delay. There is simply no doubt as to this. I'm not saving it up for some big finish. On the contrary, it is our starting point. It's where things begin to get interesting.

Provided this is accepted, we are now free to speculate as to what the seemingly inexplicable truth might be. Maybe Crippen is still guilty of murder, just not the one of which he stood accused? Or maybe he was guilty of both, or of some deeper, stranger, darker crime still. Or maybe he was, as he always claimed, completely and utterly innocent, not only in law (which has been proven) but in fact as well. The questions that remain are the following:

a) Was a crime committed?
b) If so, what crime?
c) If so, was Crippen innocent or guilty of it?

That the body in the cellar was not Belle's certainly helps to explain Crippen's blind and seemingly baffled protestations of innocence. But it does not actually *demonstrate* innocence. And this is complicated by the various secondary links to the Crippens found with the body. If he had nothing to do with it at all, how to explain the hair curlers, the nightwear fragments and the presence of hyoscine? Whose body was put in the cellar, when, by whom, and why? Is it evidence of a murder, or some other more or less illicit activity? And what did happen to Belle? If alive, why did she not come forward to confirm his story?

Possibilities

In his introduction to the Crippen volume of *Notable British Trials*, editor Filson Young put forward what he considered the only three possible solutions to the mystery. First: 'Crippen murdered his wife simply that he might indulge his guilty passion for Ethel Le Neve.' This was essentially the view taken by the prosecution, and Young wryly notes that it is 'the kind of motive which is always good enough for a jury'. Young rules it out because Crippen's relations with the two women had long been settled: 'When a man is in love with a woman who is not his wife, the time at which he is most likely to desert his wife for the mistress is at the beginning of the new relationship; not when it has been going on for years and become, as it were, regularised. And if that is true of mere desertion, how much more true is it of murder, which requires so much stronger a motive, so much more impulsive a passion.'

Second: the 'Marshall Hall defence', so called because the famous advocate was sure that had he been Crippen's lawyer, and allowed to pursue it, it would have avoided a capital sentence. This posits that Crippen was using the hyoscine either to pacify his wife, in light of her supposedly insatiable sexual demands, or to render her insensible while he entertained Ethel. Then, one time, he accidentally gave her too large a dose, killed her, and panicked. This is the version of events that is dramatised in the 1962 *Dr Crippen* film, with Donald Pleasence. It seems to me to be dubious for the same reasons it did to Young. It is hard to believe Cora did not know about Ethel,[1] and the pair seemed to do most of their illicit coupling in the afternoon: Crippen stressed that he always came home at night. And Cora's demanding of sex from Crippen is another of those stories that everyone knows to be true but which doesn't seem to have any evidential foundation. They certainly had separate rooms by this time.[2] One highly unexpected endorsement for this theory, however, comes from Ethel herself, who in the 1920 version of her memoirs wrote: 'he was in the habit of taking small quantities [of hyoscine] from the office and administering them to his wife when he thought she was likely to break into one of her fits of passion.'[3]

Lastly, the theory Young himself favours: Cora tells Crippen she is leaving and taking their money, furs and jewellery: he kills her in a red mist. There is now, of course, a further reason for ruling out all of them: so far as we know, Crippen did not kill Cora. And clearly, in the light of the new evidence, any hypothesis that posits as a given that the remains were Cora's is no longer valid. So before we can speculate anew, we need to reformulate the possibilities, using the correct evidential framework. The four basic hypotheses are:

1. *Crippen innocent of all*
   Crippen was entirely genuine – he was in complete ignorance of any crime being committed on the premises *and* had no reason to think Cora was not still alive.

Traditional contradictions to this theory:

   (c1) the additional physical evidence found with the remains linking them to the Crippens;
   (c2) the fact of his flight seemingly indicating guilt;
   (c3) his inability to explain how the remains came to be there seemingly during the period of his tenancy;
   (c4) the fact that Belle did not come forward to clear the mistake up;
   (c5) his lying to her friends concerning her death and his suspicious behaviour prior and subsequent to her disappearance;
   (c6) the evidence of hyoscine in the remains linking them to Crippen's purchasing of hyoscine.

2. *Crippen his wife's murderer, but innocent of all connection to the remains in the cellar*
   Crippen was genuine with regards to the remains found – but he had killed his wife separately and put her elsewhere. This would explain his flight, his lies and Belle's non-reappearance but not c1, c3 or c6.

3. *Crippen not his wife's murderer, but responsible for the remains in the cellar*

Crippen knew the corpse was not Belle because he did know more than he was telling about the remains. If so, what was his connection to them? This would possibly explain c1, almost certainly explain c6 and definitely explain c2 and c3, but reintroduces c4 and c5.

4. *Crippen his wife's murderer, and additionally responsible for the remains in the cellar*

Crippen knew the body was not Belle because he knew Belle was dead but somewhere else – and he did know about the other remains too. This hypothesis accounts for all the contradictions because it presupposes complete guilt.

Objections

Our job now is to attempt some form of reconstruction of events that might logically fit any of those four hypotheses, and to decide if any seem more or less likely than their brothers. This will involve considering the validity in context of the seeming objections to innocence listed above as c1 to c6. Before we do so, it may be worth reminding ourselves what Crippen's own explanations for c1 to c6 were, and considering how credible they might be.

(c1) Crippen had no explanation for how the secondary physical evidence came to be there, on the grounds that he had nothing to do with the primary physical evidence either. He was later trapped into error regarding the date his pyjamas were purchased, to counter the objection that the remains might have been placed their earlier. But Crippen never denied the pyjamas were his, he only made – and stuck to – the assertion that he had no idea how they came to be there. This would be the case whenever the remains were interred. This will be discussed presently.

(c2) Crippen said that he feared being detained pending an investigation by Dew. This would stymie his efforts to start again with Ethel, and disgrace her in the eyes of the media, as she had told of all of her intimates that they were already married. He decided, there and then, 'to take her away out of the country where she would not have this scandal thrown upon her'. This strikes me as both understandable as motive, and sensible as a course of action. Clearly, he and Le Neve were planning to go away; he had given up the lease of the flat and already begun packing. Some intrusive criminal investigation might well tie him to England, reveal his lies about Cora and expose his relationship with Ethel to censure and ridicule. He said he thought if he and Ethel ran away the scandal would eventually die down and they would be left alone: in other words, he felt himself embroiled in a compromising and unethical marital scandal, not a murder. That all seems more than enough reason for an innocent man to run off, and I genuinely can't understand why anyone would think it is not. Yes, a guilty man would act as Crippen did, but so, surely, would the man Crippen claimed to be.

(c3) Again, we are looking at this the wrong way round. A clever killer, an experienced liar, a man with months to come up with a story, would have something more convincing to say about this than Crippen. His suicidal protestations of absolute confusion do not betoken guilt, unless it is the guilt of a village idiot.

(c4) This is a very important objection and must be taken seriously. I will look into a few of the possibilities below. Unless there were reserves of hatred flowing below the surface waters of the Crippens' marriage to a degree that even his own account do not hint at, I cannot easily believe that she would have willingly done nothing and allowed him to die. So I believe we are limited to explanations of why she could not speak rather than merely did not.

(c5) Crippen tells Dew that this was because he wished to avoid prolonged questioning from Cora's friends, and to deflect any scandal, both for his sake and Cora's. He also – this is very important – wanted to have Ethel legally recognised as his wife. If Cora was merely missing he would need to wait for years for her to be declared dead, and he would have no reason to think she wouldn't pop up and spoil it all for him in the meantime. No, it was vital to the future of his relationship with Ethel that Cora be thought dead. As with c2, this seems so obvious to me I can't imagine why anyone would see it as suspicious at all. A murderer, by contrast, would have no reason to embellish a perfectly good story about her going away. The pawning of the jewellery and flaunting of his relationship with Ethel again, to my mind, suggests the crass insensitivity of an innocent man, not the discretion and calculation one would expect of a guilty one. His behaviour around the time of the dinner party with the Martinettis does give me pause, however, and I will discuss that presently.

(c6) Crippen explained that he had purchased hyoscine for use in his medical preparations, which is not at all unlikely or suspicious in itself. However, his only defence for the fact that a drug he had recently purchased was found in lethal doses in the remains was that it was a coincidence. It could hardly be anything but that, when his position regarding the remains was that he knew nothing about them. Coincidences do happen, of course, but it is very difficult to accept this. Any coherent defence, therefore, is obliged to account for it.

Thus the evidence and the arguments; let us now try out a few theories.

An accident?

Might the remains be of someone Crippen had killed accidentally, and then panicked into concealing all evidence of? This was a popular suggestion when the remains were still believed to be Cora's, which is why we have theories such as the suggestion that she had become demented by the effects of the hyoscine and he had been forced to shoot her in the head. The issue, of course, is the problem of accounting for why anyone confronted with the evidence of one crime would then go on to commit a worse one. Poisoners usually poison so as to create the illusion of death by natural causes: it seems oddly pointless to poison someone and then dismember the body and hide it. Another popular suggestion was that Crippen may have been performing abortions, and the remains were of a woman who had died during the procedure. That would have made sense – in that instance he would have committed a capital offence, and it would have been very much in his interests to remove all trace of it. Obviously, the discovery that the remains were male put paid to that one.

But what about one of his patients? An accidental overdose in that case would give us a Crippen with a dead male body on his hands, and an explanation for the presence of hyoscine in the remains. At the trial,

Crippen was asked of the patients he made these preparations for: 'Did you see them personally, or was it conducted by correspondence?' To which he replied: 'Very few personally; most by correspondence.' 'Very few' not being the same as zero, it follows that he was saying he did on rare occasions see patients personally. An accidental hyoscine overdose by a male patient then becomes a possibility. Unfortunately, this runs up against the same old problem and one new one. As before, it seems hard to understand why a doctor with a case of accidental overdose on his hands should risk mutilating and concealing the corpse rather than just coming clean. And second, Crippen's remedies were homeopathic, and, as became embarrassingly clear at the trial, the active quantity in these remedies was nil. We can, I suppose, posit the kind of freak accidental overdose as is seen to be given to Cora in the 1962 *Dr Crippen* film – in which Crippen, startled by a noise, accidentally spills a lethal dose of the powder into a sugar bowl – but this would be a flight of fantasy merely.

A different murder victim?

Could the remains be of somebody else murdered by Crippen? Conceivably, yes – but who? Might it have been one of the lodgers; even Tom Cullen's hitherto imaginary man that Crippen found in bed with Cora? Unlikely. For one thing, it was to Crippen's advantage that Cora be unfaithful: it enabled him to maintain the moral high ground with regards his relationship with Ethel, and made it more likely that they might eventually divorce. At the very least, he would have none of the passion needed for such a murder. Further, if the remains are of a murder victim they seem to be of someone who has been poisoned. That presupposes premeditation, and rules out a killing in anger or the heat of the moment. Further, if he had murdered one of his tenants – or anyone other than Cora prior to Cora's disappearance – he would have had to have done all of that dismembering and burying while she was still resident in the house. Even if logistically possible at all – which I don't think it is – she would surely have put two and two together and never stood for it.

How then might we get around the fact of Cora's presence if we are to propose Crippen killing, dissecting and entombing somebody in the house? I suppose we could posit a double murder, and have Cora discovering evidence of the cellar murder, threatening to expose Crippen to the law and thus ensuring her silencing also, by some means never discovered. Maybe Ellery Queen could make something out of that; I'm not sure I can. Then there is the suggestion by 'Perth Ethel' (see Chapter 7) that Crippen had killed Cora in a rage, with a glass of poisoned champagne, after she had threatened to shoot Ethel. The story, obviously, is a fiction (in fact it very much recalls the motive in the film *The Suspect*, see Chapter 6), but it underlines a relevant point: that if we wish to retain the claim that Crippen killed Cora we need to posit a very specific, perhaps even imperative catalyst that would have prompted him to so grievously shatter the status quo and make risking his neck seem the best option.

Another decidedly outré possibility would account for the fact of the remains, the fact of Cora's presence in the house *and* the fact of her disappearance: if the remains were of a person *she* had killed. A lover on the verge of leaving her, killed out of jealousy or in a drunken rage? Some kind of terrible accident... well, then we would still need to explain the hyoscine away. But we would at least have Crippen recognising a chance to get rid of her once and for all, agreeing to cover for her, and to deal with all the messy business, provided she runs away and keeps her head down, with no further interference in his life with Ethel. This is a pleasing fiction, not least because it is the only theory, other than sheer romantic whimsy (she banged her head and lost her memory!), that could account simultaneously for Cora being both alive and unable to come forward to clear Crippen's name. But would Crippen take such a risk, especially knowing that if the body were found he would end up in exactly the predicament as did befall him? Surely not. And it's hard to imagine someone mutilating a corpse on behalf of a spouse they weren't in love with. A rival for Ethel's hand, then? Another inconvenient John Stonehouse? That's better – but it is hard to come up with a scenario for that which would have the body end up in the vicinity of Hilldrop Crescent, getting poisoned. More likely Crippen would push him under a train.

A limited conspiracy?

So was the whole thing a gigantic hoax? Some of the recent, post-DNA articles and documentaries have darkly hinted at the possibility of it all being a police frame job, and, as noted in Chapter 6, even at the time, some papers argued that it may have been a publicity stunt, cooked up by Crippen and Cora together, the latter of whom would eventually reappear after reaping the publicity benefits.[4] An enterprising thriller writer, it seems to me, could make good use of that one, especially if at the last minute the husband reveals it was all an elaborate double-cross and kills her anyway!

Needless to say, there are no grounds for suspecting anything like the latter to be the case, with or without my Movie of the Week coda. But an official fix-up? If we accept the prosecution case, then Crippen killed his wife, mutilated her with exceptional precision somewhere where no physical evidence was left, successfully disposed of the head, limbs, genital organs and skeleton elsewhere, never to be found, and then put the easy-to-dispose-of remainder – with a telltale scar on it – in his cellar, with various articles of his and his wife's linking him inarguably to it. On the face of it, such an argument seems very hard to believe, and the fact that we now know the body was an unidentified male makes it start to smell very bad indeed. So given that the remains were not Cora's, which not only removes all evidence that she was murdered by Crippen but must render questionable the various pieces of secondary evidence that seem to link the body with Cora, how entitled are we to speculate that the entire crime scene was a fraud?[5]

At first, it does seem the logical jumping-off point from the new DNA findings, and it is only fair to begin by saying that, in reconstructing the narrative, a number of points seem oddly suggestive of such a proposition. Some writers have noted that bodies would have been relatively easy to obtain – found in the sewers or pulled from the Thames – and could easily have been placed there surreptitiously. Well, perhaps. More pointedly, Dew and Mitchell's repeated visits to the house, and indeed to the cellar, which by their account they examined *three times* before returning a fourth time with the idea to look under the floor, could be seen as their opportunity to lay the groundwork for such a deception: first digging up the cellar, then returning to bury the remains and conceal them again, and then finally returning and 'discovering' them. Otherwise, there seems to be an odd contradiction between the frequency with which they returned there and their dawdling response having done so. Alternatively, those mysterious twin coffins that arrived at the scene (see Chapter 3) might be deployed as a possible means of bringing the remains sneakily to the house, and then out again!

My feeling is that conspiracy theories of this sort become less likely the more people are required in order to sustain them. When there is a chain of deception, taking in everything from high-ranking officials to numerous rank-and-file men and representatives of sundry other related professions, it starts to look unlikely, not because I have a rose-tinted faith in human nature, but simply because there are too many weak links in the chain to presume it will hold.[6] There are any number of reasons why any link might break, exposing the whole: someone's integrity and sense of moral duty being only one of them. There's also the temptation to brag of one's importance, the pursuit of celebrity, the financial possibilities of having a story to sell, even the temptation of blackmail. It might even be accidental: a careless word spoken out of turn, or lips loosened when their owners are in their cups. It feels like too great a risk.

Of course, such things do happen, and Dr Eline M.J. Schotsmans, whose expertise on the subject of bodily preservation and decomposition I have drawn from extensively in this chapter, is one of several reasonable authorities I have discussed the matter with who see no particular reason to rule it out. She argues that a combination of deference, fear and financial inducement might be enough to pull off such a stunt. So I certainly do not rule it out without consideration. Nonetheless, *if* the mortal remains had been planted by the police, all of the following would need to have happened. The remains would have been secured and spirited away, either from a morgue or a medical lab. They would then have been skilfully mutilated to remove anything that might make (an accurate) identification possible (unless taken from a dissection room where, deliberately or incidentally, such work had already been done). Somehow, they would then have been hurried into a moderately advanced state of putrefaction, unless found that way, which would make the previous tasks even more grotesque. Then they would have been transported to the site, and taken in without being seen. The cellar would have to be dug up, indeed it would probably have had to have been dug up in advance, both to minimise the length of time the remains were present elsewhere in the house during the exercise, and to see if under the cellar floor was acceptable as a place of concealment in the first place. The pit dug, the remains would then need to be inserted (recall that they smelled revoltingly). Then either at least six policemen and a pathologist would have to knowingly lie, or Dew and at least one accomplice, probably more, would have to not only insert the remains, but replace the earth and clay, reset the bricks, dry and cover the floor, apply fake dust, and then indulge in a humiliating acting charade as, with the assistance of the other, duped policemen and under the partial supervision of the duped pathologist, they pretend to unearth them again. Notice how many individuals would need to be knowingly involved for this to work. Consider how physically disgusting it would be. And all this before we willingly assume the right to blacken the name of Inspector Dew, and so many others working under and alongside him.

Lastly, consider the risk of exposure they would be running, and what the ramifications of that would be. If the whole crime scene was a fabrication they would have no reason to be sure that Belle wasn't still alive somewhere, and might appear at any minute to discredit them all. She might even have been killed by Crippen, just as they had supposed, but buried somewhere else. Indeed, they would surely have assumed that she was. If these real remains were then subsequently found, and who would presume they would not be, the result would be the same: they would be revealed as despicable criminals. Serious criminal proceedings would ensue, and the scandal would shake all public confidence in Scotland Yard.

I can think of only two reasons why anybody would have even entertained taking the risk. One would be when a thorough search of the house and grounds, and the vicinity, had turned up nothing, and it might be feared that Crippen would slip the net through simple lack of evidence. But this decision, if it were taken, would have been taken far later in the day than when the find was made, long before all possible burial locations had been fully searched.

The only reason I can think of why it might have been planted so early would be if it was feared that without immediate hard proof of murder there would be no real grounds for launching the manhunt against Crippen. But that is to look at things exactly the wrong way round. Indeed, galling to Dew though it must have been for Crippen and Le Neve to have fled as they did, there was still no particular reason to cook up evidence of a crime that nobody seemed sure had even occurred. The scandal, such as it was, would have died down, and the public would likely have had very little lasting interest either way. On the contrary, it was the find itself that made a major case out of a minor intrigue: had it not been made, it seems unlikely to me that there would be any particularly strong pressure on Dew – from any direction – to go much more deeply into it. By now, only music hall historians would recall it, as a curiosity at best. So it is hard to imagine Dew chancing his arm so rashly, partly because it would be *such* a risk, and partly because the case as it stood hardly seemed worth it.[7]

For these reasons, weird and suspicious though Dew and Mitchell's interminable bumbling about in the cellar unquestionably seems, I still lean towards exoneration. And the two coffins, I suspect, reflect what was then Dew's certainty that there would be more still to be found somewhere on the premises, and that they were likely to find them imminently: in other words, establishing his complete innocence of planting the first set.

If, however, we are able to make a case for a much more limited conspiracy, it is precisely *because* of Dew's knowledge that the scene was genuine, and his sureness that the body was Cora's. Given that the remains *were* already in the house, and that Dew *did* discover them legitimately, it becomes much easier to accept the following. Dew, in the absolute certainty that these are Cora's remains (for what else could they possibly be?) and that Crippen is her murderer (for who else possibly could be?) notes with a sinking feeling that so thorough a job has been made of obliterating their identity they may never be positively identified. With no risk whatever in his mind, therefore, that he might be framing an innocent man, but merely helping prove the case against an indisputably guilty one, he gingers up the evidence very slightly with a few items he could easily have obtained in the time he was completely alone in the house. Though obviously not playing fair by the laws of evidence and proper procedure, this doesn't reflect *too* badly on Dew, given his understandable feelings at what he thought he had discovered, and his valid desire to see that the fiend responsible should not go scot-free. This could account for the hair curlers, likely still on Cora's dresser, and the nightwear items, likely in the upstairs drawers. (The fact that such personal items were still on the premises not only made the planting of this evidence easy, it would have also further reinforced Dew's certainty that foul play had been committed against Cora, otherwise why not take her personal items with her?)

Another small indicator emerged at the trial. As Charles Dawson discovered when he engineered the Piltdown Man hoax two years later, the best way to get your planted evidence believed is to have someone else discover it. Thus it is notable, and on the face of it surprising, that none of the really questionable evidence found at the Crippen cellar seems to have been spotted by the police. First the testimony of Dr Augustus Pepper, brought to the site, the day after its discovery, by Dew.

> In the cellar I found that part of the floor had been taken up, and in a hole in the ground I saw what appeared to be animal remains, including in the word 'animal', human... I also found some articles in the hole; some of these were taken from the hole and put on a tray. Among them there was a tuft of dark brown hair in a Hinde's curler... I also found a small piece of fair hair lying in a large handkerchief...

On 15 July, at the mortuary, eagle-eyed Dr Pepper's discoveries continued:

> I also found a portion of a woman's woollen or cotton combinations... I also found portions of a pyjama jacket.

Dr Thomas Marshall was the divisional surgeon of police for Kentish Town. Ten days later, he made a find of his own:

> On 25th July I made a further examination of the remains other than those which were in the jars at the mortuary. On that occasion I found a second Hinde's curler...

Then he made a discovery that Dr Pepper had somehow missed, over a month later:

> On 14th August I made a further examination of the remains at the mortuary, and on that occasion I found a third Hinde's curler...

As Pepper only too keenly noted at the trial:

> Taking a mass of human remains by themselves – without anything else like Hinde's curlers and so on – it is quite impossible to tell the sex, except upon anatomical grounds. There are no anatomical grounds in this case to enable me to say with certainty the sex.

What a lucky find those curlers were, then! In his book *Doctor Crippen*, Nicholas Connell repeatedly cites the hair curlers as conclusive evidence, firm enough to rule out of contention any number of theories, even as evidence against the DNA findings! My feeling is that one need not doubt that the police found the human remains as claimed (as I certainly believe), one might still believe that whatever the source of the remains they were put there by Crippen, or that Crippen murdered whomever they belong to; or even (incorrectly) that the DNA evidence is somehow wrong and the body really is Cora after all. But the notion that Crippen, after having removed the head in a different part of the house, and successfully disposed of it elsewhere, accidentally dropped hair curlers into the grave pit with Cora's hairs wound round them is so utterly ridiculous as to beggar belief. It was all but impossible to believe when it was presumed it was Cora's flesh down there. That he would somehow get his wife's hair curlers mixed in with the viscera of an unconnected man is sheer raving madness. They were always very dubious evidence of Crippen's guilt; now they are rather compelling evidence of corruption.

Now remember those early reports (see Chapter 3) that claimed there was a necklace around the small portion of throat still attached to the remains. I have made the case that we should expect the detail in these reports, which are usually in line with the canonical version, to have been informed by genuine hints and tip-offs from the police, and I see no reason to think that several different newspapers would suddenly indulge (all on the same day) in wild fancy about a necklace. So I am inclined to see it as evidence that the police were indeed engaged in strengthening a weak, possibly losing case of identity with a bit of circumstantial proof. But if so, why does the necklace abruptly disappear, only to be just as abruptly replaced by the (canonical) hair curlers? Here's my guess. Once it became obvious just how cavalier Ethel had been in her use of Cora's clothes and jewellery, any piece of jewellery placed with the body, sourced from the house while only the police were present, ran the risk of being identified as something Ethel had been wearing in the months subsequent to the alleged crime, giving the whole game away. The substitution at that point of the hair curlers and nightwear, almost certainly left completely untouched since Cora's departure, made such a risk much less likely.

The pyjama jacket seems slightly more questionable, because we cannot be sure at this distance how decayed it was. Connell certainly strongly implies that its condition told of its having been attached to the remains far longer than would be the case had it been planted. (He describes it as 'putrid', presumably with irony intended.) But the jacket was savoury enough to be brought into open court and examined by all, where its patterning and the words on the label were clear to see. It is also even harder to imagine how Crippen could have made the error of leaving it in the pit than is the case with the hair curlers. A desperate theoriser might, with luck and a favourable wind, argue that Crippen somehow transported the hair curlers (but not the head) to the scene, and then allowed them to drop in, all without his realising it. But the pyjama jacket sample was a torn fragment, and the remainder stayed outside the pit. So he is either the biggest moron of all time, tearing off a piece of his jacket to transport the remains, and knowingly using the portion showing the maker's label, somehow thinking this would not in any way incriminate him, or we are forced to suggest, as with the curlers, that it ended up in there accidentally. But that won't work this time. True, Crippen was never going to miss his wife's hair curlers. But he would have instantly been reminded that he had a pyjama jacket with an incriminating chunk missing. Indeed, such is the prosecution's case, because according to the evidence Dew claimed to find upstairs, the rest of the jacket had already been disposed of. (And yet he kept the trousers, despite having two other identical pairs. Why? When would he wear them?) In other words, he saw the damaged jacket and threw it away. But if a piece was clearly missing, why would he not guess exactly where it was and retrieve it? Re-excavating the remains would be disgusting, but hardly more disgusting than putting them there in the first place. Are we really positing that, when confronted with the remains of the jacket, it did not occur to him that the missing portion was in the pit? Or are we saying that he did realise, but was too lazy to go back in and retrieve it, even if, as proved the case, it helped put a rope around his neck? For these reasons, whatever condition the fragment was said to be in, I think we have to regard it as dubiously as we must the curlers.

The evidence of hyoscine

The one piece of evidence that does not immediately satisfy the requirements of this strictly limited conspiracy is the detection of hyoscine in the body. Other than straightforward evidence of guilt, this can only be explained unsatisfactorily: as forensic error, forensic deception, or coincidence. Our rational natures rebel at the thought of both honest error and sheer coincidence, while our 'limited conspiracy' model rightly rebels at malicious deception. Straightforward evidence of guilt, in such company, seems to be the only sane option. But let's not forget exactly what that 'straightforward evidence of guilt' would have to be: it would mean that for some reason nobody can think of, Crippen poisoned and dismembered an unknown man, got rid of most of him elsewhere but put some of him in his cellar, and then denied all knowledge of it. And totally *regardless* of what did or didn't happen to his wife. There's not much worthy of being called straightforward there. So let's hear out some of the other possibilities.

First, the known facts. Crippen purchased hyoscine on 17 January 1910, from Lewis and Burrows of New Oxford Street. His buying poison is not at all strange in itself: he bought all kinds of weird stuff – cocaine, belladonna and more – for use in his patent remedies. The problem with the hyoscine is, first, that its presence was detected in the remains, and second, and just as important in its way, that Crippen was unable to present evidence of his having used the quantity he did buy in any homeopathic preparation (much scepticism has generally greeted his claims that it might have been used for such a purpose), or to account for it in any other way. Gilbert Rylance, his partner in the Yale Tooth concern, William Long, his assistant, and Marion Curnow, who worked for Munyon's, all confirmed that he routinely made up private prescriptions. Long, in particular, gave very detailed information on the matter:

> I could not say whether he had any general practice during the time I was with him, but I knew that he used to make up special prescriptions. He would have to buy the drugs for those prescriptions. He used to buy bottles, which he kept in a cupboard or cabinet in the room that was used as the office after he joined Dr. Rylance. During the period up to November, 1909, when he was manager for Munyon's, he used to prescribe for patients, making up drugs and posting them off. During that period he would be likely to have bottles, but I could not say where he kept them. During the period between November, 1909, and 1st February, 1910, he used similarly to prescribe for patients, and he would be likely to have bottles. These bottles were kept in the office of the Yale Tooth Specialists, where he used to make up the prescriptions.

Crippen said that by this means he had used some two thirds of the supply of hyoscine he purchased. (The remainder, he says, he left in his office with his other poisons, but all had been removed without his knowledge.)

For the reasons given above ('A limited conspiracy?'), I don't like the deception option. I simply can't believe that reputable pathologists and chemists would willingly prostitute their integrity in the services of a crude police frame-up. But there is a milder version, somewhere between genuine error and wilful deception, altogether easier to accept, which is *confirmation bias.*

In the evidence concerning the supposed scar on the flesh in the cellar, we clearly see confirmation bias in action. Of course it is not necessary in logic that it not be a scar simply because we know the remains are not Cora's but an unknown man's. Men have been known to acquire scars, after all, and Pepper himself nominated the removal of stones from the bladder as one of a number of potential medical reasons why a man might have a scar in the same location as Cora's ovariectomy. Nonetheless, it does appear that the much-derided defence claim that it was merely a fold in the skin *was* correct, and the incorruptible and omniscient prosecution experts found a scar simply because they were looking for one. (For neither the first nor last time in the trial the supposedly hobbled and bumbling defence had landed an uncanny bullseye, much good it did them.) This shows the relevance of confirmation bias, and we need to be especially on guard against it in the Crippen case because there was hardly a single piece of revealed evidence that wasn't already being searched for.

John Trestrail notes that confirmation bias shaped the toxicological analysis from the first. Due to the publicity surrounding the enquiry, a staff member at Lewis and Burrows had become suspicious and checked the Poison Register. He then contacted the company chairman, who called a meeting of the board of directors to decide what to do with the information. A member of the board knew Dr Pepper, and wrote to him with his suspicions. From this point on, the quest was on to find hyoscine in the remains.[8] Nonetheless, unless we are positing a conscious act of conspiracy – which I am not – it has to be remembered that confirmation bias can only get you so far. It is only possible if genuine error is possible in the first place, because we have ruled out knowing deception. So the important question is: is it even possible to mistakenly detect hyoscine at all? Both John Trestrail and David Foran are far more confident on this point than I am, and their views, it goes without saying, carry far more weight than mine. Trestrail notes that the toxicological analyses used no controls, nor did they test for the purity of the isolated compound. He argues that the amount of hyoscine in the tissues could not even be accurately calculated, and may well have been a therapeutic dose rather than a fatal one. None of these concerns emerged in the trial. Foran likewise sees abundant evidences of subjectivity in the findings, and believes the test would not hold up as valid in either methodology or conclusions in a court of law today.

By modern standards, none of the medical evidence would be admissible. One of the constables at Hilldrop Crescent was sent to get some disinfectant by Dew, which was liberally sloshed all over the site before the remains were removed. At the morgue, they would be sprinkled with carbolic powder and then covered with storeroom paper. All of this, days before a single test had been made! At the inquest, Arthur Newton had challenged the use of carbolic powder, pointing out that if it had been present it would make the chemical analysis worthless. Both the undertaker and the morgue keeper flatly denied it had been used.[9]

Trestrail also argues that there is no demonstration that the isolated substance was pure, since the melting point measurement to assess it was not undertaken. In cross-examination, Dr Willcox had offered a cogent explanation of why this test was not done, but it does not alter the fact that it wasn't: 'In the remains I did not discover sufficient of the alkaloid to apply what is called the melting point test… It is a test which can only be applied when one has a considerable quantity of the alkaloids to deal with… you can never get enough in a toxicological case to apply the test.'

The significance of the melting point test is that the three potential alkaloids detected – hyoscine, hyoscyamine and atropine – may be most decisively distinguished from each other by their melting points, which differ in all three cases (respectively, 65, 105 and 115 degrees). In the absence of this test, Willcox confirmed the presence of hyoscine – for which he had of course been made well aware he was looking – on altogether less decisive grounds:

> The careful observation, with a lens and microscope, of the alkaloid itself, as to whether it is crystalline or gummy; also the bromine test, which has already been mentioned – the obtaining of crystals. From a careful examination of the alkaloid I found it to be gummy, which is a characteristic of hyoscine. Gumminess is not characteristic of hyoscyamine and atropine; they are crystalline.

Dr Blyth, appearing for the defence, rejected this assertion. He was also highly sceptical of Willcox's belief that the traces could not be of an animal alkaloid occurring naturally during putrefaction, which he believed would be far harder to distinguish from vegetable alkaloid than Willcox suggested. In fact, he opined that even to distinguish between the two concepts at all was misleading. In this he was supported by Thomas Lauder Brunton's *Textbook of Pharmacology, Therapeutics and Materia Medica* (1885):

> From decomposing organic matter substances can be separated which have all the characters of alkaloids.
>
> The alkaloids produced by putrefaction are usually known by the name of ptomaines. It was at one time supposed that they were different in their chemical nature from the alkaloids which occur in plants, and they were supposed to have a much greater reducing power than the latter. It was therefore proposed to distinguish between ptomaines and other alkaloids by the addition of potassium ferricyanide: if the alkaloid changed this into ferrocyanide, so that a precipitate of prussian blue was obtained on the addition of ferric chloride, it was supposed to belong to the class of ptomaines; whereas non-reduction was supposed to show that it belonged to the vegetable alkaloids. It was soon found, however, that this test was not trustworthy, for such important alkaloids as morphine and veratrine produced reduction. Later researches, especially those of Brieger, have shown that some at least of the so-called ptomaines are identical with vegetable alkaloids.
>
> We may indeed now regard alkaloids as products of albuminous decomposition, whether their albuminous precursor be contained in the cells of plants and altered during the process of growth, or whether the albuminous substances undergo decomposition from the presence of microbes, either outside or inside the animal body, or by the simple process of digestion by unorganised ferments such as pepsine.
>
> The alkaloidal products formed by the putrefaction of albuminous substances, vary according to the stage of decay at which they are produced. At first the poisonous action of these products may be slight. As decomposition advances, the poisons become more virulent; but after a longer period they appear to become broken up and lose to a great extent their poisonous power.

A recent (2009) study summed up some of the complications attendant to analysis of this sort:

> There are numerous biochemical and biological processes that occur after death that may have a significant influence on post-mortem drug concentrations. These processes may render the quantification of particular drugs unreliable, or even result in drugs being undetectable in some instances, despite the use of several methods. Problems may occur with changes in the drug concentration via bacterial degradation, residual tissue enzymatic activity, or via post-mortem redistribution from tissues of a higher to a lower concentration. Many analytical techniques can suffer from interferences due to co-extracted putrefactive compounds that mask or alter the way a drug is detected, depending on the analytical technique utilised.[10]

At the trial, Tobin summed up:

> Was the alkaloid found in the remains hyoscine? Dr Willcox said there was not enough of it to use what he said would be the most certain test of all to ascertain which mydriatic vegetable alkaloid it was. As he did not apply this test, he asked the jury to say that the matter remained in far too much doubt, whether, even if this was a vegetable alkaloid at all, it was hyoscine rather than hyoscyamine or atropine. He would go further and ask the jury to say that there was not enough to enable a man to determine whether the alkaloid found in the body was vegetable, introduced during life, or animal, produced after death by the natural process of putrefaction.

Might Crippen really have purchased the drug in all innocence, for use in his quack remedies? It is certainly telling that he purchased it under his real name and from his usual suppliers: again, hardly the behaviour of a calculating murderer. That he also signed the poisons register became doubly significant in the trial, when Harold Kirby, the assistant who oversaw the transaction, revealed in cross-examination that he did so *voluntarily*:

> I have known Dr Crippen since about October of last year. He has bought large quantities of poison from our shop. As a rule he did not sign the poisons book. We did not require him to do so, because we knew him, and knew him as a medical man. When he signed the book for the hyoscine he did not raise the slightest objection.

There is nothing *less* that a sly killer, keen to take necessary precautions, could have done, nothing more likely to expose his guilt. All arguments about him using hyoscine because it was a rarer and possibly harder to detect poison than the 'classic' ones, that it might more readily be taken for natural causes, shrivel and die in the light of this testimony, which shows him making no effort of any sort to distance himself from his purchase. A murderer who wanted to get caught would have done no different, or could have done no better.

Though an attempt was made to suggest that hyoscine was a relatively unknown drug with relatively few legitimate applications, a casual glance through the record suggests it was well known in medical circles, used widely and for many different reasons.[11] In 1892, a Dr Lionel Weatherly is singing its praises in the treatment of violent psychosis.[12] ('He says that under the administration of repeated small doses of hyoscine such a patient becomes a changed man; violence and abusiveness give place to an amiable politeness, and he subsides into silence.') Also in 1892, a Dr Usher advocated using it for alcoholism in a book called *Alcoholism and Its Treatment*; the *Lancet* wrote that 'the most useful part of Dr Usher's book is that dealing with the use of drugs in the treatment of alcoholism.'[13] In 1893, the *New York World* is reporting on its efficacy as a treatment for insomnia.[14] In 1914 it is being used to induce what is termed 'twilight sleep', a form of partial general anaesthetic used during childbirth, leaving the patient nominally conscious but calm and insensitive to pain.[15] Elsewhere we hear great things said in its favour for use against delirium,[16] seasickness,[17] drug addiction,[18] epilepsy,[19] Parkinson's disease,[20] lockjaw[21] and even rabies![22] As far back as 1885, one newspaper was noting its use as being so prevalent it was itself proving addictive: 'The New York Medical Society has lately made the discovery that there are a large number of people in that city becoming addicted to the use of hyoscine, a drug more deadly in its effects than opium or chloral. It is obtained from a German plant, and the discovery of the use to which it is being put was made from the increased demand for it at the drug stores, and the advance in its price.'[23] Users were said to be predominantly 'medical students, drug clerks and others acquainted with its soporific qualities'. In Philadelphia in 1915, three men were pronounced 'raving maniacs' as a result of sniffing it.[24] Crippen himself noted in the trial that he had seen it used to pacify mental patients in London (this is almost certainly true), and that he had been using it as an ingredient for a 'nerve tonic', which makes sense, but any credibility was soon dissipated by an agonising session in court as Crippen tried to find evidences of the customers for whom he claimed to have made up the preparations:

Is there any letter that you know of which refers to anything that you prescribed containing hyoscine?

There should be plenty of letters with registered on the back 'Special nerve remedy'. There should be plenty of those; it would not refer to 'hyoscine'.

I have a number of letters here; you know what they are?

Yes.

They relate to prescriptions?

Yes.

The point is this, do any of those letters that I have got here, so far as you know, refer to prescriptions made up by you, containing hyoscine?

There must be some there. ...

Can you tell me by looking?

I think I can.

I want anything which refers to a prescription containing hyoscine. Could you tell by looking?

I should by looking.

These are letters from patients, are they?

Yes. (A number of letters were handed to the witness.) No, these are not the letters that would refer to that.

But if we can account for the supposed hyoscine traces in the cellar evidence, *and* Crippen is not to be believed that he was using hyoscine in homeopathic capsules, why did he buy it in the first place? The most popular explanation, other than for murder, is the Marshall Hall defence that he was drugging Cora. Perhaps he was in the habit of using it to simply calm Cora down of an evening? (See 'Possibilities', above.) Or maybe she had a drinking problem, and he was making the tonics for that reason? The official version certainly portrays her as an excessive drinker, but again, there is little real evidence for it, so all of these options remain minor possibilities only. He was asked outright at the trial if he had ever given hyoscine to Cora and he said no, though one can almost hear the cogs turning in his mind here, deciding which would be the least incriminating answer. Either, I suspect, could have been the truth: it was an impossibly incriminating question to answer, honestly or not.

Crippen's inability to produce any remnant of the hyoscine he had purchased presumably indicates that, by some means or other, it had all been used, or, for some unknown reason, it had been destroyed. Ironically, he may have disposed of it because he thought that being in possession of it would have brought suspicion on him, never dreaming that he would seem more suspicious by virtue of *not* being in possession of it. If he was innocent of any involvement with the body in the cellar then he would have no reason to suppose hyoscine would be found in it. On balance, in that position, one might think it better to get rid of a known poison than to hold on to it. And it stands to reason that, having destroyed it, he would seem even more suspicious again if he admitted that during the trial.

But if, on the other hand, it had all been used, what (other than murder or a new preparation) might it have been used for? Perhaps the most obvious possibility, albeit never considered to my knowledge, is that Crippen was taking it himself, like all those medical students in New York. 'He was a drug addict, and most of the drugs he bought as a doctor were consumed by himself,' claimed Crippen's sister-in-law Louise Mills.[25] And it's worth noting how many of the characteristic behaviours of drug users match up with Crippen, and in particular with his unnaturally calm reaction to the stresses of interrogation, pursuit and cross-examination: that 'amiable politeness' noted by Dr Weatherly, above, in his descriptions of hyoscine's effect on the violent, the long periods of silence, the lethargy, and a general apathy interspersed with moments of grandiosity. He certainly admitted to being troubled by stress and anxiety: it would only be natural to prescribe something for himself. His own description of hyoscine being used as 'a nerve tonic' may hint that he himself was the patient, pacifying his own nervous state. Why, though, would he not come clean about this at the trial? Perhaps because he felt it was somehow belittling of him, especially before Ethel and the world? More pertinently, perhaps, because he thought it would be of no use as a defence anyway: the prosecution would only say that if he was beset with such nervousness that he needed to purchase hyoscine to remedy it, then maybe he had something very considerable to be nervous about. (Ethel's otherwise baffling comment to Ursula Bloom in the 1950s – 'We seldom used hyoscine, it was new and he had never liked it' – only seems to make sense if Crippen, or both of them, had been taking it themselves.)

There is one very strange sentence in an otherwise accurate account that appeared in newspapers shortly after the arrest: 'Crippen, who is in a state of extreme nervousness, confessed to the prison doctor that he was addicted to the use of spirits.'[26] Note the nervousness again, and again remember his talk of using hyoscine in a nerve tonic. But no other account suggests he was alcoholic; many of Cora's friends recalled him as more or less teetotal. Of course, he might have taken to drink more recently, or it might have been a long-term problem he had been hiding; again, there is a long history of hyoscine being used for the treatment of excessive drinking. Alternatively, if not true, he may have said it as an excuse for being in possession of hyoscine, at a time when he felt it would seem suspicious, in order to deliberately prompt that connection. But if so, what was it really for?

If he *was* still in possession of it at this point, there is one slight indication to follow up, which opens a further channel of supposition. When Crippen was arrested on the *Montrose*, he was found to be in possession of two notes, scribbled in his own hand on the back of business cards. One, presumably for Ethel, read: 'I cannot stand the horror I go through every night any longer, and as I see nothing bright ahead, and money is coming to an end, I have made up my mind to jump overboard tonight. I know I have spoiled your life, but I hope some day you can learn to forgive me.' The other gave no indication of who it was for, but it cryptically read: 'Shall we wait until tonight, about ten or eleven? If not, what time?'

Crippen claimed he had no intention of taking his life; it was all an elaborate rouse to create that impression. The first card was a fake, to give the police a false lead, the second was to a quartermaster who had warned him of his fate and offered to help hide him and spirit him away. Most people who have given an opinion, then and since, reject this story derisively, concluding that Crippen would have killed himself, if he had time to, should his capture seem certain. (A suicide attempt *was* thwarted shortly before his execution.) But in that case, if the suicide note was sincere, what did the second message mean? The smart money, we are told, is on it being evidence of a suicide pact between him and Ethel. The only problem with that is that it doesn't read anything like one. What doomed lover, giving notice of the fulfilment of a suicide pact, would offer a choice of two times an hour apart? What was she going to say? 'Eleven's better for me'? No, it reads much more like the kind of secret plan Crippen claimed it was. It is hard to believe he could have been unaware of the heavy-handed conspiracy unfolding around him, especially with Kendall doing his corny detective act every time they encountered each other. But if he was making some arrangement with Ethel he could have simply spoken to her about it. The only reason for scribbling it on a card was so as to covertly pass it to someone. And we know he wasn't a very inventive liar. I think the quartermaster story was true.

But suicide may still have been Crippen and Ethel's understood plan of last resort. And that might have been the purpose of the hyoscine.[27] One report surely indicates they knew all was not well: 'Both [Crippen and Le Neve] are sleepless and spend much time in their cabin. They show signs of worry when alone.'[28]

Some fanciful news stories appeared after the arrest. All those journalists rushing on to the ship, nothing exciting to be seen, Dew unforthcoming, each one looking for the scoop – it was inevitable that some fast and loose reporting would ensue, even from the sober ones. Crippen pulled a gun and had to be wrestled to the ground! Hardly. But this one is interesting, specifically because it seems to want to pull back on the craziness – yet it still has something very interesting to tell us:

Detective Dennis, one of the Canadian police officers who on Sunday boarded the *Montrose* to assist Inspector Dew in the arrest of Hawley Crippen, denies that the alleged murderer attempted to take his life with a revolver, or that there was any struggle for a weapon in the cabin. Crippen had no revolver on him when arrested, but a search revealed a phial containing some unrecognised liquid and a paper of yellow powder. Detective Dennis adds that Ethel Le Neve threw something through a porthole when the police entered the cabin.[29]

Likewise the *News of the World*:

'I found,' said Mr Dennis to a pressman, 'no revolver and no knife – only £2, a small watch and some trinkets. But,' and here Mr Dennis became very impressive, 'he had a small phial with some sort of unknown liquid and a folded paper containing a white, yellowish powder that looked very suspicious.'[30]

In one of Crippen's letters, the one in which he advises Ethel to take up his latest remedy and market it, he refers to 'what was taken from my pockets at Quebec', further evidence for the liquid and powder.[31]

Might we have just accounted for the missing hyoscine?

A trial run?

But before we rule out murder, or at least very foul play, there were two mysterious occasions when we might argue that we are seeing the drug in action. First there is a story told by Melinda May of the Music Hall Ladies' Guild at the inquest that sometime around Christmas of 1909 Cora had complained of a burning in her throat and of feeling so ill she feared she was dying. This, of course, pre-dates Crippen's known purchase of the drug, which may be why it was not taken up at the trial, but it does sound like poisoning, all the same. More curiously, there is the strangest (and most strangely overlooked) feature of the fateful final supper with the Martinettis: the illness that befell Paul Martinetti. Perhaps the main reason this is so often missed is because we know that Martinetti was not a well man in general; indeed, the reason he was not present when Crippen arrived at his home to invite them, and why Clara thought it might not be possible to come, was because he was visiting the doctor that day, and he always returned from his medical appointments tired and below par. Nonetheless, there is nothing to indicate an ailment as severe as the one that overtook him at the Crippens' house when they did attend, and Crippen's behaviour throughout the episode is peculiar. First, he appeared at their home during the day (around 4.00 pm, 31 January) with the invitation to dine at his house that night. Clara was clearly in two minds on Paul's behalf, and all Crippen needed to do was suggest a different evening. Instead, the famously timid and uncompelling Crippen urges her to reconsider (she says he said, 'Make him come'). Two hours later he was back again, this time to attempt to convince Paul personally.

Clara says he was unenthusiastic, and it took all Crippen's powers of persuasion to change his mind. He seems most curiously keen to get them to the house that night. Oddly, the prosecution had argued it was so that they could confirm Cora was 'in the best of health and spirits' and the couple 'on their usual affectionate terms' immediately prior to the murder. While the second consideration might make a rather crude sense, the first is curious: surely it would be far less suspicious, if poisoning were to follow, for Cora to have seemed ill than well. And that has been the position of later writers, who have argued for the supper being a set-up designed to have the Martinettis witness the first effects of the hyoscine on her, thus strengthening his then claiming that she had died in the night. Melinda May suggested that the inordinately long time Crippen took getting the carriage to take the Martinettis home was intended to have him away from the house when she sickened and died. As we know, if that was the plan, not one part of it worked out. But that is to jump ahead. Back at the Martinettis', Paul eventually acquiesces to Crippen's entreaties and suggests they all go back to Hilldrop Crescent together. At this point Crippen suddenly demurs, and says he'd better go ahead on his own since he hadn't as yet even let Cora know they might be coming! It feels very much indeed like he is (pretty cackhandedly) setting up *some* kind of a scenario (it's like an episode of *Columbo*) – but the trouble is, it's no scenario that I can make sense of. It feels like a carefully worked out plan, but its intricacies lead in no clear direction; it is disordered, obtuse.

Crippen serves drinks throughout the evening, giving him plenty of opportunity to put a small amount of the drug in Cora's so their friends can see her ailing. Instead, this is not what happens – it is Paul Martinetti who becomes ill, with symptoms that, again, strongly suggest poisoning. Suddenly he needs to visit the toilet, and returns white-faced and shivering. Crippen is sent to fetch a carriage and, as noted, took a suspiciously long time finding one, even to the extent of returning empty-handed and having to set out again. A cab eventually secured, Paul is bundled into the back, Clara and Cora kiss goodnight and the two couples part at 1.30 am. It is essential to the prosecution's case and to the standard version of the story that Cora's murder followed more or less immediately, yet the next day Crippen is back at the Martinettis – hotfoot, if the standard account be believed, from cutting off his wife's head, legs, arms and genitals and removing the bones from around her guts – to find out how

Paul is feeling.[32] (He was still in bed; he gradually improved over the course of the next few days.) A week or so later, he called to check *again*. Is this solicitousness, or more by way of a scientific enquiry? Weirdly, the explanation for Martinetti's being taken ill offered at the time – that he caught a chill from the open lavatory window – is still repeated as if it meant anything in books published in the twenty-first century. I shouldn't have to stress, but it seems I do, that people do *not* get instantly and seriously ill by catching a chill from an open lavatory window.

There are three possibilities regarding Martinetti's illness. First, it is a complete coincidence. We know he was not in the best of health anyway; it might have been food poisoning or any one of a hundred other complaints. The second, which seems to make no sense, is that it was due to poison that was intended at all times for Paul Martinetti. Hold that thought: we will return to it. The third is that he was somehow accidentally exposed to poison that was meant for Cora. If so, Crippen got the dosage wrong as well as the recipient, because he survived and soon rallied, but this line of thought does open up further possibilities. There is a very intriguing passage in Filson Young's introduction to the trial, in which he writes:

> there is a very important fact which did not and could not come out at the trial, but goes far to explain what is otherwise inexplicable. It is known that Mrs Crippen had more than once in the month of January told one of her friends that if Crippen did not give up his association with Miss Le Neve she intended to leave him, and to take her money with her.

I have never come across this piece of information – vitally important if true – nor anything that even hinted of it, anywhere else. I have no idea who the friend was: the only testimony I am aware of in which Cora is said to have commented on Ethel was the ambiguous statement of Maud Burroughs, the wife of the Ladies' Guild doctor, who had recalled a conversation in which Cora had told her: 'I don't like the girl typist Peter has in his office.' It most certainly did not come out at the trial, because if it had it would have caused a sensation: here would be the undoubted motive for which the prosecution had been scrabbling, and an overwhelming challenge to Crippen's assertion under oath that so far as he knew Cora was not even aware of his relations with Ethel. Alternatively, the defence would have pounced on it as corroboration for Crippen's version of events, since it independently shows Cora threatening to leave and take their money with her – something that we know she did attempt to do shortly before her disappearance. Now – what if she was planning this grand gesture, and Crippen, acting to prevent it, decided to kill her? But instead of doing so, as the police believed, she found him out. Say the poison intended for her was served, accidentally, to Paul Martinetti, and she put two and two together. *Then* she might have fled, just as Crippen described, with all that strange urgency and disregard for her possessions that made that story so hard to credit. The only thing he would have left out of his version would have been the true reason. (She might have assumed, probably correctly, that if she took the story to the police it would simply be a domestic dispute and her word against his. He would say he didn't mean it, and wriggle free.) Does this allow both sides to have their cake and eat it: Cora still alive and on the run, just like the defence said; Crippen still basically a murdering fiend, just like the prosecution said (only an unsuccessful one)? But why does Young say not only that this *did* not come out at the trial but also that it *could* not? Why couldn't it?

Or, might the dinner have been some sort of bizarre test run for the murder, to see exactly the effects of the drug in a non-fatal dose, and whether they might be compatible with a diagnosis of natural death? In that case, might Martinetti have been the intended victim the whole time? Crippen's constant checking on Martinetti's recovery almost gives the impression that he is using him as a guinea pig for the drug, perhaps because he is someone who is known to have health problems, and also someone that no jury in the world could come up with a reason for Crippen to poison. The main problem with that is that if he had killed Cora he had done so already, so unless he was genuinely concerned for a man he had accidentally poisoned, the two threads do not tie. Hard to get around Crippen's morbid fascination with it all, though. Even the reason he gives for Cora's last and decisive row with him – that he hadn't accompanied Martinetti to the toilet – shows it to be uppermost in his mind. So maybe Cora had run away, as Crippen alleged, but at this stage he was assuming she would, sooner or later, return? Then he would have good reason to continue monitoring Martinetti's progress.

The 'test run' theory, though pretty far out, is interesting because a test run might work as an explanation for the evidence in the cellar too. Was *this* also a dummy run for Cora's death? And yet, again, we should rein ourselves in. If it were a test run for the murder, that would certainly account for the hyoscine, but there is something absurd about a killer so keen to ensure no slip-ups in one murder that he blithely commits another to check his methodology, thus doubling the risk of apprehension. (And, indeed, ending up executed when that one was discovered and the 'real' murder was not!) The only glimmer of a possibility here is if the victim was someone that would never be looked for. The villain in the Sherlock Holmes adventure *The Norwood Builder* lures and kills a vagrant so as to fake his own death. Then there is an odd comment made by Mrs Gillatt, the neighbour whose sound testimony is generally relied upon by subsequent historians:[33] 'It was after the statement that Mrs Crippen had gone to America that a woman with a baby in her arms was seen leaving the house. Latterly there was a lady in black there, and last week there were also two lads staying with Dr Crippen.'[34] Another report stated that 'Crippen had occasionally been seen in the company of a foreign-looking youth.'[35] The mother and baby were probably Ethel's sister Nina and her child, but who are the lads? Ethel's brother Sidney came to the house on the day of her disappearance, but he would not have been described as 'foreign-looking', neither would he have been recalled as in Crippen's company, since Crippen was not there. And in any event, Mrs Gillatt speaks of 'lads' in the plural. Could it be one of these in the cellar?

Given the evidences of medical expertise and the nature of the dissection, I remain drawn towards the view that the flesh was a remnant from a dissection lab. It is permissible to speculate that, through some contact he had made in his many years of moving in quasi-medical circles, Crippen might have had access to such a thing. And if it originally came, as these things often did, from a prison or an asylum, it may well have been someone who had been given hyoscine. The thing that is very satisfying about the idea of the body coming from a dissection room is that it relieves not just Crippen but anyone of the responsibility for so expertly dismembering and filleting the remains before interring them, and us of explaining how such detailed, messy work could have been conducted in the house without any evidence being left behind. But what would he be using it for? And why would he not admit to having done that if he was facing a much more serious charge?

A surgeon after all?

Before we abandon all this 'test run' business, one last imaginative flight. Maybe it was a test run not for the murder, but for something else? Round up all those possibilities we've already discussed – the dissection room cadaver, the foreign-looking boys (this is all madly speculative, so you can make it as sinister as you like). And we might be able to factor the hyoscine back in, too. Might it have been for use as a sedative or anaesthetic during some medical procedure? We have seen it being used for this reason before in the medical literature, after all, including during childbirth. Let's go back to the odd claims made by the brother of Crippen's first wife. The very strong suggestion here (see Chapter 2) was that he was forcing her to have operations, possibly illegal, to make it impossible for her to have children. Was he, perhaps, lining up to do the same for Ethel? If so, now in England, with no intimate friends in genuine medical circles, might he have considered performing the surgery himself? Did he maybe practise with a cadaver, to check his eye was keen, his hand steady?

What about the hyoscine? Crippen would not have observed the effect of hyoscine used in homeopathic doses: he must have known that the minutely small quantities used in such remedies had no real effect because the key ingredients are reduced to a point of literal non-existence. If he was thinking of using hyoscine as a sedative-cum-anaesthetic for Ethel, he would have needed to see the effects of a medically (as opposed to homeopathically) small dose. Naturally unwilling to test it on Ethel herself, why not slip a little into Paul Martinetti's whisky? And when that dosage proved near-disastrously high, and with Cora now out of the way – why not acquire a permanently accessible guinea pig, one who would never be missed if things went wrong? What was it that Inspector Dew had said? *Valentine Lecocq had no friends in London...*

Crippen and Le Neve had gone all the way to Boulogne to acquire the services of 17-year-old Lecocq, towards the end of May 1910. I cannot think of any good reason why Crippen would suddenly want a live-in maid, something he had managed without the whole time in the past, right when he was readying to leave the house and start a new life with Ethel elsewhere. Stranger still to go all the way to France to acquire one. If he knew there was a rotting corpse in the cellar it begins to defy all comprehension. Where did Valentine sleep? Tom Cullen says it was on the very top floor,[36] although he gives no source, and it wasn't mentioned during the trial. In the famous police photograph of the basement we can see the door of what must have at one time been a servant's room – there is a bell above the door – and it is right next to the coal cellar! If Valentine *was* staying in the basement it becomes incredible to imagine Crippen would be unconcerned about her proximity to the body. And even if she did sleep upstairs, she would certainly have spent most of her working hours down there, in the kitchen and back garden. It cautiously argues for his not knowing the body was there at all. Unless Valentine was being sized up for the same fate. *Then* it wouldn't matter. If all he wanted was a bit of short-term help to keep the house clean he could have found a million eager girls with good references in London. One reason for traipsing all the way to France to secure one might be to find someone who would slip beneath the radar, just like those foreign-seeming boys. If any enquiry did find its way back to him, all he would have to say is that she ran away with a young man. Such things probably happened all the time. Then there is always the possibility that a sacrificial lamb of this sort might be intended for use in a dummy run for the operation itself. Might *that* be the intended use for the hyoscine?

Okay, okay. This is getting very Roald Dahl, I admit. I am not convinced, and I doubt I'm convincing you. I offer the theory not because I am keen on it, but because it does not conflict with the facts and has the satisfying result of tying together some of the oddest and most disparate ones: the strange repetition of the surgeries performed on the wives, the suggestion of coercion made by his former brother-in-law, the possibility that the torso was the result of some practice surgery, the strange malady that befell Paul Martinetti, and the odd arrival of Valentine into the story, willingly brought to the house by Crippen, right at the moment when he should want an inquisitive girl in his basement less than just about anything else in the world. Is it at all possible, anywhere this side of fiction, that Inspector Dew's unexpected discovery of the remains saved Valentine from ending up among them?

Beginnings of a case for Crippen's innocence

The happiest alternative to the gruesome scenario outlined above is that Crippen had no compunction about hiring a maid at what should have been the most closely guarded and stressful time of his life, and no concerns about allowing her to spend her time in the basement, simply because he had no knowledge of anything untoward down there and nothing to be stressful about. And that he hired Valentine for the reasons usually proposed: because he wanted Ethel to be spared too much housework, and she wanted to learn French. The latter, of course, might be of some use in their future life in Canada. Maybe I am being unduly suspicious: perhaps the best way to secure a French maid really was to go over to France and get one. This is therefore the right time to put aside Crippen the fiend and instead consider Crippen the innocent man. How might a case be made for him?

Innocence was, after all, his only defence from the day of his arrest to the day of his death. In a sense, the DNA discoveries have only made things harder for him. We now need to clear him of two potential crimes instead of one. The hyoscine still links him to the remains as surely as when we thought they were Cora's, and his story about Cora's disappearance still doesn't hold up. And yet, just consider his behaviour; how little it conforms with the expected actions of even a moderately careful guilty man. Would a man who had murdered his wife parade his mistress in her jewels and furs? Consider his response to being arrested: *he wanted to know what the charge was*. If you were a murderer on the run, keen to escape the consequences of your crime, there are any number of bluffs you can come up with at the fatal moment of apprehension. But 'What is the charge?' is an odd one. The only interpretation I am able to place upon it is that he wanted to know what the charge was. Then, scanning the warrant, he says: 'Murder and mutilation, oh God...' There is an incredible *subtlety* to this, if it is all performance. It has the force of truth. And Crippen's dogged adherence to the story that he knew nothing whatever of the remains in his house, even after it's been fixed up with his wife's hair curlers, also has the force of truth. It is the most unwise defence a guilty man could possibly come up with. But I see neither a mad man nor a suicidal one. I see a flailing, profoundly confused one, trying to make sense of an impossible nightmare, in which definite facts seem to contradict reality itself.

A laboratory specimen?

Should we be picturing Crippen doing a bit of amateur anatomy practice on a corpse already divested of its extremities? Often in the vanguard of progressive theories, the *New York Times* is also ahead of us with this one, opining way back in 1910 that 'it might merely be a body which Crippen, in the desire to perfect himself in his studies, had procured for the purpose of dissection'.[37]

Recall our earlier scurry round the literature of hyoscine and its use on the violent, the insane, the drunken – if we *are* positing the remains were of a medical specimen rather than a murder victim, it becomes considerably more likely that hyoscine might be legitimately found in them. Specimens must have been taken from dissection rooms from time to time: they were there to be used, and there is much anecdotal evidence of doctors and students working on them at home. And thefts from morgues and labs *did* happen.[38] An interesting passage in Cullen's book helps to put this in very valuable perspective: he tells us that workmen digging an excavation in 1962 unearthed the skull of a woman, thought to be roughly Cora's age, about 300 yards from Hilldrop Crescent. 'However, after examining the skull, pathologist Dr Francis Camps pronounced that it was a specimen of the type that is used in teaching anatomy.'[39] There is a bizarre finality to that explanation; clearly it was felt to require no further investigation. That in itself tells its own story about how strange or unusual such an eventuality was felt (not) to be. So if a head can escape from a dissection room and turn up in Camden Town without explanation, nor seemingly the need of one, can not a torso do likewise?[40]

Ah, but then – if it was just a lab specimen, and Crippen knew anything about it, it seems very unlikely he would continue to deny all knowledge if circumstantial evidence abounded to link him to it and given that he was standing accused of a far worse crime than illegal burial of a dissection room corpse. We can go round and round in circles coming up with ways around that, but the prosecution couldn't shake him down and neither, quite, can my imagination. No matter what theory we think of, no matter how ingenious, no matter how slanted it is toward his innocence, I still see him standing placidly in the dock *denying all knowledge*, and expressing only helpless bafflement.

Quicklime and bodily decomposition

But *could* someone else have done it? Crippen was asked this in the trial, and the correct answer is of course the one he gave: yes. 'It doesn't seem probable,' he said, 'but it is a possibility.' No fairer summing-up could anyone have made than that most unjustly ridiculed answer. It's weird and unlikely – but the fact that such remains were *ever* there is weird and unlikely. Once you arrive in France, there is no point in being surprised to find people driving on the other side of the road. If there was no reason to have ever suspected Crippen's responsibility then thoughts would naturally turn to who might have done it instead, and how, and when. Such questions are far from illegitimate. They are as essential to demonstrating Crippen's guilt as they are to demonstrating his innocence.

How about one of the students who lodged there? Might they have stolen a torso from the dissection lab as some grim prank, panicked, and hidden the evidence? And what about the previous occupants? Any budding anatomists among them? Le Neve suggested that previous tenants might provide a key to some of the house's mystery in conversation with novelist Ursula Bloom in the 1950s, confirming, as had others, that an unpleasant smell in the basement had been noticeable long before Cora's disappearance. It seems that the tenant before the Crippens was a mechanic with a wife and four children, plus a lodger.[41] Doubtless we should go cautiously with the irresistible scenarios this evokes, but still, one wonders where the criminal courts of England would be without husbands, wives and lodgers. Or how about Crippen's landlord, Frederick Lown?[42] He would have had easy access to the house. Crippen had told him on 16 March that he would be leaving the house on 24 June. Though he later changed his mind and requested the tenancy be extended until September, Lown's men were on the scene during the week of 24 June to fit a new stack pipe, giving free access to the house's every recess.[43]

Of course there is no reason to suspect any of these people, but given that the remains were not Cora's, there's little reason to suspect Crippen either: literally the only thing left to incriminate him is his access to the space. So these questions, far from idle speculation, become absolutely imperative. It is *vital* to discover who else may have had meaningful access within a meaningful time frame, since there is no reason we know of why Crippen should have murdered any unknown male and put a senselessly small portion of him in a house he was about to vacate.

The idea of someone else secreting the remains there has one additional point of value: it explains both the absence of the majority of the body and of any physical evidence of the elaborate job of dismemberment that would have had to have been conducted on the premises. In this scenario we simply have someone with access to the house, and keen to have the remains buried far from where they presumably originated – the *opposite* of a Crippen, in that case; a rational criminal, in other words – gaining entry to the property with, let us say, a suitcase full of flesh, hiding it there and leaving again. Ultimately, though a fantasy cut from whole cloth with no evidence to support it, this makes no less sense than Crippen doing it, *provided* we are able to cover the logistics.

The main potential argument against the remains *predating* Crippen's tenancy – I say potential because I don't think anybody has felt the need to seriously make such case (so childishly satisfied are we by those pyjamas!) – concerns the degree of decomposition. But this is far more complex than the prosecution or most later writers would have you believe, and much previous writing is coloured by two points of contention: one concerning the properties of quicklime, and one, in consequence of the first, concerning whether or not it was used in the first place. All the reports from the police and at the trial seem unanimous that Crippen used quicklime on the remains. But for some reason it has become one of the major bullet points of the crime that he did not. Cullen here speaks for many:

> Take such a simple matter as the destruction of the remains, which Crippen was so foolish as to leave in a shallow grave beneath the cellar floor. For this purpose Crippen employed what he thought was quicklime, sprinkling it liberally over the pieces of flesh he buried. Now Crippen had paid his way through the University of Michigan's School of Homeopathy by working as an assistant in the school's chemical laboratory. Later, as general manager of Munyon's Homeopathic Remedies, he had acted not only as the firm's advisory physician, but had been in charge of its chemical laboratory as well. However, his knowledge of chemistry apparently did not enable him to distinguish slaked lime, which preserves human flesh, from quicklime, which destroys it. By mistaking the former for the latter, Crippen made certain that most of Belle Elmore's organs, notably the heart, were in an excellent state of preservation, when eventually they were dug up.[44]

The issue is preservation. The myth of the 'wrong kind of lime' seems to have grown because the organs were reasonably well preserved, and quicklime is commonly understood to be flesh-destroying: ergo, he must have used ordinary lime. At the trial, Augustus Pepper argued that Crippen had used quicklime but that in damp environments quicklime was apt to turn into slaked lime. Chemist Alfred Lucas experimented with dead pigeons in 1921,[45] and concluded that 'the act of slaking lime in contact with a dead body, whether slaking is brought about gradually or done all at once, does not destroy the body'.[46] Crippen (or whoever) did not confuse two types of lime: he was well aware of the understood properties of quicklime and used it correctly – the problem was that the common understanding was ambiguous. Mortuary archaeologist Kathryn Meyers Emery expounds:

> Quicklime does have uses for burials. In the Red Cross Emergency Relief Items Catalogue, quicklime and lime are listed as a tool for aiding in proper disposal of human remains that cannot be afforded a deep burial. However, the goal of the product is not to destroy the body but rather to prevent putrefaction that create odor, and attracts flies and animals. Quicklime was often used over plague or cholera burials to prevent the spread of disease, thought during this period to be transferred through noxious bad air known as miasma… Again, in practical usage quicklime is being used not to destroy but to prevent disease from spreading.
>
> Lime is one of the major finds in many forensics cases dealing with clandestine burials due to this popular notion of its ability to remove the identity of the deceased and destroy the remains. A new study… used pig corpses to test different types of lime to see how it changed the remains. The pigs were put into graves, covered with different types and amounts of lime, buried, and were left for six months. Two pigs were buried with lime as the control group. The pigs buried without lime were mostly skeletonized and highly decayed, the two pigs buried with hydrated lime were very well preserved and had little decay, and the two pigs buried with quicklime were fairly preserved with some decay within the body. In general, they discovered that the lime was highly effective in preventing decay and protecting the body, rather than destroying it.[47]

So it seems that instead of Crippen the bumbler we have Crippen acting in perfect accordance with the general consensus of the times, albeit unaware that the general consensus of the time was wrong. The question now, therefore, becomes how good a preservative *is* quicklime? If we discount the dubious secondary physical evidence supposedly found in the pit (and treat cautiously the hyoscine evidence), are we now in a position to argue that the remains could well have been placed in the cellar prior to the commencement of the Crippens' tenancy in 1905?

Dr Marshall happily agreed in the trial that 'it is impossible to give any certain opinion as to the length of time that a body has been buried in the earth', adding that 'different bodies undergo putrefactive changes with very different degrees of rapidity, even when they have been buried under similar conditions.' If buried in lime and clay, as these had been, he affirmed that remains might enjoy 'an excellent state of preservation for some years'. To the question, 'Do you agree that it is impossible to give any certain opinion as to the length of time that a body has been buried in the earth?' he replied: 'Yes, it depends upon circumstances.' Dr Pepper willingly conceded the same.

But it should be obvious that this uncertainty is still bounded by definite limits. Put trivially, the remains could not have been there for less than a minute, or more than a million years. It is deciding what the *reasonable* limits are that is our task, and for the reasons given by Dr Marshall, it is not easy. It was not a task that was felt necessary at the trial because it was never seriously doubted that the remains were those of Cora Crippen. The calculation of between two and eight months thus evolved as a natural corollary of that prior necessity (another example of confirmation bias). With it now established for definite that the remains are those of an unidentified male, the question again becomes imperative. Pepper's testimony:

> I formed the opinion that those remains had been buried from four to eight months. In forming that opinion I took into consideration the place where they were buried, the surrounding materials, the lime and the earth, and the depth at which they were buried. In my opinion they were buried very shortly after death.

> *In your opinion is it possible that those remains could have been buried there before 21st September, 1905?*

> Oh, no, absolutely impossible.

But various studies have found surprising anomalies in understood decomposition rates.[48] The most important factor in such cases is the formation of adipocere. Sometimes called 'corpse wax', adipocere is a greyish substance that can spontaneously form in bodies when the soft tissue decomposes. The effect it can have on decomposition rates can be striking:

> The unrestrained decomposition of a corpse involves the consecutive processes of autolysis, putrefaction and decay. Ideally, decomposition is completed within the regular resting time (15–25 years) and leads to the entire skeletalisation of the corpse. Adipocere, a greyish fatty substance formed during decomposition, is regarded as a spontaneous inhibition of post-mortem changes; it makes the corpse almost entirely resistant to decomposition and makes it impossible to use the same graves again. This creates problems for local governments with regard to the generally growing demand for burial ground. Apart from corpse-specific characteristics (e.g. sex, age, physique, cause of death), method of burial (e.g. material of the coffin, depth of grave, individual or mass grave, clothing) and time of burial, the conditions of the resting place (geology, topography, soil properties and frequency of use, air, water, and heat budget), in particular, have a special impact on adipocere formation.[49]

The Crippen cellar remains were buried shallowly, according to the prosecution 'closely packed in clay and lime, five inches of such stuff above them, and a depth of three inches'. Augustus Pepper described the soil as 'composed partly of loam and partly of clay, with some lime mixed in it'. When asked if lime or clay would retard putrefaction, he replied: 'There are two kinds of decomposition taking place in dead bodies – one where it is freely exposed to the air and warmth, and the other where it is damp and largely excluded from the air, and that is what happened in this case.'

It was made clear at the trial that adipocere was present in the cellar remains, attributed by Pepper to their being packed in wet clay:

> The presence of damp clay would favour the change which happened in this case. It would not be putrefaction in the ordinary sense. It is a peculiar change which takes place; the tissues become converted into a type of soap, the technical name of which is adipocere. Buried in clay,

adipocere would be created more quickly and ordinary putrefaction would be retarded... there was very decided formation of adipocere.

Repeated studies have underlined both the astonishing preservative properties of adipocere and the range of conditions in which it is formed:

> The formation of adipocere slows further decomposition and preserves corpses for decades or even centuries. This resistance to degradation is a serious problem, especially with regard to the reuse of graves after regular resting times. We present results from an exhumation series in modern graveyards where coffins from water-saturated earth graves contained adipocere embedded in black humic material after resting times of about 30 years. Based on the assumption that this humic material resulted from in situ degradation of adipocere, its presence contradicts the commonly held opinion that adipocere decomposition only occurs under aerobic conditions.[50]

At the trial, Dr Marshall formulated the prosecution's estimate of how long the remains had been buried, based on a consideration of these conditions and factors:

> In certain cases it is very difficult to tell how long bodies have been in the ground. I formed an opinion of my own as to how long those remains had been in the ground, and I stated that opinion at the first inquest before any other witness. I formed the opinion that they had been in the ground several months... I formed the opinion on two grounds, these two grounds being that on first observing those remains buried, where we found them, I was somewhat surprised with an appearance of freshness – a redness and freshness – not the appearance of corruption that might be imagined, but when I came to examine them in detail at the mortuary I found the presence of this adipocere – certain parts where there had been masses of fat, a considerable amount of adipocere, and at other parts much less. Forming an estimate to the best of my power of the time that would be required for the formation of that adipocere, I reckoned it as a matter of several months – four, five, or six, I would say. With all the knowledge I have got, the result of all my examinations, I could not say precisely how long those remains had been in the ground. All I say is that they might have been in the ground several months, up to six or possibly up to seven months.

Dr Eline M.J. Schotsmans has conducted a number of research projects to determine the effects of lime and quicklime on the rate and nature of bodily decomposition.[51] She shared some of her conclusions with me, and introduced several new disquieting suggestions:

> People often think that quicklime accelerates decomposition (I assume that that was the reason why it was applied to the remains in Crippen's cellar), but quicklime slows the decay down and the end result is skeletonisation. In my experiments with pigs, the limed pigs were in an advanced stage of decay after 17 months of burial, and completely skeletonised after 42 months. Normally, quicklime causes an initial acceleration because of the exothermic reaction with moisture, which is good for bacteria. In my quicklime burials the organs were not preserved anymore. Once that initial raise of temperature reaction is over, quicklime becomes slaked lime and in the long term decomposition is slowed down.
>
> Normally decomposition is slowed down in a clay soil because of the lack of oxygen. But I doubt it was a pure clay soil in Crippen's basement; it was probably a city soil. The rate of decomposition depends how much oxygen and access to insects there was under the house. Even if we assume that the location of the torso slowed the decay a little bit down, the fact that the remains were found in a good state of preservation, and that even the internal organs were well preserved, makes me agree that the remains were not buried for a very long time. It is very hard to put it on a timescale, but organs do not preserve that long. I would also say that they were buried for a maximum of one year or so; maybe a maximum of a year and a half. Five years is too long to keep organs well preserved.[52]

The presence of adipocere was uncontested and vital to the prosecution's case. But according to Schotsmans, the whole question is more problematic than it seems. She told me: 'Adipocere is certainly another factor that can preserve the body and make it look fresh. In a case study that I did in Belgium the individual was very well preserved and in fact buried for 9 months. The problem with adipocere is that it doesn't go well together with lime.' An experiment on the effects of various burial conditions on the preservation of pig carcasses found:

The lime burial environment considerably inhibited decomposition and the formation of adipocere... The most likely reason for the retardation was the ability of lime to prohibit the survival and proliferation of bacteria due to its extremely alkaline nature. A lack of bacteria in the surrounding environment would significantly affect the rate of decomposition and/or preservation of soft tissue as demonstrated in this study. Retardation of the decomposition process combined with the inhospitable bacterial environment would thus have reduced the likelihood of adipocere formation.[53]

Schotsmans continues:

The presence of adipocere can indeed make the burial look younger than it is. But what strikes me is the fact that the remains were only flesh and skin with organs and no bones or extremities. I am not sure how well adipocere preserves 'a pile of flesh'. Also, the quicklime or hydrated lime effect becomes different if it is applied to 'a pile of flesh' (than if applied to a complete body). I can imagine that it dries the tissue out, as I saw on experiments with lime on cubes of tissue.

Clearly, then, this is a subject on which there is a wide spread of opinion; just as clearly, it is not a debate in which I am qualified to give any casting vote. Certainly Dr Schotsmans' observations, based on extensive research into just these questions, are compelling, and throw the whole matter wide open. Based on my entirely lay reading of numerous studies (which even taken together can offer only a partial glimpse of the full range of options, and of the various subtleties and fine distinctions that can all too often reverse a certainty on a sixpence) I would cautiously conclude that, while it *may* yet be possible the remains pre-dated Crippen's tenancy, the *likelihood* still seems to be that they did not. This was Dr Schotsmans' conclusion, and it would mean that they were either placed in the cellar by Crippen himself, or by someone else entirely without Crippen's knowledge. But for the reasons already given, I feel less compelled than most to rush from that conclusion to the certainty that Crippen was the guilty party and that to suggest otherwise is to clutch wildly at straws. Ultimately neither side has a case convincing enough to discredit the other here, and the only certain take-home point, I would suggest, is that this is a million miles from the open-and-shut matter the prosecution, and prosecution-minded historians, would have you believe.

Disposing of the remains

Which brings us to Crippen's 'big blunders'. Raymond Chandler famously observed that Crippen 'was a man who apparently had the means and opportunity and even the temperament for the perfect crime and he made all sorts of mistakes'.[54] Almost all original chroniclers agreed. It is indeed a puzzle that needs to be solved, and the usual self-contradicting portrait of Crippen as the alternating master-criminal and bumbler will not do.

The first of these, mistaking lime for quicklime, we have now shown to be neither a mistake nor a true description of what he[55] actually did. On the contrary, we have opened the possibility, at least, that the evidence of preservation, directly related to the use of quicklime, does not preclude the remains having remained in situ since before the Crippens' tenancy.

Of the other mistakes, the primary one was again identified by Chandler: 'I cannot see why a man who would go to the enormous labour of de-boning and de-sexing and de-heading an entire corpse would not take the rather slight extra labour of disposing of the flesh in the same way.' The onus is on his prosecutors to answer that one. They didn't at the trial, and the few attempts I have seen by later historians have been desperate. It makes no sense, and it rightly stands in the way of our accepting his guilt. Some books have suggested he may have dumped the rest piecemeal in the nearby Regents Canal. But this idea was as old as the case, and the police of the time *had* considered it. The following is from 20 July 1910:

> Scotland Yard found what is believed to be a clue to the disposition of the bones which, with the flesh unearthed in the cellar in Hilldrop Crescent, once formed the body of Belle Elmore, the American actress wife of Dr Crippen.
>
> As the result of a tireless search among the friends and known acquaintances of Ethel Claire Leneve, the typist who disappeared recently with Dr Crippen, the detectives found a woman who said that Miss Leneve had been her friend and had talked to her in confidence.
>
> The typist, the woman said, had spoken to her of mysterious visits paid by Dr Crippen to the neighbourhood of Regents Park.
>
> The theory woven from this information by the police is that the bones of the dead woman may have been carried in small parcels to Regents Park and thrown into the Regents Canal.
>
> The authorities ordered that the canal be dragged.[56]

In his 'iron bar' interview (Chapter 1) Dew confirms the police had attended to this theory, and we know that locating the rest of the body was at all times the police's top priority in terms of evidence gathering. Thus we may assume it was investigated fully and concluded to be a dead end.

Some have said that having put all the identifiable remains elsewhere he may have felt safe to deposit the remainder closer to home. *But it is not his home!* It is not his cellar. It is a rented property he knew he would shortly be vacating. And as Chandler says, why not take the slight extra labour anyway? Was he *so* sure that the other parts had been disposed of beyond all chance of retrieval? If so, how? If not, they might be discovered, and the last thing he would want is so direct a link between he and them as the missing parts in his cellar. This is risk enough had he owned the house.

And why the cellar? Temporarily wrapped in sacking, the relatively small portions could easily have been secretly buried in the garden, where he would have known they had a much stronger chance of rotting away to nothing quickly than they would inside the house. And the remains were not 'the unidentifiable parts' anyway, as the trial soon showed: if there *had* been any truth to the scar evidence, Crippen would have known that the torso was fully as incriminating, perhaps more so, as the bones or legs. No, there seems no way of reconciling the fact of the partial burial with any rational, unforced decision.

Was there, then, some reason why he was forced to put the remains there? None that I can think of, and the only suggestion I have seen along these lines (not counting the classic 'being scared by a milkman') – maybe he was almost caught on one mission to dump remains in a river and thought it too risky to continue – is thin indeed. This would mean it was merely coincidence that the parts in the cellar were the semi-unidentifiable ones because they just happened to be what he had left to get rid of when he had nearly been apprehended: it might just as easily have been the head. No, this will not do, either. The most likely explanation, in my opinion, is that there was no secondary site of burial or destruction, because there was nothing else to get rid of in the first place. If the torso had come from a dissection room, all that messy work – so difficult to not leave traces of in the house, so difficult to dispose of – may have already been done. And because that would to my mind rule out Crippen – because otherwise he would have admitted to it when confronted with a murder charge – I think it more likely that it was done by somebody else.

Most important of all, *any* theory of this being a murder committed in the house runs up against the huge problem, totally fudged in the trial, of just what the killer *did*, and how, why and where. If it were Crippen, could he, with his at most extremely limited surgical expertise, dissect a corpse so expertly? As Dr Pepper confirmed in the trial, there was no sign in the remains of any slips of the knife, ragged cutting or hacking. And quick, too – the earliest he could have started work was in the early hours of Tuesday, 1 February. He went to work as normal on Tuesday, and by Wednesday he was inviting Ethel back to Hilldrop Crescent. Dr Marshall stated in evidence that 'whoever did it must have taken his time about it, for it was a most deliberate and long process'. Crippen, a surgical dilettante at the very best, seems to have managed it, and removed all traces, over the course of two nights, while holding down a full-time job in the daytime. And where in the house did he do it? Some have said the bath, which deals with the issue of blood, but it doesn't take much imagination to see how inconducive a bathtub would be for doing so expert a job. Anywhere else in the house raises the question of why there was no trace of the enormous quantities of physical evidence it would have left behind. And all this *before* we add the absurdity of Crippen using an easily identifiable piece of clothing to transport the flesh he had decided to leave in the cellar of a house he knew he would soon be vacating, and then leaving it in the pit with the remains, *and*, despite not bringing the head anywhere near the pit, tossing in a few hair curlers for good measure. If it was the result of a murder, I suspect it was some other murderer's work, transported to the site specifically because it had no meaningful connection with the location either of the crime or of the remainder.

Suspicious behaviour

Crippen's other 'mistakes' are more nebulous, and usually amount to 'behaving inappropriately': lying to his friends, pawning the jewellery, installing Ethel in the house incautiously and allowing Cora's friends to see her in her clothes and jewellery, running away when it looked like he would be the centre of an ongoing missing persons case. This all seems like incriminating behaviour only if you start from the premise that he is guilty. Then yes, it looks like suspicious behaviour of a sort, albeit the suspicious behaviour of a quite exceptional fool. But if you instead suppose that he is innocent, that he is not guilty of a murder that so far as he knew hadn't even taken place, then his behaviour *is not in any way difficult to understand either*. It would be *perfectly normal behaviour*, the way we might expect any oblivious person to behave. So which is it? Innocent and rational, or guilty and stupid beyond belief? Those, I believe, are the only options.

The pawning of the jewellery and the giving of some of it to Ethel makes perfect sense if it is understood that these items were not exactly Cora's, but rather the couple's shared assets. Crippen had bought them as an investment, obviously allowing Cora to wear them for as long as they were in his possession, but always on the understanding that they were his to cash in should the need arise. Tom Cullen notes: 'The couple put nothing aside in the way of savings, but began at this time to invest their surplus cash in diamonds, about which Crippen now became an expert. He could talk knowledgeably about the intricacies of cleavage and refractivity in diamonds, knew the difference between table-cut, rose-cut and brilliant-cut stones, could appreciate the subtle beauties of the pinks and sapphire blues.'[57] At his trial Crippen was asked what he would have done if Cora had got in touch to say she wanted him to send the trinkets on to her. 'I should have kept them,' he replied. 'I paid for them.' When asked why he had pawned his wife's jewellery, he was emphatic: 'I refuse to accept the idea that it was my wife's.' So it is perfectly understandable that he might have pawned them and given some to Ethel if he were innocent. But it is not something we would expect him to risk doing if he were guilty.

As for why he and Ethel fled when they did, Crippen again made perfect sense. It was entirely reasonable for Crippen to fear a criminal investigation without it being necessary to assume that he was a criminal. The truth is that most people fear the police, *especially* the innocent, who have only an outsider's view of how criminal investigations work, and are accustomed to nets of coincidence closing around the innocent in popular fiction. Add to this the scandal and media condemnation to which Ethel in particular would be subjected and it is hard to think what else they even might have done.

I explained this to her; she told me, of course, that she had made a statement, the same as I had; I explained to her that that statement involved her in describing that she lived with me, and that my statement gave the same, and that there would be a scandal which would turn her folks against her, and that Mr. Dew had said that if I did not produce Mrs. Crippen there would be trouble for me, and the only way I saw for us would be to escape this by going away to another place where we could be alone and start a new life together.

Both of you disguised?

Both of us disguised.

Before leaving Hilldrop Crescent after his first visit, Dew suggested that it would be in Crippen's interests to place an advertisement requesting that Cora get in touch, and they promptly wrote one together. But Crippen, already planning to move away with Ethel, wanted nothing less than for Cora to put in a reappearance. The arrival of police on the scene changed everything. The case against Crippen is predicated on the belief that if he was innocent he would be in no way inconvenienced by a police investigation. This is so blatantly silly, on so many separate counts, that it's hard to know where to start. In the trial, Muir tried to embarrass Crippen into admitting he predicted being arrested for murder and fled to avoid rightful justice. Not so, said Crippen. 'Inspector Dew was very imperative in pressing upon me that I must produce my wife,' he replied, 'or otherwise I would be in serious trouble.' A pretty straightforward summation of the position Crippen found himself in, you might think. Apparently not. Dew, in high dudgeon, railed: 'Obviously this was a thing I should never have dreamed of doing.' Author Nicholas Connell, taking up the cudgels on Dew's behalf, is somehow in no doubt either: 'Dew had not told Crippen that he would be in serious trouble if he did not produce his wife.'[58] Connell obviously has no idea what Dew did and didn't say and is simply taking his word here – an irritating tactic. In fact, the evidence, as so often, is on Crippen's side. How else do we account for that advert Dew and Crippen drafted? It plainly reads: 'Will Belle Elmore communicate with H.H.C or authorities at once. Serious trouble through your absence.' Serious trouble. Absence. Absence. Serious trouble. 'Inspector Dew was very imperative in pressing upon me that I must produce my wife, or otherwise I would be in serious trouble.' What am I missing here? *Ah, but maybe this is Crippen exaggerating his position in the advert just as he was exaggerating in the trial?* No, in his testimony at the trial, Dew is emphatic: '*Together* we composed an advertisement,' he says. *He then reads it aloud.* Such was the topsy-turvy universe of the Crown v. Crippen.

The opening speech for the defence, in my imagination, is accompanied by an insistent whistling wind, its defiant trumpet sounding for reason in a wilderness of disinterest, echoing noiselessly on the walls of a citadel built upon sensationalism, and tolerant of no other sustenance:

> It was said he pawned her jewellery and gave away her clothes, and therefore must have known she was dead. It would be idle to pretend that when she went Crippen was overwhelmed with grief. Not at all. They had not been on good terms at home. Under those circumstances he was not in the least keen or anxious to find out where she had gone. He was not grieved – he was not concerned to advertise in the papers to inquire from any of her relatives in America or elsewhere where she had gone. He had his mistress, Miss Le Neve – who had been his mistress for some few years – and in those circumstances Dr Crippen saw no impropriety whatever in giving to his mistress his wife's jewels and furs, and in pawning others. He had earned the money; he had paid for the things. No inference adverse to the prisoner was to be drawn from that. It was all done openly. The jewellery was worn by Miss Le Neve at the ball which people who knew his wife were sure to attend. Such things as he pawned openly at a pawnbroker's where he had been before, and where his name and address were known. He did not go to a pawnbroker who did not know him, where he might have given a false address. He pawned them in his own true name. There was no secrecy about it. He saw no harm in it at all.

And on inviting Dew to the house:

> Here was a supposed murderer readily and willingly going with the chief inspector to the house where, if he were the murderer, he knew that part of his wife's remains were buried. He went into all the rooms with Dew, and they went into the cellar together. If he were a murderer, if he had buried those remains in the cellar, he knew the spot in the middle of the cellar, there under his very eyes as he stood there! Yet he never turned a hair, never showed the slightest

sign of agitation, or fear, or terror. Was it possible that he was the murderer and was standing within three feet of the hole where his own hand must have put the remains if he was the murderer? Was it not beyond all powers of belief? Let the jury remember that on 8th July, at Albion House, a representative of the law had said to him at Hilldrop Crescent the same evening, 'Crippen, I must find your wife.' With those words ringing in his ears picture what Crippen's thoughts must have been. Crippen must have realised that the lies he had told to cover up the scandal, the lies he had in his folly told, must have raised a mountain of prejudice, and formed clouds of suspicion which it would be for him to dispel. During the night he wondered how he could remove that mountain of prejudice and dispel those clouds.

So he resolved to do what hundreds of men had done before. Feeling there was that high mountain of prejudice which he had erected by his lies against himself, he did what innocent men, threatened with a charge, have done before. He resolved in his folly to fly. Experience taught that the very threat of any criminal charge often made good, strong men take their own lives. He did not do that, or attempt it, but in his folly he resolved to fly. What more natural than that he should take with him his mistress? The rest followed as a matter of course – the disguise, the shaving off his moustache, the dressing of Le Neve in boy's clothes. He went away from the inquiries of the officer as innocent men had fled before.

And the whistling wind whistled on. Tobin should have saved his breath.

What really happened to Cora?

If she is not in the cellar, and if Crippen did not bump her off in some other, as yet undetected manner and location, why can we not produce Cora Crippen? We no longer have evidence of her murder, but we still have a very strange and suspicious disappearance. One obvious possibility rarely considered is that she may have taken her own life. Imagine if Crippen had told her that night that he was leaving her, starting a new life with Ethel, taking all their savings, leaving her with nothing? And in a new country: a new start, scandal be damned. Might she have seen her entire life crumbling to nothing, run away in extreme distress, and, say, thrown herself in the river – a suitably theatrical last flourish for one who spent half her life dreaming of dramatic acclaim? Such things happened: it's certainly a more commonplace fate than dismemberment. Bodies were constantly being dredged from the Thames, some of them in an advanced state of decomposition. With a few heavy stones in her pockets she would be even less likely to be found, or, if eventually found, to be identifiable. And nobody was looking for Cora in such a scenario anyway. Without any positive clue to her identity she would have simply been an anonymous female. One of many, move along, nothing to see here.

But apart from some other murder scenario, or suicide, do we have any other reasonable options? What seemed to be an extremely tantalising hint was recently raised in a television documentary: the discovery that in the 1920 census a 'Belle Rose' appears, apparently living with Cora's sister Bertha, listed as her cousin. There is no other record of Bertha having a cousin by so provocative a name. Where had she suddenly come from? Could this be the evidence of Cora in America after 1910 we've all been searching for? Sadly, no. Whoever Belle Rose may have been, she's living with the wrong Bertha. Bertha Marsenger was by this time Bertha Smith, present and correct on the 1920 census, living with her (second) husband and daughters.[59] The 'Bertha Messinger' who is living with Belle Rose in 1920 has nothing to do with Cora, or her family, or our story.

If nothing else, this error helps to remind us that any evidence of Cora being alive after 1910 would leave two major questions unanswered. It would be no surprise if she had intended to leave. She was an American, trapped in a loveless marriage in a foreign country, and not even fulfilled professionally. The last communication her family had received from her seemed to suggest this was her intention: she complained that her house was too large for two people, and that although she had many friends, they could never mean as much as her 'own people'.[60] But why, if she was alive and well, did she not come forward to save Crippen from the gallows?[61] And why leave in such mad haste? Would she really not have arranged for her most valued clothes, jewellery and other items to go with her? We do know that she had called at the Charing Cross bank in December of 1909 and asked the manager if she could withdraw all her personal savings and the £270 in their joint account, suggesting she was planning something along these lines. Unless we consider one of the more fanciful ideas I have already advanced – such as that she found out about Crippen's plans to kill her (see above, 'A Trial Run?') – her hasty departure and invisibility thereafter is, along with the true identity of the cellar remains, one of the case's two biggest mysteries. And if she had gone, even in a hurry, we should still hope to find some trace of her passage and arrival. Did she travel under an assumed name? Where was she headed? Not to Bruce Miller at any rate. Everyone knows that was one of Crippen's more desperate lies. We ruled out his involvement decisively, back at the trial.

Well… actually, no. We didn't, at least not quite. Of the true identity of the body in the basement, alas, we have no clue. As to what really happened to Cora, however, we do have a small, nagging *hint* of a possibility. And it may just involve a certain shadowy character who has been hiding in plain sight in the Crippen saga all this time, but whose manifestly untrustworthy nature has, in the rush to confirm Crippen's status as Britain's public monster number one, been whitewashed for over a century.

The time has come to find out a little more about Bruce Miller.

'Mr' Bruce Miller

When and where Bruce Miller died does not seem to have been established hitherto, and it was no doubt for safety's sake that he is referred to as Bruce Martin in the 1962 *Dr Crippen* film.[62] But we can do better now. It's no surprise he eluded researchers – I suspect he very much wanted it that way. And it would appear that whatever the facts of his association with Cora were, Crippen was in no way maligning his character.

He was born on 14 April 1865 – the day of Lincoln's assassination – in Quincy, Illinois, making him around 35 years old in the period in which he knew Cora Crippen. Tom Cullen describes him as a former prizefighter, but prior to taking to the stage he was no pugilist. Bruce Miller was, in fact, a doctor.

In the 1921 Alumni Record of the University of Illinois College of Medicine, from which he graduated in 1886, he is described as physician and surgeon.[63] A photograph of his graduating class shows a ruminative, even intense young man, looking not at the camera but distractedly off to the middle distance. He looks, in short, like a bit of a dreamer.

Cullen also says that his stage act was a one-man band, in which he played banjo, harmonica and drums. Miller was, it is true, noted for his ability to play the banjo and harmonica simultaneously,[64] but his one-man band act at this time was much more elaborate. It was an entire miniature orchestra, in which multiple instruments are played simultaneously by mechanical automata. Here are its origins in 1899:

A Chicago genius claims to have created an automatic orchestra, which will be operated by a musician seated at an organ. The inventor is Dr Bruce Miller, who, after much study and experimenting, believes he has produced a startling novelty. Dr Miller's present orchestra consists of twelve figures, representing young women playing various instruments. These figures are life-size, and it is the purpose to have them produce the effect of a real orchestra by means of pneumatic tubings and other connections operated through the mechanism of an organ. An account of the invention in a Chicago paper states that the figures, which are of papier mâché, are first filled with wind, and when the musician wants a certain figure to toot her part he has simply to open the valve and the figure does the rest. Just how the stringed instruments are made to 'toot' is not explained.[65]

An engagement at Hammerstein's Roof Garden in New York the same year brought some more information: the figures are attired in white satin costumes, and will 'get up and sit down, [and] tune their instruments, every finger moving as in real life'. It took Miller ten years to perfect, and 'is exceedingly intricate. It includes 3,000 bellows, a mile and a quarter of tubing, and 6,000 valves. The operating force is a gigantic affair. Mr Miller performs the music and directs the figures from a central keyboard resembling an organ.'[66]

The young Miller, apparently, was 'literally absorbed in music. It was the one passion of his life, and he almost lost his mind over it':

His father forbade him to follow its study and placed him in the College of Physicians and Surgeons, whence he graduated in 1886. For three years he practiced his profession, but soon he returned to his first love, music, and soon invention in that connection became a positive hobby with him. To invent something new, something that would be so far removed from the ordinary productions in music that it would set the world talking, became his sole purpose and ambition... To a person at a distance everything looks bona fide. Indeed it would never be suspected that figures of papier mâché did the blowing, for the fingers of the violinist, the flutist, the picoloist and other players move up and down the instruments with every note. Now and then a solo or a duet is played. The figures taking these parts arise, bow to the audience, and then proceed with their part. It is done so real and lifelike that one is easily fooled thereby. Of course, the musician-operator at the organ works the whole contrivance... Miss Mamie Frey, an expert watchmaker at 556 West Madison Street, manufactured the delicate machinery which moves the heads, arms and eyes of the figures. She also completed the mechanism of the snare drums and violins after repeated failures by other parties. Dr Miller's work has been conducted for over a year past in an empty store on the West side. He has frequently had as many as a dozen workmen helping him.[67]

There is something a bit creepy about this. It hints at a solitary, obsessive personality, inward-focused, and imaginative in not altogether healthy ways: he doesn't seem to want to bring joy to an audience with his orchestra so much as show them how clever he is. And in the photographs, reprinted here for the first time, the act itself has a rather spooky quality to it too. Miller's platoon of identical, obedient, silent women unnerves as much as it charms. His decision to look at the ground in a promotional photograph, as if concealing his face, also registers. In his long black coat, his head lowered, he looks more like a shady undertaker than a music hall artiste.

Later Miller would dabble in carpentry, contracting and real estate, before returning to medicine (or the pretence of it). But it was with his weirdo orchestra that he set sail for England on 19 August 1899. *Reynold's Newspaper* announced his imminent arrival, musical marvel in tow, on 13 August, and an appearance at the Earl's Court Exhibition is confirmed by the London *Evening Standard* on 29 September 1900. But I would find it hard to believe it had been his intention to stay in England, drifting around the halls, for the next four years. I'm much more inclined to believe that something unexpected caused him to change his plans and stick around. For all we know the intoxication of being a free man in a different continent from his wife may have inspired him to any number of shifting dalliances. Cora was certainly among them, though: their continued acquaintance years after his return to the US surely proves that. The 1901 UK census, listing him as an American musician with his own act, puts him in lodgings at 18 Colville Place, St Pancras, London. This is no more than a five-minute walk from Store Street, where the Crippens were living at the time.

His return to America is recorded on the passenger list of the SS *Oceanic*, sailing from Liverpool to New York on 20 April 1904. Advance publicity promoted his return, and another new invention:

> A few years ago an orchestra of twelve life-size automata, invented by Dr Bruce Smith[68] caused a sensation in London. He is now bringing out a yet more ambitious device, the pneumultiphone, which is to enable one man to play twenty-four musical instruments at once... The machine is worked by compressed air.[69]

This ties with the fact that his wife Edith is living with their son Bruce at her parents' house on the 1900 census, but in 1910 the family are together again. This was their situation when British justice came calling, much to the inconvenience of Miller, who was now out of show business and patching things up with Edith. 'I have no grudge against Crippen for slandering me,' he told the press. 'It was a case of a drowning man clutching a straw.'[70] All very magnanimous, I'm sure. So off he goes to London, delivers the spiel, and hurries home. And that's where the official record of the case, satisfied with his story, bids farewell to him. We, however, will stick around. We're about to hit a curve.

In 1915, a Chicago woman named Valerie Ordner gave birth to a daughter called Jeanne. Then, in 1917, she had a son, called Barry. Their father was Bruce Miller. And the 1920 census reveals something very interesting indeed. Miller had *not* left his wife for another woman. He was leading a double life. He is listed resident at two households, one with Edith (on 12 January) and one with Valerie (on 7 January).[71] In both households he is described as married.[72]

Miller seems to be turning into Crippen before our very eyes! But wait, we're just getting started. Miller then reappears on the medical scene in 1924, decades after bidding it adieu, and this time as a full-fledged and unequivocal quack. Claiming to be 'medical director of the National

Cancer Research Institute' (not to be confused with the reputable National Cancer Institute, which wasn't founded until 1938), he is hawking a 'yellowish salve' which a horse doctor called Hoxie had successfully used to treat the cancer of a circus pony, but which also cures most known cancers in humans, and the secret of which Hoxie's son has now given to Miller, who wants to share it with the world.[73] Dr Miller has already treated twenty patients, including a police sergeant, and promises to treat anyone who comes to Chicago, whether they can pay or not. 'I don't want fame, money, or anything. All I want is a chance to apply my treatment on cancer sufferers. I know I have a positive remedy, and reputable men say the same thing.' Connoisseurs of cheap crooks and their tactics will be well aware of that classic. ('Professor' Munyon was another who only wanted to help people.)

Very well buried in the piece is the information that Miller's claims have incited 'the condemnation of the American Medical Association, which brands it just a variation on the old-time arsenical escharotic of a century ago. An escharotic is a caustic agent used to burn away unhealthy tissues. Dr Miller of course denies this. He points to an authenticated book full of cases that have been cured with his cancer-killing preparation.' By 1947 he is president of something called the National Medical Society, which sounds grand, but proves to be the usual nest of snake oil salesmen, the giveaway being his description of the organisation as 'a united front against the menace of regimented medicine (and) the arbitrary, monopolistic and oppressive leadership of the American Medical Association'.[74]

All very sleazy, for sure, but *why* did Miller suddenly make another bid for medical glory in December of 1924, after decades of doing almost everything but? Had he suddenly come into funds? We know that at some point he and his first wife Edith divorced. Whether this was because she became aware of his second life it is impossible to say, but we do know the time window: they are definitely still married in 1920, when Miller splits into two like a bisected worm on the census, and they are definitely divorced in 1922, when Miller and Valerie Ordner finally marry for real. Then, in 1924, *right before he re-emerges in funds as a bogus cancer specialist*, that rare stroke of fate experienced with such disproportionate regularity by bigamists and two-timers occurs to Dr Bruce Miller: his first wife dies in a strange and tragic accident.

The circumstances are quite something. First, she suffered what crime fiction readers know to be the world's least-accidental accidental fate: ladies and gentlemen, I give you *the fall down the stairs*. Does this *ever* actually happen, outside of novels? Well, it did here. Was it the loose stair rod? The hole in the carpet on the second stair from the top? The broken bannister? That insecure handrail they always meant to have fixed? We don't know. But down the stairs she fell.

And an even nastier surprise waited for her at the bottom. She landed on a broken bottle. How, exactly? Again, we do not know. But – and just imagine the odds, here – the splintered glass of this bottle, which she somehow landed on after an accidental fall down her stairs, somehow managed to slice into her left buttock and *sever her femoral artery*.

What happened after that, we *do* know. On 21 February 1924, Edith Sophia Miller bled to death.

News reports described her as 'prominent in the social life of East Chicago', and her death 'a shock to many friends'.[75] Not remarried after Miller, and divorced from him for at least two years, one might therefore assume she was independently wealthy. Maybe she hadn't got around to cutting Miller out of her will. Or if not convenient in death, perhaps she had been inconvenient in life? Perhaps that Chicago social life she was so prominent in was funded by Miller's alimony? One must presume the police investigated fully, though one wonders if they might not have been extra curious had they known about that little discrepancy in the 1920 census, or the man's past in the Crippen affair. This is all, of course, speculation, and if the dead have been libelled here, I give sincere apology. But the parallels with Crippen and Cora are chilling, all the same.

And so it seems they *could* have referred to him by his real name in the movie, though only by a whisker, because 'Dr Bruce Miller, retired physician' died at the age of 95 on 12 March 1961.[76] The role he had played over fifty years before in one of the most famous trials in the history of crime was long forgotten. But where does what we now know of him take our understanding of that crime?

Nowhere specific, alas. Once again we are struck by how Crippen seems to make some wild, absurd, desperate stab in the dark, without rhyme or reason, like a child caught with his hand in the cookie jar claiming no knowledge of cookies, or jars… and, without anybody realising it when it mattered, is completely and utterly vindicated. What do we now know for certain about Miller that the jury could have neither known nor suspected when assessing his evidence? We know that he was reckless and feckless, a reprobate, a liar, a serially unfaithful husband, and a repulsive conman who peddled fake cancer cures. We know he was from youth somewhat of a misfit, a young man with something to prove and perhaps a chip on his shoulder, dissatisfied with the impositions of convention and accountability, and built for something better. A man who buried himself in intricate, extravagant, oddly eldritch creative projects; a mysterious, vain, mercurial character, and one who, all things considered, made for about as unreliable a witness in a murder trial as can be imagined. That's enough to be going on with. Anything more than that, conceded, would be only supposition. There is no evidence the death of his first wife was anything other than the utterly *bizarre* accident it was, somehow, officially deemed to be. There is certainly no evidence that Cora ran to this man.

But my God, *if* she had! *If she had, there is no reason to think for a single second that he would have told the truth about it.*

We know she still displayed his pictures. We know they still wrote to each other, after so long apart – and regularly, so she certainly knew his address. What might happen if an unwanted and inconvenient old flame *did* appear on the doorstep of such a man as this? It is *just* possible that we may have arrived, against all the odds, at the most elusive missing link in the whole Crippen saga: a plausible reason why that old flame may not have been heard from again.

As Miller so cockily told the American press: 'She is dead. You may rest assured on that.'[77]

A tentative summing up

And so we arrive at a kind of stalemate. Tempting though it is to join the final dots in some grand and speculative synthesis, this is as far as I feel the present evidence allows me in good conscience to go. On one hand, I feel that question marks must still hang over the rate of decomposition of the remains (and whether it is possible for them to predate the Crippens' tenancy), the fact of Belle's non-reappearance, Crippen's behaviour before, during and after the supper with the Martinettis, the report of the boys at his house and his hiring of Valentine Lecoq, and the unexplained elements of his first wife's death (specifically the repeated references to operations performed on both wives, and the behaviour of Ethel that could suggest the repeating of this admittedly confusing cycle). In *these* regards, I feel his behaviour remains alternately suspicious, anomalous and contradictory. And I remain of the belief that the portrait of him as a man too kind and caring to get involved in murder is not helped by the nature of his professional life, and its clear evidences throughout his career of a blithe disregard for the well-being of others, other than as sources of profit and loss.

On the other, I *strongly* feel that Crippen's conduct throughout the period after his arrest and to his death, very much including (I am tempted to say especially) during the trial, was genuine. Psychologically, I cannot shake the conviction that we are, somehow, by some chain of circumstance still to be fully untangled, watching an uncomprehending man trapped in a Kafkaesque nightmare. I do not feel remotely challenged in this opinion by any of the following points, all of which I consider either wrong or grossly flawed in their common interpretation: the hyoscine evidence (sloppily arrived at and met with eminently reasonable objection at the time by experts of equal stature), his brazen behaviour with Ethel after Cora's disappearance (the last thing a guilty man would do), his pawning of Cora's jewellery (ditto), any suggestion he had a gun in his pocket when Dew made his first inspection of the cellar (silly nonsense), his flight or his and Ethel's use of disguise (possibly naïve and foolish but therefore, again, the opposite of what a conniving murderer would do), the scar evidence (always flawed; now discredited), the hair curlers and pyjamas (now more than ever suggestive of police tampering, indeed close to inarguably so), the phony reports of gunshots and screams (wholly without merit). All of that I either dispute entirely or consider by no means incompatible with innocence, and in some cases actually suggestive of it. And with these subtracted, what is left? Not a whole lot.

As for Cora: might Crippen have been telling the truth? Had she still nurtured an undimmed love for the odious Miller? The court had forced him to own up to stolen kisses and letters addressed 'love and kisses to Brown Eyes'. They still communicated regularly, *six years* after they last met. It doesn't *sound* like a trivial dalliance. *Might* she have run to him, covering her tracks with false names on her journey,[78] unable to take her belongings with her, pathetically besotted, intent on making trouble just when he was getting his marriage back on track and actually making a go of some conventional business? That business was real estate: might there, even now, be something nasty in the concrete foundations of some Chicago house, built around 1910, its keys once entrusted to Bruce Miller? What we now know of his life subsequent to the trial makes this a question worth asking, at least. For what it's worth, by far the most elaborate of the Cora sighting hoaxes in the immediate post-arrest period emanated from Chicago. It still gets us no nearer to putting a name to the remains in *Crippen's* cellar, but why should it? That is a completely different mystery now.

One thing is certain: there is no longer anything close to sufficient evidence for Crippen's conviction. Most of the evidence judged persuasive at his trial was wrong, and some of it frankly stinks. It is not simply that his accusers had no access to the DNA evidence that would have stopped them completely in their tracks. That's going too easy on them. The Crippen case pushed a predetermined narrative for all it was worth, and predetermined narrative is the reason why Crippen was hanged. Predetermined narrative is the reason why entirely eminent experts with entirely reasonable objections to the Crown's scientific evidence are virtually inaudible in the record; why the jury seems almost literally to have *not heard them*; why this is the first study to have even granted them the courtesy of letting them make their points in full. Predetermined narrative is the reason why Crippen and Le Neve's wholly understandable decision to leave the country is permitted to seem sinister, and suggestive of guilt, when it manifestly was neither. Predetermined narrative is the reason Bruce Miller was allowed to slither into court and slither out again, without leaving so much as a single shed scale in the witness box to mark his passage. We shall permit no excuses along the lines of: *how could the jury have been expected to guess he might have anything to do with Cora's disappearance when it had already been decided that Crippen had bricked her up under the floor of his cellar?* Because it *hadn't* been decided: the jury alone could decide that. Had they wished, they could have rejected every inadequate and circumstantial part of that claim. Instead, they chose to sit back and watch the show, and then, after a few insulting minutes – twenty-seven of them, to weigh the worth of a man's life – they chose narrative over doubt, and made the wrong call. But before we pardon Crippen, don't we need to find out who that really was, in partial form, in his cellar? No. With all due respect to British justice, that should be the least of its worries at this point.

So let us at last return to our four hypotheses. Is there a theory that fits hypothesis 4: Crippen guilty of both the body in the cellar and the death of his wife? Not in good conscience, no. We know the remains are not Cora and we have no evidence as to what happened to her. Crippen may have killed her and got rid of the body somewhere else, and his behaviour regarding the dinner party with the Martinettis *is* suspicious, but no court would entertain such a flimsy case for a single second. Thus I conclude there are no grounds for maintaining this position, and for all the other reasons outlined above I consider it incredibly unlikely. Not guilty.

The same goes for hypothesis 2: Crippen innocent of involvement with the body in the cellar, but guilty of murdering his wife. For the reasons just given, Crippen has no case to answer, only a suspicion to live down. Not guilty.

What then of hypothesis 3: Crippen innocent of his wife's death but responsible for the remains in the cellar? There is evidence for this: the presence of hyoscine in the remains, if we believe it, to some degree ties the corpse to Crippen, and it remains a considerable case to argue that it was placed in the cellar prior to his tenancy. But both contentions can at least be sincerely questioned, the first very persuasively indeed, and I don't think the prosecution would get a conviction on either anymore. Crippen's relative incompetence at surgery remains as big a stumbling block to his responsibility for the state of the remains now as it should have been at the trial. The idea that it may have been a test run for some gynaecological operation on Ethel is worth considering, but the sex of the corpse argues against it. For this, I like that halfway verdict that is peculiar to Scottish law: Not Proven.

Which just leaves hypothesis 1: Crippen is entirely innocent. We need to overcome a lot of suspicion, and shake off many decades of conditioning, to arrive at this conclusion, but *unlike the other three*, it *can* be done. As to Cora, there is no evidence linking Crippen to any crime, and no proof that she died at all. Suicide remains possible, and it's a fair bet that Bruce Miller's evidence was worth not the smallest fraction of the amount he was paid for it. As for the remains in the basement, we need not worry about the secondary physical evidence, which certainly gives the impression of having been planted, and the hyoscine evidence is, to put it mildly, unsafe. A canny lawyer would be able to junk both with ease, given that there is now no possibility of the remains being Cora's. There seems no plausible reason why Crippen would have murdered anybody else, and the fact of multiple lodgers, previous tenants and others with legitimate access must make it at least permissible to argue that it may have been effected without his knowledge, provided we get the pyjamas and hair curlers thrown out of court, as any half-decent barrister would now do with flourish and ease.

Further, evidence and logic argues against so elaborate a murder, dismemberment and interment having taken place in the house without detection in the time frame provided, *or in any possible alternative.* Had he done it before Cora's disappearance, he would have needed to complete the filthy business without her being aware of it; afterwards, the same problem would have arisen with Ethel on the premises (and that, don't forget, a matter entirely of his own choosing). I think a good case might be made for the remains originating, in already dissected form, in a medical lab, and if so, for absolving Crippen of responsibility. It is perfectly possible he might have taken a corpse to practise on, but I can't think why he wouldn't admit to that when facing a murder charge. A slight paradox thus emerges. If it was Crippen's doing, it would probably *have* to be a murder. If it is *not* a murder, it's probably not Crippen. But if it *is* a murder, it *can't* be Crippen! Only possibility remaining: *it's not Crippen.*

Was he good at lying or bad at lying? We can't have it both ways. If he was good at lying he'd have come up with something a damned sight better than the unsatisfactory banalities that tied the rope around his neck. Bad at lying, then? No, sorry. Nobody is *that* bad at lying. His story was tantamount to pleading guilty, and thus could not have been the story of a guilty man feigning innocence. No truly guilty man would be so stupid as to behave the way Crippen did in court. Crippen was not stupid, and I think his responses during the trial only *begin* to make any kind of sense if he is innocent.

Shortly before his death, Crippen wrote the following:

> I desire to make a last appeal to the world not to think the worst of me, and to believe words now written from the condemned cell. I beg them to remember that I have been condemned on inconclusive evidence, and chiefly by evidence of expert witnesses who were

contradicted by other experts upon the most vital points of the case…
Face to face with God, in whose presence my soul shall soon stand
for final judgement, I still maintain that I was wrongly convicted, and
my belief that facts will yet be forthcoming to prove my innocence.
I solemnly state that I knew nothing of the remains discovered at
Hilldrop Crescent until I was told of their discovery by my solicitor
Mr Arthur Newton, on the next day after my arrival at Bow Street.

I am struck by the fact that even here, with death at his elbow, he is
not making some vague statement about having been undone by love,
or condemned by fate. He's still right down among the actualities and
specifics, disputing the evidence, questioning the experts, and begging not
to be forgiven but to be *believed*.

Clearly there is much about the case that remains puzzling and insoluble,
and the full story could be as far from our grasp now as it ever was. The
big question remains unanswered. How *did* that hideous mess end up
under a London basement floor? And when? And why? And by whose
hand? There are no likely answers, only varying degrees of unlikely ones.
But whatever the ultimate truth, one conclusion seems to me – wholly
unsatisfactory though it may seem, and despite a century of melodrama
pulling us the other way – to be *less unlikely* than any other.

That it had nothing to do with Crippen, or Cora, or Ethel, and no
connection with the sad, awful tragedy these three lonely people made
for each other, fell headlong into, and then unwittingly shared with the
world.

Notes

Prologue

1. In recent years they have also been attributed to press photographer James Jarché.
2. He is now in storage: Madame Tussaud's insist that they never melt a statue down.
3. *The Argus* (Melbourne), 20 March 1925.
4. Nicholas Connell: *Doctor Crippen*, p. 170.
5. Some reports say in four.
6. *Times* (London), 7 June 1931.

Chapter 1

1. *Daily Mail* (London), 14 July 1910.
2. Nobody has ever come up with an explanation for this nickname, which doesn't seem to have predated Crippen's marriage to Cora and was never used by Crippen in any professional connection.
3. Connell, p. 13. Original report 12 January 1930.
4. *Evening News* (Sydney), 30 August 1910.
5. Ibid.
6. Crime historians who suggest Crippen may have used this opportunity to take some bits and pieces of Cora with him and throw them over the side of the ship during the journey have far more imagination than he did.
7. This is an important point to bear in mind whenever theorists try to suggest that he placed some of the remains under his cellar on the grounds that he would have presumed they would not be disturbed: it was *not* his cellar, and he knew he would not be living there much longer, so it would have been a lunatic thing to do.
8. Quoted in Oliver Double: *Britain Had Talent*, p. 42.
9. Quoted in Matthew Sturgis: *Walter Sickert: A Life*, p. 198.
10. The transition, already begun, between music hall and variety involved the smoothing away of much of this insalubrious 'authenticity'. By 1913, one Charles E. Hands wrote to the *Daily Mail* to complain that 'the conquering hordes of the upper and middle classes' had 'taken away our music halls from us'. Among the dubious new developments: 'the only place left for us was a gallery two miles high, and that at a price that made a hole in the week's spending money', and, worst of all, 'they won't let us have any beer'. (Double, p. 42.)

11. *Arrow* (Sydney), 19 August 1932.

12. Ibid.

13. Connell, p. 14. This is the great artist usually referred to these days as 'George Formby Sr'; not his more famous but less innovative son, who should, by rights, be referred to as 'George Formby Jr'.

14. You're going to have to get used to this as we proceed through this story: on small points, big points, trivial points and vital points, on occasions when it is imperative and occasions when it is of no importance whatsoever, we will constantly catch Crippen out telling the exact and honest truth.

15. There *is* a story, supposedly emanating from Formby's wife Eliza, that Belle *saw* Formby performing in 1902, and was so impressed that she contacted Ted Granville, who would give Formby his first London booking at the Royal Albert Music Hall in Canning Town, urging him to see his act. The idea that Cora would have the ear of a man such as Granville is incredibly hard to believe, and this story is not to be taken too seriously either; nonetheless it seems to be the origin of the later mutation that Cora and Formby shared a bill.

16. Cora was the Guild's treasurer. After her disappearance the accounts were scrupulously checked in case embezzlement might have been her motive to abscond: everything was in apple-pie order.

17. *Variety*, 1 September 1916. By very curious coincidence, Atherstone also ended up the victim in an unsolved 1910 murder.

18. *The Era*, 23 July 1910.

19. That Kelly's corpse lay naked on the bed is confirmed by the medical notes of Dr Thomas Bond, made at the scene but lost until 1987. Until that time, the only official testimony was that of the supremely unreliable Bagster Phillips, who told the inquest she was clad in a linen undergarment. Ripperologists have tended to endorse Phillips, partly because they're suckers for authority, and partly because in the crime scene photo what looks like the puffed sleeve of a chemise is visible at the top of Kelly's arm. But look again (on a clear, large reproduction). It is not a sleeve at all; merely part of the sheet she is lying on, pulled up and over her shoulder. (See Bruce Robinson's *They All Love Jack* for a cogent if chilling explanation of why Phillips was playing fast and loose here.) Bond was right, Phillips was wrong, and Dew seems to be referring to inquest notes, not his 'as if it were yesterday' personal memory.

20. Later in the statement he says: 'My belief is that my wife has gone to Chicago to join Bruce Miller.'

21. For some reason I imagine Dew exhaling deeply after Crippen told him: 'I had been married to her some little time when she told me her name was not [Corrine] Turner, but Kunigund Mackamotzki.' I then hear Sergeant Mitchell wearily interrupting: 'Could you spell that for me, sir?'

22. In early July, this would still be in bright daylight.

23. He may not have realised at this point that this would not be contested by anybody, nor that it was not in the least suspicious. Neighbours had confirmed

that Crippen was not averse to a little target practice in the garden; he had even been seen teaching Ethel the finer points of marksmanship. Several accounts note with ominous significance that Sergeant Mitchell found a box of .45 cartridges in the basement; not many have the generosity to add that there was a pile of well-peppered paper targets alongside them.

24. *Evening News* (Sydney), 30 August 1910.

25. What was Crippen thinking of when he decided to try to pass off Ethel as a boy? Did he really think that would work? He may have had unrealistic expectations based on many years of immersion in the world of theatre. Cora had appeared in male disguise on stage; witnesses also recalled an occasion on which Crippen had dressed as a woman for fun, apparently making a fine job of it.

26. The prosecution and later writers would make a silly pantomime out of this point, implying that only a guilty man would read such an inference into the events and only a guilty man would need to worry about it: we will come to it in time, but note here its complete disingenuousness.

27. And there's another object on the wall that is hard to make out: it is three-dimensional, irregularly shaped, and seems to be hanging from a hook. It might variously be a bundle of dried flowers or herbs (a form of Edwardian air freshener, perhaps?), some sort of doll, a ceramic posy or peacock, a sconce for a candle, even a dog lead holder shaped like a dog's head. If so this might be more evidence for Crippen's disappearing bull terrier. The dog is mentioned anecdotally by both Clara Martinetti and Ethel Le Neve, but seems to disappear thereafter. John Trestrail thought that the dog would notice the smell of a corpse in the basement, which he thought suggested the remains were planted by police. Alternatively it could be argued that it was made to disappear by Crippen, for that very reason. Likely he gave it away, as he did the ornamental fish. Likewise there is no certain knowledge of what happened to Cora's two cats: some have claimed that these, too, were slain by the wicked Crippen. The writer J.B. Booth recalled that he was once strolling in the Caledonian Road Market when he was approached by a man who offered to sell him 'Dr Crippen's favourite cat, rescued from the garden of Hilldrop Crescent, for a couple of bob and a pint of ale'. The man was chased off by a policeman who told Booth that 'some forty or fifty of "Dr Crippen's favourite cats rescued from the garden of Hilldrop Crescent" have all found good homes from this market'. (*The West Australian*, 25 November 1933.)

28. *South Wales Daily Post*, 19 September 1910.

29. *Los Angeles Herald*, 31 July 1910.

30. Smith, pp. 144–5.

Chapter 2

1. *The Advertiser* (Adelaide), 29 November 1910.

2. *Lethal Witness: Sir Bernard Spilsbury, Honorary Pathologist*, p. 21.

3. Tom Cullen: *The Mild Murderer*, p. 31.

4. *Los Angeles Herald*, 23 October 1910.

5. Why 'Yale'? So far as I know the reason is unknown, though it may have come from a mental association with 'Madame Yale's Tooth Powder', a quack remedy produced in Philadelphia, where Crippen had spent many years.

6. *San Francisco Call*, 23 February 1896.

7. Ibid., 6 October 1895.

8. *Stockton Record*, 26 December 1901.

9. *San Francisco Call*, 6 October 1895.

10. *Mirror* (Perth), 5 May 1951.

11. Cullen: *The Mild Murderer*, p. 9.

12. There was a moment of sad humour when a juror requested that Crippen state the therapeutic dose of hyoscine. The question was relevant because Crippen had said he was using hyoscine in his mail order remedies, but cited as his authority for so doing a book he had not seen in fifteen years. Surely he could not remember the correct dosages after all that time? Crippen was made to look suspicious, when all that had really happened was that he had been revealed as a quack: 'They do not recommend the doses in those books,' he squirmed, 'the allopathic books give you a specific dose, but the homeopathic books simply say, "an infinitesimal dose", which means a very minute dose, like the 10,000th of a grain.' What he was struggling to convey, of course, is that the active dose of the medicinal elements in homeopathic preparations is nil.

13. Connell, p. 52.

14. *San Jose Mercury-News*.

15. Ibid, 15 March 1912.

16. Connell, p.52.

17. *Morning Press* (Santa Barbara), 17 July 1910.

18. *Daily Star* (Brooklyn), 16 July 1910.

19. Cora's sister, Teresa Hunn, would give the following evidence at the trial: 'The first time I saw the accused was when he came to my father's house with my sister about 1892 or 1893. My sister showed me a wedding card, but the accused was not with her when she showed me it. He was with her when she spoke to me about his having married her. She introduced him to my father and mother as her husband.'

20. In his statement to Inspector Dew from which much of his biography is gleaned, Crippen is uncertain of the year both of Charlotte's death and of Otto's birth. He makes two guesses for each, and gets Otto's birth year wrong both times.

21. The suggestion that she was pregnant with Crippen's child at the time of his death, occasionally advanced, including in the play *Miss Elmore* shown in 1981 as part of the ITV *Lady Killers* series, has no basis in known facts.

22. *Lloyd's Weekly News*, 28 August 1910.

23. For this hypothesis I am indebted to David James Smith's book *Supper with the Crippens*.

Chapter 3

1. *St Pancras Chronicle*, 15 July 1910.
2. *Sacramento Union*, 18 July 1910.
3. *Press Democrat* (Santa Rosa), 15 July 1910.
4. Or sometimes both: 'the battered body of a woman was found buried in the cellar. It had been placed in quicklime and was burned beyond recognition...' (*San Bernardino Sun*, 15 July 1910.)
5. Another strange anomaly, never to be repeated, is the suggestion in the initial Associated Press account (e.g. in *Humboldt Times*, 14 July 1910) of the discovery that number 39 was the property of 'a North London undertaker'. Given the nature of the find, this would be of enormous interest to the defence team, but it seems to be entirely untrue and therefore quite inexplicable. The property's owner, a Frederick Lown, resident of 12 Ashbrook Road, Highgate, was a building contractor. It is possible that the implication that he was a funeral undertaker was not intended, and all that was meant was that he was an undertaker in the archaic sense of one who *undertakes* a contract to provide labour or materials for building work.
6. *Evening News* (Sydney), 30 July 1910.
7. *Daily News* (Perth), 27 August 1910.
8. *Santa Cruz Evening News*, 14 July 1910.
9. Ibid.
10. *Daily Mail* (London), 15 July 1910.
11. Ibid., 16 July 1910.
12. *The Sun* (Sydney), 22 July 1910.
13. *San Diego Union and Daily Bee*, 23 July 1910.
14. Ibid.
15. *The Advertiser* (Adelaide), 18 July 1910.
16. *Morning Press* (Santa Barbara), 16 July 1910.
17. *Illustrated Police News*, 6 August 1910.
18. E.g. *San Diego Union and Daily Bee*, 24 July 1910; *Bathurst Times*, 25 July 1910; *Illustrated Police News*, 30 July 1910.
19. *San Francisco Call*, 19 July 1910.
20. *The Sun* (Sydney), 22 July 1910.
21. *Sacramento Union*, 21 July 1910.
22. *San Diego Union and Daily Bee*, 22 July 1910.
23. Ibid.
24. *San Diego Union and Daily Bee*, 23 July 1910.
25. *The Sun* (Sydney), 22 July 1910.
26. *San Diego Union and Daily Bee*, 22 July 1910.
27. *The Times* (London), 21 July 1910.
28. *Daily Telegraph* (Sydney), 21 July 1910.
29. Dew, p. 25.
30. *The Advertiser* (Adelaide), 18 July 1910.
31. *Daily Mail* (London), 16 July 1910.

32. *San Diego Union and Daily Bee*, 16 July 1910.
33. Ibid., 17 July 1910.
34. *The Advertiser* (Adelaide), 18 July 1910.
35. *San Diego Union and Daily Bee*, 16 July 1910.
36. *The Advertiser* (Adelaide), 18 July 1910.
37. *San Diego Union and Daily Bee*, 16 July 1910.
38. Bruce Robinson's *They All Love Jack* gives superb demonstration of how the coroner's inquests were used to control the evolving narrative of the Ripper murders.
39. Newspapers and even present-day accounts of the case repeatedly but wrongly refer to Pepper as 'Professor Pepper', apparently confusing the eminent pathologist with a well-known music hall conjurer. (Andrew Rose: *Lethal Witness.*)
40. *The Sun* (Sydney).
41. Associated Press (*San Diego Union and Daily Bee*).
42. *Evening News* (Sydney).
43. *San Jose Mercury*, 20 July 1910.
44. *San Francisco Call.*
45. *San Diego Union and Daily Bee*, 23 July 1910.
46. *Bathurst Times* (NSW).
47. *The Sun* (Sydney).
48. *Daily Mirror*, 27 July 1910.
49. *Daily Mail* (London), 30 July 1910.
50. Ibid., 26 July 1910.
51. Syndicated, e.g. in *The Voice* (Hobart), 5 & 12 September 1942.
52. *Sacramento Union*, 2 August 1910.
53. *Daily Mail* (London), 25 July 1910. There may have been still another, unless this is more information on the same one: 'It is stated that a steward on the *Montrose* frequently played billiards in a public house in the vicinity of Hilldrop Crescent, and must have seen Crippen, who was an habitual customer there.' (*Daily Telegraph*, 29 July 1910.)
54. 27 July 1910.
55. *Sacramento Union*, 2 August 1910.
56. *Daily Mail* (London), 27 July 1910.
57. *The Sun* (Sydney), 1 August 1910.
58. *Queensland Times*, 2 August 1910.
59. *Lloyd's Weekly News*, 28 August 1910.
60. *Newsletter* (Sydney), 6 August 1910.
61. *Daily Mail* (London), 30 July 1910.

Chapter 4

1. By the time Cora became world-famous in 1910, Mary Schmidt had died, having already been widowed and remarried to a Frederick Marsenger (for some reason usually spelled Mersinger in most accounts of the case; once

again variations abound in the various documents), but a brood of sisters and half-sisters remained to watch the tragedy unfold, some of whom will feature in the ongoing saga.

2. Cullen, p. 79.
3. *Arrow* (Sydney), 19 August 1932.
4. More accurately to a Polish father and German mother, as we have seen.
5. *Daily Express* (London), 15 July 1910.
6. *Daily Mail* (London), 30 July 1910.
7. Crippen came from fiercely Protestant stock; Cora was Catholic. Tellingly, it was he who converted, and with sufficient sincerity to go to his death clutching his rosary.
8. *Daily News* (Perth), 15 August 1910.
9. Cullen, p.39. Munyon may not have been the most objective of witnesses on this score, however. Himself married four times, he was in the midst of his third alliance at the time of the Crippen tragedy, to a Vaudeville actress named Pauline Neff, 24 years old to his 60 when they married in 1908. Less than a year later she had filed for divorce because he had locked her out of their house. (*Humboldt Times*, 16 July 1909.) Five months after that, and apparently reconciled, they had an argument 'in an automobile near City Hall, and many persons saw her strike Munyon, tear his clothes, and throw his belongings into the street'. (*Philadelphia Inquirer*, 8 July 1916.) In 1913 she told the *Los Angeles Herald* (7 January) that she was glad to have abandoned the 'artificial atmosphere' of the stage and had now decided to run a farm, having already acquired 'a nice fat Jersey cow and a pig', adding: 'I shall learn to milk in time.' She signed off the interview with the enigmatic declaration: 'My wisdom teeth have all come out and I feel that my real affinity is with my farm.' This intoxication with the bucolic was affirmed in January and seems to have lasted until June, when she began another action for divorce and told the same paper that she was returning to the stage after all. (23 June: 'She has joined the stock company which is playing in the Harlem opera house and will appear as a member of it today, when it presents Mr. Winched Smith's comedy *The Only Son*.') This divorce too was called off, but in 1916 it was Munyon's turn to file, this time for keeps. 'Papers in the suit were impounded, and the ground for the action was never made public,' noted the *Philadelphia Enquirer* (8 July 1916). It may be presumed, therefore, that Munyon's views on theatrical wives were not likely to be characterised by any overabundance of robust impartiality.
10. *Los Angeles Times*, 15 July 1910.
11. In fact, the record shows some modest activity thereafter, for example a week in Boston in October 1905, then at Brooklyn in December, and Pottstown, Pennsylvania, in early 1906. (*New York Clipper*, 28 October 1905; *New York Clipper*, 30 December 1905; *Variety*, 27 January 1906.)
12. 'I became an estate agent because I was tired of the show business and I saw a chance of making a little more money,' he testily told the court at Crippen's

trial. 'I was not a failure on the music hall stage!' Nobody had even suggested that he had been, but Miller is permanently on the defensive – a point to hold on to.

13. 19 July 1910.
14. 20 July 1910.
15. Nicholas Connell, staunch advocate for Crippen-guilty-as-charged, deserves unequivocal applause for being generous enough to suggest that Miller's pseudonym when travelling to England for the trial – C.C. Brown – might be interpreted as 'Cora Crippen Brown-Eyes'. Although more likely the inspiration was his East Chicagoan brother-in-law C.C. Smith. But why did he feel the need to use a pseudonym in the first place?
16. *Morning Press* (California), 9 November 1910.
17. Otto Hawley, that is, but Hawley seems to have been preferred.
18. *Sacramento Union*, 15 July 1910.
19. *Los Angeles Herald*, 15 July 1910.
20. Connell, p. 158.
21. Ibid., p. 157.
22. *Bathurst Times* (New South Wales), 3 August 1910.
23. E.g. *National Advocate* (Bathurst), 2 August 1910.
24. *News of the World* (London), 17 July 1910.
25. At Ethel's trial she would change the date under cross-examination to sometime in January, thus removing any suggestion that Ethel's agitated state might have been informed by Cora's fate. Though, as later writers have pointed out, this could instead suggest it was part of the impetus for it.
26. This is a reference to Ethel's miscarriage.
27. *Los Angeles Herald*, 20 September 1910.
28. *Queensland Times*, 9 September 1910.
29. As indeed it may not have been: see Chapter 2.

Chapter 5

1. *Sacramento Union*, 3 August 1910.
2. *San Diego Union and Daily Bee*, 4 August 1910.
3. *The Telegraph* (Brisbane), 21 June 1911.
4. *Lloyd's Weekly News*, 28 August 1910.
5. 4 August 1910.
6. *San Francisco Call*, 2 August 1910.
7. *San Bernardino Sun*, 4 August 1910.
8. *Sacramento Union*, 2 August 1910.
9. *Santa Barbara Weekly Press*, 4 August 1910.
10. 27 July 1910.
11. *San Francisco Call*, 2 August 1910.
12. *Los Angeles Herald*, 15 July 1910.
13. *The Sun* (Sydney), 13 August 1910.
14. *Clarence and Richmond Examiner*, 2 August 1910.

15. *Sacramento Union*, 7 September 1910.

16. Ibid., 9 September 1910.

17. Ibid., 15 September 1910.

18. Lieck, *Bow Street World*, quoted in Rose: *Lethal Witness*, p. 25.

19. Dornford Yates: *As Berry and I Were Saying* (pp. 244–6 in my edition [House of Stratus, 2001]).

20. Lest it be felt I am being too hard on Mr Mercer, here is another sample of his insight: 'Crippen wasn't human. I once saw him laugh in court – throw back his head and laugh, at something his solicitor said. He opened his mouth wide and bared his teeth. He looked like a cat, or a tiger – you know, how a cat, when it cries, will open wide its mouth and bare its teeth. I was quite close to him, and the startling similarity hit me between the eyes. Crippen was an animal.' Compare this with the testimonies of people who knew him at the start of Chapter 3.

21. There were slight variations of course: Ingleby Oddie, who appeared for the Crown, preferred to believe that Crippen had shot Cora in the head, on the secure grounds that there was no head to contradict him, and one of Crippen's neighbours had claimed to hear screams and a gunshot ninety minutes too early.

22. *Sacramento Union*, 9 September 1910.

23. Quoted in Andrew Rose: *Lethal Witness: Sir Bernard Spilsbury, Honorary Pathologist*, p. 69. Rose adds: 'Spilsbury's very presence in court, giving his testimony on the side of the prosecution, was powerful ammunition for the Crown.'

24. Though as early as 1925, an unheeded voice of dissension in the *Law Journal* expressed 'profound disquiet' over 'the more than Papal infallibility with which Sir Bernard Spilsbury is rapidly being invested by juries'.

25. Simpson: *Forty Years of Murder*, p. 26.

26. Ibid., p. 26.

27. Rose believes Fox was guilty as charged of starting the fire in his mother's hotel room, and the subsequent mendacity that it was designed to facilitate, but that the evidence points overwhelmingly to his having done so callously and opportunistically after returning to the hotel and finding his mother dead of natural causes. I agree with Rose in this reading of the events: others, numerous and occasionally contemptuous, do not.

28. Rose: *Lethal Witness*, p. 183.

29. Ibid., p. xx.

30. Turnbull was explicitly told he would not be called at the trial if he gave an opinion, then was. Irritating for him, certainly, but for the life of me I cannot see how virtually every writer on the case gets from there to 'his expert opinion can therefore be discounted'. Yet, somehow, they all do.

31. Rose: *Lethal Witness*, p. 30.

32. *San Francisco Call*.

33. *The World's News*, 3 December 1910.

34. *San Francisco Call*, 23 October 1910.
35. *Los Angeles Herald*, 23 October 1910.
36. Ibid., 6 November 1910.
37. Also on his shipboard reading list was *The Pickwick Papers*: one wonders if he saw any parallels between his fate and that of the book's hero – a short, bald man in round glasses, hung out to dry by the British justice system after being found guilty of an entirely false charge.
38. *Chico Record*, 23 November 1910.
39. *Tasmanian News*, 13 July 1911. Wallace, meanwhile, seems to have gone to his grave genuinely believing that he had merely punched-up an otherwise genuine document.
40. *The Macleay Chronicle*, 21 December 1910.
41. *Los Angeles Herald*, 19 November 1910.
42. *Leamington Spa Courier*, 25 November 1910.
43. *Chico Record*, 23 November 1910.
44. 24 November 1910.
45. *The Humboldt Times*, 23 November 1910.
46. *The Advertiser* (Adelaide), 25 November 1910.

Chapter 6

1. *San Francisco Call*, 13 June 1911.
2. *Sausalito News*, 12 August 1911.
3. *Forty Years of Murder*, p. 26.
4. *The Advertiser* (Adelaide), 29 November 1910.
5. In 1940, the English variety comedienne Jennie Howard was touring Australia when she picked up a Melbourne newspaper and discovered that her London home had been destroyed in the blitz. Howard's house was in Hilldrop Crescent, directly opposite the former Crippen home. Far from a faded memory, even then, Howard said that sightseers would stop her every weekend to ask 'Which was the murder house?' *The Truth* (Brisbane), 9 February 1941; *Mirror* (Perth), 27 July 1946.
6. *Macleay Argus*, 23 September 1910.
7. *Barrier Miner*, 26 October 1910.
8. *The Register* (Adelaide), 26 October 1911; *Burrangong Argus*, 20 September 1911. It was all very different in 1997 when Crippen's pocket watch was auctioned. The successful bidder, David Gainsborough Roberts, who claimed his uncle had lived next door to Crippen, beat off several other keen bidders and took it home for $16,000, ten times the estimate. (*Santa Cruz Sentinel*, 2 May 1997.)
9. *New York Times*, 26 October 1910.
10. One of the odd inconsistencies in her various serialised memoirs is her attitude to Crippen's criminality. For the 1910 version, Philip Gibbs, one of the two journalists hired to transcribe her recollections, recalled that 'she had no doubt of his guilt'. By 1920, she was of the opinion that Cora died accidentally and Crippen was guilty only of panicking and hiding

the evidence. To Ursula Bloom, who met her in the fifties, she expressed complete faith in his innocence, and implied that the omnipresent bad smell in the basement might indicate that the remains predated Crippen's tenancy.

11. In December, though, I'm not sure even America – Hunn lived just outside Queens, New York – would have offered bright sunshine. It sounds as though she is considering Australia. Although she seems never to have gone there, she for some reason frequently claimed she had in her semi-fictional newspaper memoirs in the years that followed. Maybe it had been her original idea, and then remained her default when offering the embroidered version. An Australian Mrs H?

12. Connell, p.143.

13. *Southern Star*, 22 February 1911.

14. *The Sun* (Sydney), 1 August 1910.

15. Bernstein went into the movies and built Universal City. He died on 19 October 1944, just over two months before his studio released *The Suspect*.

16. 26 November 1910.

17. *Sunday Times* (Sydney), 2 October 1910.

18. *San Diego Union and Daily Bee*, 8 November 1910.

19. *The Leader* (Orange), 9 November 1910.

20. *San Francisco Call*, 8 November 1910.

21. *Los Angeles Herald*, 13 November 1910.

22. *Moving Picture News*, 18 February 1911.

23. *Evening News*, 29 June 1932.

24. *Mirror* (Perth), 28 April 1952.

25. *Evening News*, 29 June 1932.

26. 28 June 1932.

27. 12 August 1932.

28. *Mirror* (Perth), 5 May 1951.

29. 21 April 1951.

30. *Mirror* (Perth), 5 May 1951.

31. *Daily Telegraph* (Sydney), 19 August 1951.

32. *Mirror* (Perth), 11 August 1951.

33. *Chico Record*, 31 July 1912.

34. 24 December 1910.

35. *Daily Post* (Hobart, Tasmania), 29 April 1911.

36. *Southern Cross Times*, 22 June 1912.

37. *Saturday Mail*, 1 August 1914.

38. *Arrow* (Sydney), 19 August 1932.

39. E.g. *Bathurst Times*, 11 March 1925.

40. *Northern Herald*, 21 March 1918. According to Walter Long, the purchaser at Crippen's request, Ethel's suit had been obtained from Charles Baker's, a menswear shop on Tottenham Court Road. There was no sack.

41. And it would be adding innuendo to injury to read any significance into the fact that his wife was the sister of Tom Terriss, one of Britain's most

prolific and imaginative liars – see my book *Egyptomania Goes to the Movies* for more.

42. *Sporting Globe*, 29 July 1940.
43. *New Call* (Perth), 23 February 1933.
44. *Kalgoorie Miner*, 15 June 1926.
45. *Los Angeles Herald*, 31 August 1910.
46. Ibid., 9 September 1910.
47. Ibid.
48. *Los Angeles Herald*, 16 September 1910.
49. Cullen, p. 203.
50. Lacking the devotion of her character, Eggar told the press of her dread of having her hair cut to boy's length for the scenes on the *Montrose*, and her relief when a means was found to pin it up and still make it look like a short cut.

Chapter 7

1. In the 1875 New York state census, Cora/Kunagunde Makomarski is 1 year and 8 months old on 1 June 1875, living with her mother Mary and father Joseph, and Joseph's sister-in-law Tessa Smith. The papers in 1910 say Cora's mother remarried to Frederick Marsenger when Cora was 2 (about 1876) and that her mother was dead by 1910. Cora grew up with numerous step siblings (ten, by my count, according to the 1880 and 1900 census). Cora's half-sister Theresa Hunn said Cora was born in Brooklyn on 3 September 1873, which matches the information in the census. When Cora's and Theresa's sister Louisa was born, the mother's maiden name is recorded as Schmidt. How she ended up being called 'Wolff' on Cora's marriage certificate I have no idea, but there's definitely only one mother to the family, with children born to two fathers.
2. David R. Foran, Ph.D.; Beth E. Wills, A.D.N.; Brianne M. Kiley, M.S.; Carrie B. Jackson, M.S.; and John H. Trestrail III, B.S.: 'The Conviction of Dr. Crippen: New Forensic Findings in a Century-Old Murder' in *Journal of Forensic Science* (Vol. 56, No. 1: January 2011).
3. Correspondence with author: May 2020.
4. 1 July 2008.
5. Yet again this maddening faith in Spilsbury, though!
6. Amanda Fazi, Brianne Gobeski, David Foran: 'Development of two highly sensitive forensic sex determination assays based on human DYZ1 and Alu repetitive DNA elements' (*Electrophoresis* 2014, 35, pp. 3028–3035).
7. The one remaining doubt as far as Ethel is concerned is over the extent to which she may have collaborated with the authorities: see Chapter 6.

Chapter 8

1. Crippen would claim in court Cora did not know about his relations with Ethel, and like much of his testimony it should be presumed to carry some

weight simply because it worked to his disadvantage: if Cora knew about his affair it would have given her a good reason to leave and strengthened his case, so it's hard to think why he would say otherwise other than because it was true. Perhaps it was true so far as he was aware, he being not the most imaginative of men. Nonetheless, it is hard to believe she did not know and that by extension she did not make it known that she knew, and it is possible Crippen was just trying to be gallant here. Certainly, Maud Burroughs's recollection of Cora saying she didn't like Crippen's typist, if true, sounds like some pretty solid suspicions in the process of forming, even if it stops short of full conviction.

2. There is some dispute as to this, but no strong reasons for doubting it. Cora's sister Louise Mills noted that they co-habited when she visited them, but Crippen had already stressed that they had both vowed to maintain an outward impression of having a happy marriage, so this was likely just for show. Or it might even more simply be that they did not want to go to the effort of making up a third room.

3. Even stranger is one of the notes Ursula Bloom made of their conversations in the 1950s: 'Le Neve said "We seldom used hyoscine, it was new and he had never liked it."'

4. E.g. *Bathurst Times* (New South Wales), 15 August 1910.

5. One other possibility that perhaps should be acknowledged for the sake of completeness is that it could have been a complete hoax or conspiracy that was orchestrated by a private individual or individuals to discredit Crippen, but *not* by the authorities. We could even imagine it being done with the complicity of an incognito Cora! Needless to say, however, while there is no evidence ruling this option out, neither is there any that might reasonably point us in that direction, so it's another one for the faction files.

6. Ludovic Kennedy's reprehensible *10 Rillington Place* relies on several of these.

7. Conspiracists have read much into the fact that Dew resigned from the force after the Crippen case. Was his conscience troubling him? Or was it some oblique comment on the dirty work his superiors had forced him into doing? Very unlikely. Dew had made it known he would be retiring before the Crippen case began. And a further inducement was the pretty penny he made from suing various newspapers and periodicals associated with it for libel. Nine separate actions for libel were brought, and all paid off nicely. He received £600 from the *Montreal Star* alone! (*Ballarat Star*, 6 June 1911.) Action against the *Daily Chronicle* netted him a further £400 (*Barrier Miner*, 3 April 1911). Most reports state that his case against the *Chronicle* was that it claimed that Crippen had confessed to him after his arrest, when he had in fact done no such thing. But according to the *Sun* (Sydney, 1 April 1911) the article he objected to was one that 'severely criticized the part played by Mr Dew in connection with the arrest of Crippen'. Dew seems to have been morbidly concerned with his reputation, and even in old age continued to write peevish letters to newspapers who had commented on the case in ways

he considered unfavourable to him. He never quite seemed to be able to free himself of the conviction that the case was his property, on which only he was allowed to pass opinion.

8. Trestrail: correspondence with author, May 2020.
9. *Daily Mercury*, 22 September 1910.
10. Danielle M. Butzbach: 'The Influence of Putrefaction and Sample Storage on Post-Mortem Toxicology Results' (https://pubmed.ncbi.nlm.nih.gov/ 19946767/).
11. My all-time favourite: a chewing gum laced with hyoscine for use by rabbits who are afraid of air travel. (*Greenfield Recorder-Gazette*, 4 September 1947.)
12. *Healdsburg Tribune*, 9 June 1892.
13. *Ballarat Star*, 8 October 1892.
14. *Brisbane Courier*, 4 December 1893.
15. *San Pedro Daily News*, 8 December 1914.
16. *Illustrated Sydney News*, 31 October 1889.
17. *Manning River Times and Advocate*, 2 February 1944.
18. *Poughkeepsie Eagle News*, 14 June 1935.
19. *Evening Bulletin*, 29 September 1885.
20. *Buffalo Courier-Express*, 17 February 1949.
21. *Duluth Evening Herald*, 22 January 1907.
22. *Long Island Daily Press*, 26 May 1921.
23. *Evening Bulletin*, 29 September 1885.
24. *Syracuse Journal*, 24 August 1915.
25. Connell, p. 157.
26. *Queensland Times*, 3 August 1910.
27. In Los Angeles in 1895, a saloonkeeper named Henry Meybach attempted suicide with hyoscine (*Los Angeles Herald*, 21 June 1895), while in New York in 1910, Joseph G. Robin, a banker on trial for embezzlement, swallowed hyoscine before taking the stand, announcing, 'I am a dead man; I have taken poison tablets' (*San Francisco Call*, 31 December 1910). Both men were saved.
28. *National Advocate* (New South Wales), 1 August 1910.
29. *Evening Journal* (Adelaide), 3 August 1910.
30. *News of the World*, 7 August 1910.
31. Other mentions: 'The contents of his pockets included a packet containing powder.' (*Queensland Times*, 2 August 1910); 'The police upon searching Crippen's pockets found a packet containing a white powder. It is believed to be a dose of poison with which he intended to dispatch himself if he got the chance. Le Neve also had in her possession a small packet, which however she contrived to get rid of by throwing it out of one of the portholes.' (*The Sun* [Sydney], 2 August 1910.)
32. According to Clara's testimony, she asked how Cora was and Crippen replied, 'Oh, she is all right.' Again, this sounds nothing a million miles close to a murderer with the least interest in covering his tracks. What it sounds a lot like, however, is a husband who has just had a blazing row with his wife.

33. See Chapter 4.

34. *Daily News* (Perth), 15 August 1910.

35. *The Sun* (Sydney), 16 August 1910.

36. Cullen, p. 20.

37. 1 August 1910.

38. An especially grim story from Chicago in 1898 (*Tasmanian News*, 22 February) concerned a Dr William Smith, a demonstrator of anatomy in Missouri, who stole bodies from a morgue with the aid of a nightwatchman. He also alleged that inmates from the local mental asylum were often killed for use in dissection labs. (Plenty of hyoscine in those corpses, I'll wager.) In Calcutta in 1949, police found fourteen bodies cut into pieces and packed in bundles: they were found to be the remnants of dissected bodies stolen from hospitals by attendants. (*Daily News* [Perth], 21 July.) The thieves had soaked the bodies in water to remove the flesh so that they could sell the bones to medical students. The leftovers must have exactly resembled what was found in Crippen's cellar. As recently as 1986 in Philadelphia, a 70-year-old doctor who shipped human heads to a Colorado research centre for use by medical school employees was convicted of having bought and sold body parts for at least ten years and earning in excess of $14,000. (*Salamanca Press*, 16 October 1986.)

39. Cullen, p. 174.

40. The other thing that to me is highly suggestive that the remains were obtained in the form in which they were found is the absence of bones. Eline Schotsmans immediately focused on this element when I was discussing the case with her: for those of us who have brooded long on the mystery it is a fact that has blended with the wallpaper, but to Schotsmans it was glaringly anomalous. She wrote: 'Dismemberment is one thing, but removing the bones? That is all very difficult, and why would he do that? Why would he go through such an effort? Thinking of all the mess it makes. That is something that bothers me in this story.' Suddenly it bothers me much more than it used to, too.

41. David James Smith, p. 46.

42. Living in Highgate at the time of the Crippen affair, Lown had a wife and two daughters, and usually two servants, which may be mildly surprising for a North London builder, but nothing suggestive of a lead worth pursuing survives in the record. He died in Surrey in 1938.

43. Nicholas Connell, p. 39.

44. Cullen, p. 24.

45. The following year, Lucas assisted in the preservation of items retrieved from the tomb of Tutankhamen.

46. Alison Adam: *A History of Forensic Science*, p. 99.

47. https://bonesdontlie.wordpress.com/2013/08/08/new-morbid-terminology-quicklime/

48. In 2013, 275 complete bodies and 125 body parts were exhumed from the Tomašica gravesite, near Prijedor in the north of Bosnia. Though they

had been buried for over twenty years, many of the bodies were strikingly well preserved, 'with skin, soft tissues and internal organs still present in abundance and gross structures clearly identifiable'. (Adis Salihbegović, John Clark, Nermin Sarajlić, Svjetlana Radović, Finlay Finlay, Anes Jogunčić, Emina Spahić, Vedo Tuco: 'Histological Observations on Adipocere in Human Remains Buried for 21 Years at the Tomašica Grave-Site in Bosnia and Herzegovina' [https://pubmed.ncbi.nlm.nih.gov/29669235/].) But according to Eline Schotsmans, this is misleading in the present context: 'The example of the mass burial in Bosnia is not really applicable to this case because individuals in a mass burial decompose differently than in an individual burial. In fact, the dead in the middle of the mass are usually well preserved, and at the side they appear skeletonised. This is called the "feather" effect.' (Correspondence with author, June 2020.)

49. Sabine Fiedler, Matthias Graw: 'Decomposition of Buried Corpses, With Special Reference to the Formation of Adipocere' (https://pubmed.ncbi. nlm.nih.gov/12883770/#affiliation-1).

50. S. Fiedler, A.E. Berns, L. Schwark, A.T. Woelk, M. Graw: 'The Chemistry of death--Adipocere Degradation in Modern Graveyards' (https://pubmed. ncbi.nlm.nih.gov/26461030/).

51. See Eline M.J. Schotsmans, John Denton, Jonathan N. Fletcher, Robert C. Janaway, Andrew S. Wilson: 'Long-term effects of hydrated lime and quicklime on the decay of human remains using pig cadavers as human body analogues: Field experiments' and 'Short-term effects of hydrated lime and quicklime on the decay of human remains using pig cadavers as human body analogues: Laboratory experiments' (*Forensic Science International*, January 2014).

52. Correspondence with author: June 2020.

53. Shari L. Forbes, Barbara H. Stuart, Boyd B. Dent, 'The effect of the burial environment on adipocere formation' (*Forensic Science International*, 154 [2005] 24–34).

54. Cullen, p. 24.

55. In saying 'he' I realise I am implying that the person who planted the remains was definitely Crippen: I do so only for convenience, and 'he' should be taken to mean 'Crippen or whoever'.

56. *San Jose Mercury*, 20 July 1910.

57. Cullen, p. 38.

58. Connell, p. 105.

59. Husband William Smith dies in 1923, whereupon Bertha marries for a third time, to Otto Sternhopf. Following Bertha's death in 1926 her two youngest daughters go to live with Cora's sister, Louise Mills. None of them have any connection whatever with a 'Belle Rose'.

60. *New York Times*, 15 July 1910.

61. There is evidence of letters purportedly from Cora being sent to the authorities at the time of the trial, but they seem to have been fairly blatant fakes.

62. The same caution governs the naming of anyone who was known to be still alive or whose death had not been absolutely established. So while even

characters as minor as Mrs Jackson, Sergeant Mitchell and Marion Curnow are named correctly, Captain Kendall, who did not die until 1965, is rechristened Captain McKenzie, and Clara Martinetti, who was overwhelmingly likely to have died but for whom there was no definite information, becomes 'Mrs Arditti'. (In fact, she had died in May of 1945, in Torquay.)

63. His address (41 Baring Avenue, East Chicago) confirms that this is the same Bruce Miller who is living with wife Edith at the time of the Crippen trial.

64. 'The [harmonica], profaned in common parlance by the humble name of mouth-organ, was exalted to heights of real music with Mr. Miller's remarkably clever execution, and the manner in which he thrummed the banjo was equally a marvel.' (*Hammond Times*, 30 September 1911.)

65. *Times Union* (Brooklyn), 4 March 1899.

66. *North Eastern Daily Gazette* (Middlesbrough), 20 June 1899.

67. *Saint Paul Globe*, 19 February 1899.

68. Miller is also named Smith in at least one other source at this time: it may simply be a mistake, or it may be that he had decided to change his stage name (and then changed his mind again). Smith (originally Schmidt) was the maiden name of Cora's mother; weirdly, Miller had a brother-in-law called Smith and would later have a son-in-law called Schmidt. Which just goes to show that coincidences really do happen.

69. *Daily Independent* (Hutchinson, Kansas), 3 March 1904.

70. *Daily Herald* (Adelaide), 27 October 1910.

71. Registry of Births: Cook County, Illinois.

72. No, they are not two different Bruce Millers. Miller's death notice lists Valerie Ordner as his wife and names his children as Jeanne, Robert Bruce, Barry and John. Jeanne and Barry are the two children he had out of wedlock in 1915 and 1917. They are listed as living with Bruce and Valerie (aged 4 and 2) in the 1920 census. (John followed in 1927.) But Robert Bruce is his son with Edith, living with her and her parents in the 1900 census, then (aged 23), with Edith and Bruce in the 1910 census, moved away by the time of the 1920 census, which lists Bruce and Edith alone. The deceased Miller, married to Valerie, has the same date and place of birth as the one who lived with Edith, and is likewise a (retired) physician. This is probably also the place to stress that Valerie's birth and life before meeting Miller can also be fully traced in the documents, so there is absolutely no possibility of her being an incognito Cora.

73. *The Republic* (Columbus, Indiana), 11 December 1924.

74. *Los Angeles Times*, 17 October 1947.

75. *The Times* (Munster, Indiana), 22 February 1924.

76. *Los Angeles Times*, 16 March 1961.

77. *Evening Telegram* (New York), 8 November 1910.

78. If she had used an entirely false name she would be all but untraceable now. Even if she wasn't especially imaginative: for the record, 32 Coras, 20 Belles and (let's be fanciful) 59 Millers within ten years either side of a birth date of 1865 left Britain for America in 1910.

Bibliography

*Especially important and/or recommended books are indicated by an asterisk.

All newspapers, periodicals, journals and scientific papers cited or referred to are separately credited in the notes section.

Ackroyd, Peter, *London: The Biography* (London: Chatto & Windus, 2000)

Adam, Alison, *A History of Forensic Science: British Beginnings in the Twentieth Century* (London: Routledge, 2017)

Begg, Paul, *Jack the Ripper: The Facts* (London: Robson, 2004)

Bloom, Ursula, **The Girl Who Loved Crippen* (London: Hutchinson, 1955)

Browne, Douglas G. & Tullett, E.V., *Bernard Spilsbury: His Life and Cases* (London: White Lion, 1951)

Coniam, Matthew, *Egyptomania Goes to the Movies* (Jefferson: McFarland, 2017)

Connell, Nicholas, *Doctor Crippen* (Stroud: Amberley, 2013)

—— *Walter Dew, The Man Who Caught Crippen* (Stroud: Sutton, 2005)

Cullen, Tom, **Crippen: The Mild Murderer* (London: Bodley Head, 1977)

Dew, Walter, **I Caught Crippen* (London: Blackie & Son, 1938)

Double, Oliver, *Britain Had Talent: A History of Variety Theatre* (London: Palgrave Macmillan, 2012)

Fido, Martin, *The Murder Guide to London* (London: Grafton, 1987)

Goodman, Jonathan, **The Crippen File* (London: Allison & Busby, 1985)

Grant, Thomas, *Court No. 1, The Old Bailey* (London: John Murray, 2019)

Orwell, George, **Decline of the English Murder and other essays* (London: Penguin, 1965)

Priestley, J.B., *The Edwardians* (London: Heinemann, 1970)

Robinson, Bruce, **They All Love Jack: Busting the Ripper* (London: Fourth Estate, 2016)

Ronald, James, *No Way Out* (London: Hodder & Stoughton, 1948)

Rose, Andrew, **Lethal Witness: Sir Bernard Spilsbury, Honorary Pathologist* (Stroud: Sutton, 2007)

Simpson, Professor Keith, **Forty Years of Murder* (London: Harrap, 1978)

Smith, David James, *Supper with the Crippens* (London: Orion, 2005)

Sturgis, Matthew, *Walter Sickert: A Life* (London: Harper Perennial, 2011)

Sugden, Philip, *The Complete History of Jack the Ripper* (London: Constable & Robinson, 2002)

Wilson, Colin, *A Criminal History of Mankind* (London: Panther, 1985)
—— *Written in Blood: A History of Forensic Detection* (London: Grafton, 1990)
Wilson, Colin & Pitman, Pat, *Encyclopaedia of Murder* (London: Arthur Barker, 1961)
Yates, Dornford, *As Berry and I Were Saying* (London: Ward, Lock & Co., 1952)
Young, Filson (ed.) **Trial of Hawley Harvey Crippen* (London: William Hodge & Co., 1933)

Acknowledgements

The author gratefully acknowledges the assistance and generosity of the following: Patrick McCaughey and Helen Ellis for invaluable research, David Foran and John Trestrail for sharing their findings regarding the DNA testing of the cellar remains and reading and correcting Chapter 7, James Patrick Crippen for his correspondence and encouragement, Eline M.J. Schotsmans for sharing her expertise and the findings of her research in the decay of human remains, barrister Matthew Scott for helping to hack a path through some of the oddities of the trial and prosecution, Fran Hall of the Good Funeral Guild for her insight into early twentieth-century mortuary practice, Peter Charlton and Alison Young of the British Music Hall Society for helping map the largely non-existent contours of Cora's theatrical career, Andy Carne for talking me through the finer points of lime and quicklime, Veikko Suvanto for helping me make sense of *Dr Crippen Lebt!* in the absence of subtitles, Daryl Stafford for assistance with sources, Linne Matthews for her galvanising interest in the project, my wife Angela and son Edward for their essential love and support, and the late Colin Wilson, without whom we would not now be having this conversation.

Index